*The Death
of the German Cousin*

The Death
of the German Cousin

Variations on a Literary Stereotype, 1890–1920

Peter Edgerly Firchow

Lewisburg
Bucknell University Press
London and Toronto: Associated University Presses

Associated University Presses
440 Forsgate Drive
Cranbury, NJ 08512

Associated University Presses
25 Sicilian Avenue
London WC1A 2QH, England

Associated University Presses
2133 Royal Windsor Drive
Unit 1
Mississauga, Ontario
Canada L5J 1K5

The paper used in this publication meets the requirements
of the American National Standard for Permanence
of Paper for Printed Library Materials Z39.48-1984.

Library of Congress Cataloging-in-Publication Data

Firchow, Peter Edgerly, 1937–
    The death of the German cousin.

    Bibliography: p.
    Includes index.
    1. English literature—20th century—History and
criticism.   2. English literature—19th century—
History and criticism.   3. Germans in literature.
4. Germany in literature.   5. National characteristics,
German, in literature.   6. Great Britain—Relations—
Germany.   7. Germany—Relations—Great Britain.
I. Title.
PR129.G3F57   1986   820'.9'3520331   84-46097
ISBN 0-8387-5095-8 (alk. paper)

Printed in the United States of America

For Katti
who also wants to be known as Kathy

Contents

Preface

Writers on the subject of national characteristics notoriously tend either to confirm existing prejudices or to establish new ones. Often they do both. No doubt the rule holds true for this book as well. I can only plead, by way of justification and extenuation, that the culture with which this book deals is still, in most of its essentials, our own; and that even the terms with which one may choose to criticize one's culture remain products of that culture. This axiom is, in fact, one of the starting points of my study.

Still, it goes without saying—though, for the record, I will say it—that I have tried to be objective. Being objective is not the same as not taking sides. I freely admit that I have made judgments and committed ironies, though not, I think, shamelessly or without granting the reader insight into my reasons and sources. Hence the swarm of footnotes crowding the final pages of this book.

Though this book is long and heavily documented, some readers will be bound to object that I have omitted or neglected or skimmed over authors whose works I might have dealt with, or dealt with more fully. I accept the validity and even the value of such criticism, though not its immediate relevance. I would like to make it clear that this book is not intended to be exhaustive; it is intended to be representative. It does not try to achieve or portray a total picture of events, but rather hopes, in the memorable conception of Georg Lukács, to isolate what is typical of the whole in the most individual of extreme situations. Moreover, it needs to be said that I have deliberately confined myself to writers and books that belong to, or are at least usually considered to be on the verges of the "serious," so that subjects like popular journalism or children's literature are by and large excluded. My chief reason for limiting the focus in this way was my hope to establish all

the more convincingly the close links between literary intellectuals and
political action.

The approach this study takes, the methodological assumptions on which
it rests, are generally speaking those of "intellectual history," or what is
nowadays more often called, in some circles at least, "cultural criticism."
Here, however, the history and the culture are at any rate primarily of a
literary sort; but not the history of an abstract idea embodied in literature—
as, for example, the idea of the value of life in Erich Heller's classic *The
Disinherited Mind* (1954)—but rather the history of a way of looking at or of
conceiving another people and national culture. Inevitably, the way one
thinks of others says a great deal about the way one thinks of oneself.
Conception of others is also self-conception and self-deception.

Recently a word for precisely this subcategory of literary study has been
coined: *imagology.* (For those to whom this kind of approach may be
unfamiliar, I have provided in the Appendix a brief historical/theoretical
overview.) Though "imagology" may not be an altogether satisfactory word,
it does convey a sense of the use of the imagination—and hence of literature—to project an "image" of what another world is like. In this case that
other world is a German one, a world that, during the period with which
this book is concerned, was simultaneously perceived as a model of what
England should, and should not, be. Culturally, in terms of religion and
"race," Germany was often viewed as an ally, even as a "cousin"; politically
and militarily, it came increasingly to be thought of as an enemy. The way
English literature responded to this ambiguity is the subject of this book.

This is not, however, to say that literature is merely passive or that it
simply "reflects" the intellectual and social currents of its time. An important part of my argument is that literature is also active, that it helps to
create—or, as here, often to hinder—the mutual understanding of nations.
Literature does not only mirror national stereotypes; it shapes them,
changes them, and makes them respectable. There is a continual interplay
between "reality" and consciousness; and literary consciousness can and
does affect the way we think of the real world we live in. And the way we
think of the world affects the way we act in it. Literature matters; and the
subject matter of literature matters.

This is especially true at a time when we are once again inundated by
projections—on the screen and on the page, as well as in the mind—of an
Evil Empire in the East that seeks to destroy us. Whatever the reality behind
these projections, it is clear that we must learn to look not only beneath and
behind them, but also directly and objectively *at* them as continuous historical and cultural phenomena; and that we must learn to relativize them lest
we become their prisoners and in the end, as so many generations before us,
their victims. Wars, we are now coming more and more to realize, are not
merely the inevitable results of vast impersonal political and economic

conflicts; they are that, of course, in part, but they are also brought about by quite personal convictions, as the wars of religion amply and bloodily testify. Poetry—literature in general—does make something happen. If this book helps a few readers understand that this is true, it will have achieved its purpose.

Acknowledgments

Parts of this book have been published elsewhere, though often in somewhat abbreviated and altered form. I wish to thank the following journals for permission to reprint chapters that first appeared in their pages: "Kipling's 'Mary Postgate': The Barbarians and the Critics," *Etudes Anglaises* 29 (January–March 1976): 27–39; "Conrad, Goethe, and the German Grotesque," *Comparative Literature Studies* 13 (March 1976): 60–73; "Germany and Germanic Mythology in E. M. Forster's *Howards End*," *Comparative Literature* 33 (Winter 1981): 50–68; and "The Death of the German Cousin," *South Atlantic Quarterly* 83 (Spring 1984): 193–206. The Appendix on Imagology is based on a paper read at the Eleventh Congress of the International Comparative Literature Association in Paris (August 1985). I also want to thank the libraries at the following universities for allowing me to use their facilities: Minnesota, Harvard, Cambridge (England), California at Los Angeles, Edinburgh (Scotland), and Marburg (W. Germany). I am most grateful to the Graduate School and the Office of International Programs of the University of Minnesota for helping to fund a study whose controversial nature intimidated other granting sources.

It is a duty and a pleasure to acknowledge my debt to friends and colleagues who, over the years, have read and commented on this book, or parts of it, in one of its several metamorphoses: Wlad Godzich; Peter Keating; Larry Mitchell; Stephen Prickett; and, above all, Leonard Unger. Inga Velde's bibliographical talents were often helpful. And, as always, my wife, Evelyn Scherabon Firchow, looked over my shoulder, telling me truths pleasant and unpleasant, and giving me the courage to go on.

*The Death
of the German Cousin*

Introduction: National Character and "Race"

No man will treat with indifference the principle of race. It is the key to history.

Benjamin Disraeli

Nationalism is a state of mind.

Hans Kohn

The idea that there is such a thing as national character is as old as the idea of a nation itself, and probably even older. For it is arguable—and indeed has often been argued—that nations only begin to exist when they grow aware, whether consciously or, more likely, subconsciously, of their own identities, of what distinguishes them from other nations: in short, of their national characters. So, for instance, Ramsay Muir in *Nationalism and Internationalism* (1917) proposes that a nation "is obviously not the same thing as a race, and not the same thing as a state. It may be provisionally defined as a body of people who feel themselves to be naturally linked together by certain affinities which are so strong and real for them that they can live happily together, are dissatisfied when disunited, and cannot tolerate subjection to peoples who do not share these ties." Like all definitions in the field of cultural history, this one is admittedly loose and tentative. "It cannot," as Muir goes on to say, "be tested or analysed by formulae, such as German professors love."[1]

By a curious irony of cultural history, however, it is to a German professor—though not one much given to formulae—that this definition of nationality may be principally traced. Johann Gottfried von Herder (1744–1803), the sometime mentor of Goethe and the "father" of the German Romantic movement, originated, in his monumental *Outlines of a Philosophy of the History of Man* (1784–91), the concept of an evolutionary national character identified with the evolution of a national state. Herder was not, however, a narrow German nationalist; on the contrary, his vision was of a future in which every nation would be permitted to realize its own identity fully and in harmony with all other nations.

That vision, needless to say, has not been achieved and it does not look as if it ever will be. The full expression of one national identity is apparently not consistent, in the nature of international relations, with the equally full expression of another. One can hope to avoid dissonance among nations, but harmony can be achieved only by abolishing individual national characteristics and submerging them in a universal, international character—a consummation that even as gentle and cosmopolitan a soul as E. M. Forster feared.

National character certainly exists; and since the time of Herder, at least, it has also been acknowledged to develop and change. The nineteenth century is crowded with studies of greater or lesser pretension to scientific accuracy, in which are outlined the development of the chief Western nations, studies often but not always disguised as history. These are usually self-examinations, attempts to define the national identities of the historians themselves. In this sense, a nation's historians are not merely the chroniclers and preservers of a nation's past but the creators of a nation's present and even, to some degree, of its future. For frequently—and especially in the period with which this book is concerned—the actions of national states are not postulated on so-called *Realpolitik*, but on a perception of what a nation, given the character that it attributes to itself, should or must do.

Historians, including literary historians, play a large, even disproportionately large, role in the creation of national self-images, but they have been less instrumental in shaping the ways in which one nation views another. In this area, it is literature (of all brows: high, middle, and low) that has been most important. The British conception of the Russian national character, for instance, owes immeasurably more to translations of Tolstoy, Dostoevski, and Chekhov, than it does to any history books, Russian or British. Similarly with France or Germany. Moreover, in the case of these last two nations it is also possible to trace, over a considerable period of time, how English reactions to their national characters developed. This is especially true of Germany in the closing years of the last century and the opening years of this, a period when England felt increasingly threatened by Germany as a rival imperial power, and when, as a consequence, English writers often felt impelled to set down their impressions of the German national character.

The study of these impressions, no matter how much one wishes to be objective, can never be free of subjectivity. Inevitably one is, like everyone else, a product of one's time and of the accumulation of views—or prejudices—about the characters of other national groups. This applies *a fortiori* to any study of the German national character, which has obviously undergone considerable revision owing to the critical experience of two major wars. Certainly the example of other, supposedly dispassionate, attempts to examine this national character is not encouraging. Take, for instance, the chapter "Germany–England" in *Portrait of Europe* (1952) by the eminent

Spanish author Salvador de Madariaga, formerly professor at Oxford and sometime ambassador of republican Spain to the United States. In this chapter Madariaga compares an English sentence, "I have dropped my glove," with the same sentence in German, "Mein Handschuh ist hinuntergefallen." This is what he has to say about the German sentence: "Notice the organ-like weight and sonority of the sentence, its length and that of its words. There are nineteen letters in the English one; thirty-two, nearly twice as many, in the German one. The possessive *My* is now loaded with a heavy *N: Mein.* Instead of the light and elegant *Glove,* the German says *Handschuh,* i.e., *hand shoe,* a concept rather than a live word, and a heavy and ungraceful concept at that, without subtlety or humour. And finally, *ist hinuntergefallen,* which is over-explanatory, a whole treatise on the art of falling, of actual effective falling, here at my feet, lest you have not understood it—a word for slow minds who need a lot of explaining. . . . In contrast with this heavily weighted language, English expresses a people all muscle, bone and sinew. Much of the Anglo-German tension can be explained by this fact . . . English is to German as a dry sponge is to a soaked one. This mushy character of the German language finds expression in the superabundance of the sound *Sch,* which, as is well known, can be heard not only wherever it is written (which is often enough) but also wherever an *S* meets any other consonant; for instance in *Spät,* pronounced *Schpät.* The swelling which so much water produces adds also to the volume of the numerous syllables in um, am, em, all heavy with mush. . . .The German is moreover usually wet by temperament. Then, all this water tends to produce steam. Hence the frequency of the sound *F* in German, particularly at the end of the syllable. All *V's* are made to blow and steam and become *F's.* And as for *P's* they all end in *F's,* as in *Pferde, Pfeife.* No German can make *P* explode neatly without letting off after it the surplus pressure of the steam in his soul. Thus camp becomes *Kampf.* And the very word for steam could not be more characteristic: *Dampf.*"[2]

This, by almost any measure, is remarkable stuff. The soul of a nation is revealed here in the sound and structure of its language—and it is a spongy, clammy, clumsy soul in the case of the German nation. This idea, and especially Madariaga's metaphorical development of it, is patently absurd, but absurd with more than a touch of poetry: poetry like that of Edward Lear or Lewis Carroll. One does not quite know what to make of it or whether to make anything of it at all. It is hard to take seriously, though it was clearly meant to be taken seriously, and was once in fact (and for all I know may still be) taken seriously.

Not that this sort of "scholarship" has vanished with Madariaga. It survives in full flower in an essay by Willa Muir, half of the famous husband-wife team that translated Kafka into English. This essay, entitled "Translating from the German," is contained in a once widely used anthology, *On*

Translation (1966), edited by the late Harvard English professor Reuben Brower. As with Madariaga, the attempt to define the German national character calls forth Muir's poetic powers: "I find myself disliking the purposive control, the will power dominating the German sentence. I dislike its subordination of everything to these hammer-blow verbs; I dislike its weight and its clotted abstractions. I have the feeling that the shape of the German language affects the thought of those who use it and disposes them to overvalue authoritative statement, will power, and purposive drive. . . .A language which emphasizes control and rigid subordination must tend to shape what we call *Macht-Menschen*. The drive, the straight purposive drive, of Latin, for instance, is remarkably like the straight purposive drive of the Roman roads. One might hazard a guess that from the use of *ut* with the subjunctive one could deduce the Roman Empire. Could one then deduce Hitler's Reich from the no less ruthless shape of the German sentence? I think one could. . . .The Germans roll compound words into sausages of abstraction, and then roll these sausages into bigger ones. This predilection for the sausage shape cannot be fortuitous. It must have some relation to the German love of *Wurst* and *Dachshunds*. And why did the Germans invent the Zeppelin? Nor should we forget that the favorite German word of abuse is *Scheiss* [*sic*]. One can tell that the Germans are very bowel-conscious, or as the psychoanalysts say, anal-erotic. So the right image for the German sentence, I suggest, is that of a great gut, a bowel, which deposits at the end of it a sediment of verbs. Is not this like the Reich desired by Hitler, who planned to make mincemeat of Europe?"[3]

Neither Muir nor Madariaga makes it clear whether the German language is supposed to have shaped the German character, or vice versa; that is, whether the Germans, if they had been willing to abandon their language and begun, say, to speak English, would have been spared their spongy souls or their sausagelike determination to dominate the world. The distinction is an important one, because in the first instance these national characteristics would be innate and in the second—in the main, at any rate—environmental. The fact that the cause is left ambiguous suggests perhaps that we are to make up our minds, depending on our own experiences of Germans; but it also suggests that Madariaga and Muir, under the guise of a linguistic study of national characteristics, wish to put forward racist doctrines without having to examine the assumptions on which such racism is based. In extenuation of these views, however, it should perhaps be added that this kind of quasi-racist prejudice may be necessary to shoring up one's own sense of national identity, that one national character always requires another to be its scapegoat.

This is, admittedly, a somewhat depressing view, but it finds confirmation in even the most objective studies of national prejudice, such as the English historian's E. H. Dance's *History the Betrayer, A Study in Bias* (1960). This is a study of prejudice in history textbooks throughout the world, based partly on the results of the International Schoolbook Institute at Brunswick, Germany. Dance's credentials are impeccable, his aims laudable, but he apparently cannot help remarking, near the opening of his book, that "there has been much talk of 'objective' history—especially in Germany, where the word *objektiv*, rolled round the Teutonic tongue, often conveys an altogether false feeling of security."[4]

This particular species of linguistic/racist speculation takes its origin in a combination of Max Müller's work on what he called the "Aryan" languages and Darwin's theory of human evolution. The resulting popularized compound was to prove explosive, though in isolation each element may have seemed innocuous. Certainly Müller, who for much of his career was professor of modern languages and comparative philology at Oxford, objected unmistakably to any effort to link a linguistic phenomenon with an ethnological one. In his *Biographies of Words and the Homes of the Aryas* (1888), he writes: "I have declared again and again that if I say Aryas, I mean neither blood nor bones, nor hair nor skull; I mean simply those who speak an Aryan language. The same applies to Hindus, Greeks, Romans, Germans, Celts and Slaves. When I speak of them I commit myself to no anatomical characteristics. . . . To me an ethnologist who speaks of Aryan race, Aryan blood, Aryan eyes and hair, is as great a sinner as a linguist who speaks of a dolichocephalic dictionary or a brachycephalic grammar."[5] Nevertheless, despite these very explicit warnings from Müller, the latter half of the nineteenth century—in England as well as in Germany and France—was thickly populated with ethnographers who measured heads and sought to correlate their findings with language and national character.

Part of the problem undoubtedly arose from the very imprecise and unscientific way in which the word *race* was used by many of these researchers and by the public for which they wrote. Until relatively recently this word was more or less interchangeable in meaning with a word like *nation* or *people*. The *Oxford English Dictionary* lists, among others, the following definitions: "A tribe, nation, or people, regarded as of common stock;" and: "A group of several tribes or peoples, forming a distinct ethnical stock." For the latter definition, the *OED* cites an example drawn from J. R. Green's *The Conquest of England* (1883): "Courage . . . was a heritage of the whole German race." Similarly, it was perfectly proper to speak of an "English race" or a "French race." Inevitably, and often quite intentionally, there crept into this usage a connotation that such "races" were biologically distinct, though in the more serious studies such connotations were reserved for the so-called three European races: the Nordic, the Alpine, and the Mediterranean.

Nowadays, this type of racism is generally identified with Germany and specifically with the period of Nazi domination of Germany, but it is absolutely essential to realize that it was (and to some degree still is) a general European and American phenomenon, one that very definitely includes England. Much of the English perception of Germany—and the shifts in that perception as Germany was sensed as an ever graver threat—can only be understood in the context of a general acceptance of racist assumptions like those of Madariaga's or Muir's.

In England, where it was obvious that the English had mixed for centuries with the French, the Welsh, the Scots, and the Irish, the idea naturally arose of an "English race" in terms of a mixture of these nationalities. Aided by Darwin, much was made of this happy historical circumstance, particularly in terms of the blending of the so-called Nordic and Mediterranean peoples. Necessarily, a virtue was made of this kind of "racial" mixture, though, with an eye to recent German military successes and French defeats (as well as Gobineau's idea that the French aristocracy was Nordic, the French peasantry Mediterranean and Alpine), it was always the Nordic element that was stressed. How common the notion of dividing Europe up into three distinct racial groups was, can be seen from a highly popular collection of verses for children, Hilaire Belloc's *Cautionary Tales* (1907), which contains the following (only partly ironic) poem entitled "The Three Races":

I

Behold, my child, the Nordic Man
And be as like him as you can.
His legs are long; his mind is slow;
His hair is lank and made of tow.

II

And here we have the Alpine Race.
Oh! What a broad and foolish face!
His skin is of dirty yellow,
He is a most unpleasant fellow.

III

The most degraded of them all
Mediterranean we call.
His hair is crisp, and even curls,
And he is saucy with the girls.[6]

Hilariously enough, of course, Belloc, born in France of a French father and an English mother, was by these criteria something of an "unpleasant fellow" himself.

Belloc may have based his racist conclusions in this poem on Isaac Taylor's *The Origin of the Aryans* (1889). In this frequently reprinted work, Taylor—who was canon of York, recipient of honorary degrees from Edinburgh and Cambridge, and so well known for his work that he was sometimes called the "Darwin of Philology"—argues that England is composed of three races: Iberian, Celtic, and Teutonic (roughly equivalent to Mediterranean, Alpine, and Nordic). As with Belloc, so with Taylor, the Nordic man or "the pure Teuton is phlegmatic in temperament, and somewhat dull of intellect; but is brave, warlike, and given to field sports and athletic exercises. He is a tall, flaxen-haired, large-limbed giant, fat and stupid, like the Goths and Burgundians whom the Roman provincials regarded with fear, mingled with contempt." As for Alpine or Celtic man, his "broad, capacious forehead and the short, square chin indicate mental power and determination of character." As a result of these superior characteristics, the Celts had early subdued the Iberians, "who were plainly the primitive inhabitants of the island" and whose skulls also plainly testified to their inferiority: "the face is oval, feeble, and orthognathous; the forehead narrow; the chin weak, pointed, and elongated." Once the Celts and Teutons, and to some lesser degree the Iberians, had mingled (as the usual Victorian euphemism has it), they produced a new race, one that has "profoundly modified the physical type in Germany, France, Italy and England."[7]

How widespread these notions were even before Taylor "systematized" them emerges clearly from an examination of an elementary schoolbook like Arabella Buckley's *History of England for Beginners* (1887), where the original inhabitants of Britain are described as having "long and narrow" skulls resembling those of "a small, dark-skinned, curly-haired people called the Basques or Iberians. . . . There is even a small dark type of men among the lowest class of Irish and Welsh of to-day which is probably a remnant of this same ancient people." Eventually these people were conquered by the Celts, a "race with rounder skulls . . . a large-limbed, fair-haired race" that then began to "mingle" with the smaller and darker natives.[8]

The Welsh historian and founder of the University of Wales, Thomas Nicholas, is an even heartier advocate of mixture than Taylor. His *Pedigree of the English People* (1868), a lengthy and learned tome that within a decade went through five editions, arrives very quickly at the conclusion that "the mightiest nations have been those whose origin is traceable to mixed sources. That combination of noble qualities which culminates in national greatness, is found at the focal point where the varying but still harmonizing attributes of different stocks of race meet and blend."[9] That these harmonizing attributes are not to be discovered much beyond the confines of the British Isles is suggested by a textbook on *Ethnology* (1909) by the Cambridge Professor A. H. Keane. There, after a discussion of the mixing of the Spanish with the Indians in Latin America, the French with the Indians in Canada and the Siamese in Indochina, the Dutch with the Hottentots in South Africa, and so forth, he notes that the English are exempt from this tendency to mix. "As a rule," he informs us, "the Anglo-Saxon or British Aryans, who are by far the most numerous and widespread out of Europe, do not amalgamate with the aborigines. Hence Anglo-American, Anglo-African and Anglo-Australian half-castes are rare, and the modifications of the Aryan types undoubtedly going on in the 'Greater Britain' beyond the seas are due, not to miscegenation with lower races, but partly to the changed environment, partly (North America) to fusion with Germans, Scandinavians, and other fellow Aryans."[10]

The folly of amalgamation with "lower races" is emphasized even as late as 1927 in Ernest Barker's *National Character and the Factors in Its Formation*. After striking what seems at first a more tolerant note by contending that "British is an adjective not of race, but of nationality," and after even suggesting that it was "the sad fate of the scholarship of the nineteenth century to invent the double concepts of race and language-group—as explosive as any invention of the laboratory"—Barker returns with an easy conscience to the old themes and variations. "Our racial blend," he tells his readers, is basically a combination of Nordic and Mediterranean types "without any but the slightest admixture of the Alpine." This recipe, we are then reminded, is the same as the one followed by the ancient Greeks: "It is the same blend which produced the ancient Greeks; and in so far as we are made by race, we owe what we are to the fusion of these two strains." Having thus rediscovered scientifically modern Britain's racial kinship with ancient Greece—one recalls in this connection the old myth of British descent from Troy—Barker naturally derides those nations which are proud of their racial purity. "If they were more discerning," he observes, "they might pride themselves with greater propriety on racial impurity." Lest we interpret this as license for all sorts of racial intermarriage, however, Barker immediately reminds us that there *are* limits: "There are, it is true, elements which it is better not to mix, because they are so unlike that their offspring, with its ill-assorted mixture of discrepant qualities, will be ill-balanced and unharmonious. Miscegenation of East and West, or of white and black, has its perils. But inter-breeding of the different varieties or races of Europe, which unite a fund of similarity to all their differences, is an entirely different matter."[11]

That Barker's views were fairly representative even in the twenties may be seen by comparing his work with the more "scientific" Lowell Lectures of the distinguished English psychologist and sometime Harvard professor, William McDougall, by whom we are told that "modern science is very largely a product of northern Europe, of those countries where the Nordic blood predominates; not exclusively so by any means. But note this fact: The Greeks, who founded philosophy and science, were probably in the greatest age, compounded of the Nordic and the Mediterranean races." McDougall also includes a photograph of an African black with the following caption: "Nor is it easy to suppose that they [the most resolutely optimistic humanitarians] could contemplate with equanimity the substitution of the Anglo-American stock by persons of this type."[12]

Some of the leading intellectuals of the period were infected with similar notions—at times, surprisingly, the very same people who were contributing most toward freeing England from other kinds of prejudice. There was Havelock Ellis, for example, the author of *Studies in the Psychology of Sex* (1897–1928), the first volume of which had been banned for obscenity, a man who probably did more than anyone else (even than Lawrence, never very influential until late in his lifetime; or Freud who, until the twenties, was virtually unknown or merely laughed at) to create an atmosphere in which there could be rational discussion of sexuality. Even a man like Ellis is to be found, in *The New Spirit* (1890), mouthing clichés normally expected only from Kipling. In the introduction to this book, which is an attempt to chart the intellectual history of the nineteenth century by considering a few of its leading writers, Ellis briefly stops to consider some aspects of the future. Russia, he feels, will come to dominate Asia, for the Russians are capable of mixing "even with the fiercest yellow races and bringing them into relation with the best European influences," whereas for the English "it has never been easy to find a *modus vivendi* with lower races, or races which we are pleased to consider lower." That this last qualification is merely a matter of form is confirmed by what follows. Regretfully, Ellis continues, "the English are beginning to learn by bitter experience that they are not suited for the mission of civilizing Asia." There is all of South America for the "Spanish races" to expand in, a large part of the African continent for "those slow, yet tenacious and admirable colonists, the Germans" to settle in. But what is left for the English, since they are not given as others are to living together with supposedly inferior races? The answer, stated with brutal simplicity, is the extermination of those races. "If we English," Ellis's argument runs, "are certain to make little progress where, as in Asia, the great task is conciliation, when it is a question of stamping out a lower race—then is our time! It has to be done; it is quite clear that the fragile Red men of America and the strange wild Blacks of Australia must perish at the touch of the White man." And in Ellis's mind, logical and not sadistic, "touch" it is, not shove or even kick: "On the whole we stamp them out as mercifully as may be, supplying our victim liberally with missionaries and blankets."[13]

National Life and Character, A Forecast (1893), by Charles Henry Pearson, formerly Fellow of Oriel College, Oxford, Professor of History at King's College, London, and Minister of Education for Australia, contains a vision of the future based on analogous racist assumptions. After examining some of the dangers that will confront the white man in the future, Pearson directs himself to what divides the European nations in the present, namely imperial rivalry. "Two centuries hence," he warns his readers, "it may be a matter of serious concern to the world if Russia has been displaced by China on the Amoor, if France has not been able to colonise North Africa, or if England is not holding India. For civilised men there can be only one fatherland, and whatever extends the influence of those races that have taken their faith from Palestine, their laws of beauty from Greece, and their civil law from Rome, ought to be a matter of rejoicing to Russian, German, Anglo-Saxon, and Frenchman alike." As for a solution like that proposed by Ellis, that is no longer possible. "No one," he tells us in a tone that sounds suspiciously like wistful regret, "of course, assumes that the Aryan race—to use a convenient term—can stamp out or starve out all their rivals on the face of the earth. [Pearson has obviously not read Ellis or Dilke]. It is self-evident that the Chinese, the Japanese, the Hindoos, if we may apply this general term to the various natives of India, and the African negro, are too numerous and sturdy to be extirpated. It is against the fashion of modern humanity to wish that they should suffer decrease or oppression."

If only some other means could be found of making them go away. But this is not to be, and the day shall come, Pearson foretells, when black and yellow men will be "invited to international conferences, and welcomed as allies in the quarrels of the civilised world." And not only this: they shall move in polite society, they shall "throng the English turf" and populate the salons of Paris, they shall be permitted to intermarry. Having his "pride of place" thus humiliated will be the white man's reward for carrying "peace and law and order over the world, that others may enter in and enjoy." Small wonder then that Pearson and others of a similar cast of mind "are not sorry to think that we shall have passed away before that day arrives."[14]

Sir Francis Galton places his discriminations among races and nations in a less emotional framework in *Hereditary Genius* (1869; rev. ed. 1892), but his conclusions are not radically different. And he too is continually peering into the future. Like Nietzsche, impelled by some of the implications of Darwin's theory of natural selection, Galton looks forward to the development of a race of supermen. In his preface, he informs us that "there is nothing either in the history of domestic animals or in that of evolution to make us doubt that a race of sane men may be formed, who shall be as much superior mentally and morally to the modern European, as the modern European is to the lowest of the Negro races." Later on in the book, Galton establishes in a rather arbitrary fashion a scale ranging upward from A to G with an additional X for all classes above G, according to which he judges the intellectual ability of various regional, national, and racial groups. One of the first conclusions he arrives at is that "the average intellectual standard of the negro is some two grades below our own." Another is that, within Great Britain itself, the intelligence of the lowland Scotch and the English

North-country men is definitely a fraction of a grade higher than that of the rest of the British. But even these are but savages when compared to the ancient Athenians, who, to Galton's mind, were the intellectually most accomplished people of all time. "On the very lowest estimate," he tells us, their average natural ability was "very nearly two grades higher than our own—that is, about as much as our race is above that of the African Negro."[15]

If only, Galton speculates enthusiastically, that distance could be narrowed: instead of the paltry six men above class G now inhabiting England, a mere difference of one grade would produce eighty-two such men. And a difference of two grades, one thousand three hundred and fifty-five.

In *A Study of British Genius* (1904) Havelock Ellis undertook to reexamine Galton's conclusions from a less arbitrary perspective. His inquiry, he tells us at the very outset, is solidly based on the recently completed *Dictionary of National Biography* (begun in 1885). Of the thirty thousand persons listed therein, Ellis omitted from his investigation all hereditary notables, all women whose accomplishments were not chiefly intellectual, and almost everyone who had not rated at least three pages in the *Dictionary.* Using these criteria, Ellis came up with nine hundred seventy-five British men of genius and fifty-five British women of genius, "being in proportion to the men about 1 to 18." The information about these people already given in the *DNB* he supplemented by reading additional biographies and by visits to portrait galleries, particularly the National Portrait Gallery.[16]

On the basis of these data we are given to understand, among other fascinating tidbits, that men of genius tend to be either tall or short, but not of medium height, and that aristocrats of genius are more often fair, lower-class geniuses more often dark, a distinction also true for active and contemplative men of genius. When he comes to examining the matter of the relative geographical distribution of genius, and with England as the standard, Ellis finds that Scotland has far more than her share, Wales rather less, and Ireland far, far less.

Galton's most important and authentic disciple, however, was not Ellis but Karl Pearson (no relation to C. H. Pearson), who, aside from editing Galton's work and writing his life, eventually became the first Galton Professor of Eugenics at University College, London. Pearson was one of the most influential scientific popularizers of his generation. Like Galton and Ellis before him, his great aim was to make social anthropology an exact and empirically verifiable science. That he did not succeed any more than his illustrious predecessors is a good deal more obvious today, however, than it was to his contemporaries.

In *National Life from the Standpoint of Science* (1901), Pearson puts forward the racial doctrines of his time under the most scientific guise they had ever received. But in essence those doctrines remained unchanged. His view of the African black, for instance, is virtually identical with Galton's or Ellis's. "What I have said about bad stock (in Europe)," he writes, "seems to me to hold for the lower races of man. How many centuries, how many thousands of years, have the Kaffir or the negro held large districts in Africa undisturbed by the white man? Yet their intertribal struggles have not yet produced a civilisation in the least comparable with the Aryan. Educate and nurture them as you will, I do not believe that you will succeed in modifying the stock." Improving on Ellis's example, Pearson is also prepared to adopt the "new spirit" toward these supposedly lower races, but for him the white man's expansion will no longer be masked by Bibles and blankets. Rather than "settle down and live alongside the inferior race," Pearson would prefer to have white men either not emigrate at all or else "go and completely drive out the inferior race." While this is not yet quite a scientific rationale for genocide, it comes remarkably close. After all, in the Darwinian/Spencerian theory of evolution the extermination of one species by another is justified as the "survival of the fittest." And Pearson is nothing if not a good social Darwinian: "This dependence of progress on the survival of the fitter race, terribly bleak as it may seem to some of you, gives the struggle for existence its redeeming features; it is the fiery crucible out of which comes the finer metal." The same social Darwinian principles that apply to the colonies should also be accepted at home. In this way the national character could be established and improved—scientifically. "You will see that my view—and I think it may be called the scientific view of a nation—," Pearson asserts confidently, "is that of an organized whole, kept up to a point of internal efficiency by contest, chiefly by way of war with inferior races, and with equal races by the struggle for trade-routes and for the sources of raw material and of food supply."[17]

A later generation of Englishmen was to grow more familiar with this brand of social Darwinism in the writings and speeches of Adolf Hitler and Alfred Rosenberg, but by then most of them had forgotten the partly native English origins of such views. An even later generation—ours—was virtually to forget that such doctrines had ever been widely accepted in Britain or had even received a serious hearing by respectable people. But it is only when we realize how such ideas dominated the English intellectual landscape during the last years of the nineteenth century and the opening decades of ours that it becomes understandable how and why the British could have felt justified in their initial admiration for and subsequent condemnation of the German "race."

For it is essential to grasp that in their changing view of the qualities that distinguished the Germans from themselves, the English were defining, though only to a small degree consciously, the changing conception of their own national identity. Looking at the literary reflection of Germans, the English were peering, with increasing fascination, horror and contempt, at an image that seemed to teach them what not to be. This image, initially that of a "racially" related country cousin, harmless though clumsy, deteriorated progressively until, at the outset of the Great War, it revealed unmistakably the utterly alien features of the Hun. In the end, the image would be entirely emptied of the self and become the very embodiment of the Other.

1

The Death of the German Cousin

England and the south-east of Scotland constitute the oldest, the most successful, and the most complete of German colonies beyond the limits of Germany.

Sir Harry Johnston, Common Sense in Foreign Policy *(1913)*

Friends now, friends forever.

Toast at the "great festivities at Kiel, where the German and English fleets lay side by side, with the Kaiser in the midst of them." June 27, 1914.

George Dangerfield, The Strange Death of Liberal England *(1935)*

From the distance of three-quarters of a century it is no longer easy to grasp the complex of explosive emotions that brought civilized Europe into the Great War. Though the intervening years have not always been appreciably less brutal or bloody than 1914–18, never again (outside of Germany and the Soviet Union at any rate) has the modern European mind succumbed so completely, so uncritically, and so fanatically to an illusion. Never again was there anything like the great rush of patriotic feeling of the August days immediately preceding and following Great Britain's entry into the War; never again was there such intense public self-indulgence in national pride and hatred. By comparison World War II was for the average Briton a necessary but unpleasant business to be concluded as quickly as possible. But the Great War, when it began, was England's last and greatest crusade.

The chief reason that it was a holy war and, for that matter, the last "great" war, is that most of the people who supported (and to a lesser degree those who fought in it) still believed in the truth of great and holy wars. Now only infernal wars remain; perhaps literally and certainly literarily, war has turned into "hell." What made it so is summed up, I think most persuasively in George Steiner's argument that after 1915 the modern mind was so terribly numbed by the immensity of slaughter and atrocity that its delicate moral scales collapsed under the weight of horror.[1] Thereafter there could be little in human behavior that could truly outrage public opinion; and after the Nazi and Soviet death camps of the ensuing war, there was nothing at all. Solzhenitsyn's graphic accounts of over a hundred million killed by Lenin and his heirs have burned no holes on intellectuals' bookshelves. For whatever reason he may have written them, in the contemporary West they are understood as epitaphs, not as calls to action.

For the pre-1914 mind in Britain, however, the great abstract moral truths were still valid and could be uttered and printed unabashedly in upper case letters. God might be dead and Nature dying, but Britain and the gentlemanly values still stood. And for the British mind then, the great threat to those values came from Germany, a supposedly ruthless power bent on world domination as an end in itself, trusting to blood and iron alone. Germany haunted the British imagination of the period like an evil spirit, and in a narrow sense the Holiness of the Great War is explicable only in terms of a bitter struggle to exorcise German Satan.

German Satan, however, had once, like his prototype, been German Lucifer, one of the greatest powers ranged on the side of good and intimately—even "racially"—allied to the chief of the unfallen Archangels. As the holy war-fever mounted in the years immediately preceding the war, and of course during the war itself, Satan came to be identified specifically with the person of the German Emperor, but the identification was never wholly limited to the royal house. The "bad" German was, as he to a considerable degree still is thought to be, inherently evil, though he had once been the "good" German.

By one of those curious coincidences of history which almost appear to suggest the handiwork of a maliciously ironic humorist, England received its first German king exactly two hundred years before the outbreak of the war. However, Germany only began to impinge on the English consciousness in the mid-eighteenth century, when England supported Protestant Prussia in its protracted and eventually successful war against a coalition of Catholic powers and Russia. Then, as the century progressed and the fad for Gothic architecture and especially Gothic romance gained strength, translations of Bürger's famous ballad "Lenore" and Kotzebue's plays were placed beneath the simple altar of Frederick the Great. By the time the century was drawing to a close, Germany's reputation for poetry and philosophy was already sufficiently strong to attract men like Wordsworth and Coleridge to spend brief periods in that country trying to learn the language. But the venture proved to have little success, as we can see from the account of the two Lake poets sitting mutely across the table from the equally mute German poet Klopstock: a situation that John Mander, perhaps rightly, sees as archetypal for the relationship between England and Germany.[2]

The growing awareness of Germany reached its first peak with the juncture of the English armies under Wellington and the Prussians under Blücher at Waterloo to crush Napoleon's last bid for world supremacy.[3] When the universal bogeyman was done for and the old balance of power on the Continent reestablished, England could turn its attention to India and parts east without having to fear a serious rival in Europe. At roughly the same time, helped by Carlyle's prolific Germanophilia and the awakening interest in linguistic and racial researches, the English began to rediscover their own origins somewhere in the bogs of Schleswig-Holstein. The Germans who, with the exception of Prussia, seemed a harmless, industrious, pacific people, much given to lyric poetry, music, science, abstruse philosophy, and beer, were gradually transformed into "our German cousins." When in 1837 an eighteen-year-old girl assumed the throne, a girl who had been conceived in Germany, who spoke German at least as well as she did English, and was later to marry a German Prince, the newly rediscovered relationship seemed to be symbolically confirmed.

How deeply this sense of racial kinship infused some Englishmen, frequently highly intelligent and influential ones, emerges strikingly from an entry in Thomas Arnold's diary, written while he was touring in Germany in 1828 just prior to assuming the headmastership of Rugby: "Before us lay the land of our Saxon and Teutonic forefathers, the land uncorrupted by Roman or any other mixture, the birthplace of the most moral races of men that the world has yet seen, of the soundest laws, the least violent passions, and the fairest domestic and civil virtues. I thought of that memorable defeat of Varus and his three legions, which forever confined the Romans to the Western side of the Rhine, and preserved the Teutonic nation—the regenerating element in modern Europe—safe and free."[4] Some forty years later, in a course of lectures on *The Roman and the Teuton* (1864), Charles Kingsley expressed a similar idea—but with England rather than Germany in the foreground—in words that almost seem to echo Arnold's: "And if our English law, our English ideas of justice and mercy, have retained, more than most European codes, the freedom, the truthfulness, the kindliness, of the old Teutonic laws, we owe it to the fact, that England escaped, more than any other land, the taint of effete Roman civilization." Elsewhere in these lectures Kingsley speaks grandly of "our worthy West Goth cousins" and expresses the hope that his auditors will "hold (with me) that the welfare of the Teutonic race is the welfare of the world. . . ." In another course of lectures, addressed to an Oxford audience some twenty years later, Edward Freeman places the beginning of English history in Germany at the time of Caesar: "And now our history begins, the history of the Teutonic race in its three great homes, in the European mainland, in the great island of the Ocean, in the vaster mainland beyond the Ocean. I need tell no one here that in Caesar's day, in days ages after Caesar, the history of ourselves, as distinguished from the history of our future home, is to be sought for, not by the Thames and the Severn, but by the Rhine and the Weser. We have not very long to wait before one line of Tacitus will reveal the existence of the Angle, before one line of Ptolemy will reveal the existence of the Saxon. But as yet we stand undistinguished among the mass of our brethren. Whatever is theirs is ours also. We have our part in the great deliverance by the wood of Teutoburg; Arminius, 'liberator Germaniae,' is but the first of a roll which goes on to Hampden and to Washington."[5]

The effect of this kind of dogma on generations of impressionable schoolboys was incalculable. By the end of the century, Joseph Chamberlain could proclaim as almost self-evident the "truth" that "the main character of the Teutonic race differs very slightly from the character of the Anglo-Saxon." A few months after the outbreak of the war, Cecil Chesterton was to summarize this process of teutonizing England from a somewhat different perspective. The English, he writes in a book portentously entitled *The Prussian Hath Said in His Heart* (1914), the English had over the years "contrived a method by which in flattering the Germans we could also flatter ourselves. The Germans were 'our cousins'; they were fellow 'Teutons.' If, therefore, they were such fine fellows, there was a presumption that we were fine fellows too."[6]

But the comparison did not, in spite of Chesterton, always tend to support the idea that Englishmen were really such "fine fellows." Indeed, after the brief Franco-Prussian war—in which the English had by and large been on the side of the Prussians, happy enough to see the bellicose Napoleon III humiliated[7]—and after this dramatically abrupt conflict had revealed Prussia to be a far more formidable and awesomely efficient enemy than anyone (including the Prussians themselves) had imagined, the English began to suspect that their German brethren might soon be putting in claims for a share of the family inheritance elsewhere. This possibility loomed even more ominously when the more or less independent German states joined with Prussia to form the German Empire in 1871. In subsequent years, though Germany and the Germanic ancestry of the English continued to be popular subjects, and though it was even good form among the middle and upper classes to don mourning dress when the Emperor Frederick III died in 1888, nonetheless relations with the Germans were never again quite so jolly as they had been in the days before Kaiserdom. Henceforth, Germany was to be viewed as a potential enemy. George Bernard Shaw, looking back later amid the fury of a long-expected war, considered himself "old enough to remember the beginning of the anti-German phase of that very ancient propaganda in England," that is, in 1870 after the great Prussian victory at Sedan. And Benjamin Disraeli was very quick to perceive the consequences of 1870 for British foreign policy. "This war," he observed in February 1871, "represents the German Revolution, a greater political event than the French

Revolution of the last century. . . . Not a single principle in the management of our foreign affairs any longer exists." The next thirty years were to bear witness to the truth of Disraeli's insight, until Britain had again found security in a mutual understanding with France and Russia.[8]

Almost the first literary symptom of British uneasiness was an odd and now nearly forgotten novelette by G. T. Chesney called *The Battle of Dorking* (1871)—at one time thought to have been written by Disraeli himself. In this work Chesney envisioned a successful invasion of England by an efficiently organized German expeditionary force.[9] The lesson to be drawn from this work, and from the long line of successors it spawned, was that England was being lulled into a slumber of security from which it would be rudely awakened, too late to resist the ruthless machine of German military planning. Ironically, this fear of a German conquest of Britain often most intensely haunted those people who were otherwise utterly taken in by Germany's allegedly considerable virtues. For instance, Stanley Unwin recalled that when he was a pupil at the New School, Abbotsholme, the headmaster, Dr. Cecil Reddie, who was a firm believer in the "superior intellectual and social order" of Germany, once became so enraged at his students' incompetence that he broke his pointing stick across a table and remarked that "if we did not learn to think and to take more pains we should end by blacking the boots of the Germans."[10]

As if the prospect of a great invading German army, supported by a powerful German navy, were not enough to throw terror into the minds of the British reading public, H. G. Wells raised the specter of an aerial attack by a massive fleet of Zeppelins. Though the hair-raising story he told in *The War in the Air* (1908) pits Germany and the United States against each other as the primary antagonists, England does eventually get involved. Ironically, in view of later events, Wells describes this as occurring when Britain and France and Italy had declared war upon Germany and "outraged Swiss neutrality." However, the European and American conflicts, ruthless and destructive as they are—New York, London, Paris, and Berlin are quickly reduced to ashes—are soon dwarfed by the entry of the Oriental Empires, China and Japan, whose "secrecy and swiftness and inventions had far surpassed those of the Germans, and where the Germans had had a hundred men at work the Asiatics had ten thousand." In a single overwhelming air battle, staged, with an instinct rivaling Hollywood's, above Niagara Falls, the Far Eastern Powers utterly annihilate the German Zeppelins. The world has mercifully been made safe from the German menace, but only at the price of an even more frightful Yellow Peril.[11]

Less dramatic (and as a forecast of what would take place in the First World War much less fantastic) was another scarifying tale of imminent British disaster, "Danger," Arthur Conan Doyle's most powerful expression of his recurrent nightmare of what might happen to England if no cross-Channel tunnel were built linking Great Britain with France. This story purports to be the first-person account of Captain John Sirius, commander of a fleet of eight submarines belonging to a small, mythical European nation, Norland (presumably Norway). When war breaks out between Great Britain and his country, rather than yield to British demands, as his King and Admiral reluctantly agree they must do, Sirius advocates a bold strategy of submarine warfare. And that is precisely what he proceeds to put into practice. Placing his submarines at strategic positions around the British Isles, Sirius torpedoes every large vessel attempting to reach port. In a few weeks, facing imminent starvation, a humiliated British Empire is forced to surrender. The lesson here is clear: if tiny Norland can bring Britain to its knees, what would not mighty Germany do?[12]

Erskine Childers, who was later to die fighting the British in the cause of Irish independence, depicted in *The Riddle of the Sands* (1903) how the Germans were busily establishing a secret naval base in the North Sea, from which to launch an attack on Britain. A whole generation of schoolboys grew up under the influence of this remarkable novel, one of the few from the invasion boom that still remains readable. For these boys Childers's vision of a lonely Englishman pitting his natively English skills of sailing and sleuthing against the collective efficiency of the German military machine was to prove inspiring. It also inspired that grown-up schoolboy John Buchan, who drew on Childers for both his amateur adventurer and spy Richard Hannay, and for the German scenes in *Greenmantle* (1916). Schoolboys, and their parents for that matter, could also have their worst invasion fears confirmed in the Sexton Blake stories and novels, where another Hannay-like hero was uncovering, as a later critic observes, "with almost monotonous frequency . . . plans of the German High Command to invade Britain by sailing up the Thames, or by arriving 'the unexpected way,' from the north; or to bring Britain to her senses, and her knees, by first overrunning the Continent."[13]

Before and during the early stages of the war, the so-called boys' magazines and papers such as *Gem* and *Magnet*, had a wide readership, including such remarkable boys as George Orwell. As late as October 1914, *Magnet* was still fanning invasion flames with a story in which Germans living in Britain ("the thousands of time-expired foreign soldiers who have lived amongst us") attempt to join a German invading force to capture London and, as one of their leaders tells them, "strike such terror into the hearts of the millions of this teeming town by killing all you meet, military or civilians, that they will not dare to offer the slightest resistance." By the time this story appeared, all such "time-expired" soldiers and their wives and children were either already under arrest or else under close police observation. Still, Arnold Bennett, who lived on the exposed seacoast south of London, was alarmed in January 1915 by rumors that some thirty-thousand Germans were about to land nearby.[14]

It seems clear now that the prewar invasion stories were largely a spontaneous response to increasing German naval power and the heightened awareness of British vulnerability brought about by the Boer war. To some appreciable degree, however, the natural apprehensions of ordinary English people to keep bloody foreigners out were transformed into an unnatural hysteria—paranoia may not be too strong a word—by the yellow press. Northcliffe was the chief culprit. "In March 1906 [Northcliffe's] the *Daily Mail* declared war on Germany," writes I. E. Clarke in *Voices Prophesying War* (1966), "in a serial story which proved to be the most sensational of all the pre-1914 imaginary wars. It was written by Queen Alexandra's favourite novelist, William Le Queux; and his account of the German descent on Britain, *The Invasion of 1910*, aroused such intense interest throughout the world that it was translated into twenty-seven languages." The ostensible author of this story was Le Queux, but much of the background had been provided by Lord Roberts and the story had been conceived by Northcliffe himself. The publicity was also of Northcliffe's devising: men dressed in German uniforms and spiked helmets carrying sandwich boards with maps of the districts the Germans were planning to invade the following day.[15]

Northcliffe followed up this success by persuading the "jingo socialist," Robert Blatchford, to write a series of sensationalist articles on the German danger. These appeared in the *Daily Mail* in 1909 and 1910 and were later published in book form. In the first installment, dated December 13, 1909, and ominously entitled "The Menace," Blatchford set the tone by announcing that "Germany is deliberately preparing to destroy the British Empire." He issued a call for a strong leader—a Lord Roberts or a Kitchener—to assume direction of the British defense effort and to create an army of over a million men together with a more powerful navy. According to Blatchford's biographer, Laurence Thompson, " he did not hate the Germans. He was a Determinist, incapable of hate. He only thought that such unclean creatures should be wiped off the face of the earth." Similar determinist sentiments seem to have motivated Northcliffe, who kept up his campaign of invasion hysteria in publications for younger readers, such as the *Boys' Friend, Boys' Herald,* and *Marvel.*[16]

The literary culmination of the prewar invasion hysteria is undoubtedly Saki's *When William Came* (1913), a graphic description of England under German occupation, and a grim warning of what would happen if to a Norman William were added a Prussian Wilhelm the Conqueror. In this novel Saki makes England drink to the dregs the cup of national humiliation. Not only has Germany, before the novel even begins, completely routed the brave but unprepared defenders of the realm, but the Germans proceed to kill the British with kindness. Rather than force the defeated population to work for the conqueror, or to serve in his armies, the Kaiser's colonial administrators shrewdly ease them of the burden (and the honor) of bearing arms. Their object, clearly, is to reduce the British to a slothful, careless people that will inevitably give way to more vigorous German colonists. Hard as all this is, it is still not the worst. The intensest anguish is caused by watching "the grey cold sea outside Dover and Portsmouth and Cork, where the great grey ships of war rocked and swung with the tides, where the sailors sang, in doggerel English, that bitter-sounding adaption, 'Germania rules t'e waves,' where the flag of a World-Power floated for the world to see."

Already one of the characters, who had been away in Russia during the invasion, had noticed the difference in his treatment, the slight note of pity and contempt creeping into his hosts' voices for a man who was no longer the subject of a "World-Power." What to do in such a situation? What to do when one has been "bred and reared as a unit of a ruling race?"[17] The answer, according to Saki, is to pin one's hopes on the young. For such seems to be the import of the final scene of the novel, where the Kaiser, his generals and his retinue are drawn up at attention in a Trafalgar Square festooned with Imperial German banners, waiting to review the march-past of the Boy Scouts of Britain. In vain, for nothing happens; the Kaiser and his court are left standing, shuffling their feet in the hot sun and in silent shame. Faces, in consequence, grow red, and England, it is clear, may yet hope.

Not that this was the only answer. The game of prestige could be played for higher stakes—in real life. Witness Lord Rosebery's recruiting speeches given in Stirling shortly after the outbreak of the war. Speculating on the consequences of a British defeat, Rosebery begins by dismissing as utterly incredible the notion of Britain's sinking to the status of a mere province. "But," he goes on to say, "there is another very improbable danger which might happen, which would happen if we were defeated. It is that we would be reduced at once to an inferior Power, living at the goodwill of our superior lord, our Empire cut up and divided among the plunderers—a position so abject that we cannot realise it now." Rather than face so horrible a fate, rather than be known publicly as a mere third-rate Power, Lord Rosebery goes on to vow that "I for one would, from my heart and soul, rather that all our people as they now exist were to pass into exile or into death, and leave this island vacant for some superior race. (Cheers)." Clearly, in order to keep up with the von Schmidts, the Lord Roseberies were willing to stake everything they—or their fellow Englishmen—possessed.[18]

By 1908 the German invasion scare had reached such a pitch that even King Edward VII was worrying about his uncle the Kaiser's sending "a *corps d'armée* or two into England." In the same year Parliament concluded its hearings on a possible invasion and during that summer "national anxieties came close to panic when the Navy began extensive manoeuvres in the Channel and the North Sea with the evident intention of practicing methods for dealing with an attempt at invasion." A year later, in reaction against the latest German naval program for building additional dreadnoughts, the Government revised its own estimates upward, amid a Parliamentary debate that raised the specter of German naval supremacy and was "tantamount to a formal charge of trickery and lying by the British against the German Government."[19]

Despite its dramatic maneuvers, the Navy itself remained relatively unconcerned. Sir John Fisher ridiculed British fears of a German invasion in his famous speech of November 11, 1907 ("Sleep quiet in your beds . . ."); and Winston Churchill wrote a letter to his Dundee constituents in 1908, asserting that these fears were "a false, lying panic started in the party interests of the Conservatives." It may be that the feeling of relaxed confidence among Navy people was due to the Navy investigation of 1903—undertaken in response to the furor raised by Childers' novel—as to whether a German invasion was at all possible. The official conclusion of that investigation had been that English defenses were strong enough to withstand a German surprise attack even "at a time when we were at war with France and Russia."[20]

The real invasion hotheads were in the Army. Their spokesman was Lord Roberts who, inspired by Milner, founded the National Service League in 1905, an organization that hoped to expand the size of the British Army and improve its quality in order to meet the German threat. Roberts, the grand hero of the Indian and South African campaigns, gave respectability and credibility to what might otherwise have seemed merely irresponsible speculations of novelists and journalists. The House of Lords—and the nation—listened attentively when, in November 1908, he informed them that there were eighty-thousand Germans in Britain, "almost all of them trained soldiers. They work many of the hotels at some of the chief railway stations, and if a German force once got into this country it would have the advantage of help and reinforcement such as no other army on foreign soil has ever before enjoyed." According to Roberts and the rest of the so-called Bolt-from-the-Blue school, the Germans were planning to surprise British defenses by secretly landing a large armed force, just as Childers had warned a few years earlier. Roberts, to whom the Kaiser had personally presented the "Order of the Black Eagle," seemed, like Sexton Blake, to have access to the most confidential secrets of the German High Command.[21]

Not that it was particularly difficult to find out what would happen in the coming war. In the pages of Leo Maxse's anti-German *National Review*, Lord Percy published in 1911 an essay that outlines with breathtaking accuracy the opening movements of the war that was to take place three years later. "Of no war since the world began," he writes confidently and correctly, "has it been possible to predict with such absolute certainty what the strategical situation will be at the outset." Percy discusses in detail the plans of the German General Staff (Schlieffen, Bernhardi, and Falkenhausen) for attacking France via Belgium; he touches on the dangers to Germany of provoking British intervention by violating Belgian neutrality; and he evaluates (unfavorably) the preparedness of the British Expeditionary Force of some seven divisions to help France and Belgium repel the German attack. His conclusion is that "the day is approaching when the weary babble of politicans and humanitarians shall be drowned in the thunder of the guns."[22]

Invasion or no, it was clear that Germany had turned into an enemy. Official British foreign policy not only reflected this view but actively fostered it. Bertrand Russell, who met Sir Edward Grey for the first time in 1902, four years before the latter became Foreign Secretary, already noted his anti-German bias. In 1912 G. H. Perris, examining British policy toward Germany in *Our Foreign Policy and Sir Edward Grey's Failure*, concluded that British diplomacy was "permeated with an obstinate Teutophobia." The same year saw the formation of a Liberal Foreign Affairs Group with the express aim of improving Anglo-German relations and counteracting the Germanophobia of the Foreign Office. At the same time the Labour Party adopted a resolution condemning Grey's anti-German policy.[23]

The Government's basic policy was to isolate and "encircle" Germany with the help of Russia and France. This policy was forcefully promoted and officially formulated in a secret "Memorandum on the Present State of British Relations with France and Germany," written by a prominent Foreign Office specialist on German affairs, Sir Eyre Crowe. Crowe was half-German, was married to a German, and had been partly raised and educated in Germany. He became a tireless and vociferous opponent of Germany, a kind of Cato of the Foreign Office. His "brilliant and remorselessly penetrating brain," to quote L. S. Amery on Crowe, influenced Grey's rather more sluggish and less penetrating but equally stubborn brain to see in Germany an enemy lacking any regard for "the elementary rules of straightforward and honourable dealing." Ironically, as Paul Kennedy notes, Crowe's memorandum had been originally requested by Edward VII who "had repeatedly expressed himself perturbed by what he thought was our persistent unfriendly attitude towards Germany with our own eagerness to run after France and do anything the French asked." A further irony was that after the outbreak of the war he had foreseen—and perhaps helped not a little to bring about—Crowe himself became a victim of his colleagues' Germanophobia and was transferred out of the War Department.[24]

Though opposed by isolated intellectuals like Russell or marginal political movements like the Labour Party, the Foreign Office's attitude toward Germany was in perfect agreement with the rest of the nation. This is evident especially from those breeding grounds of opinion, the public schools.

Robert Graves, who in 1914 was to leave his school, Charterhouse, directly for the Royal Welch Fusiliers and the trenches, recalls that during the annual Officers' Training Corps summer camp in 1913, "General, later Field-Marshal Sir William Robertson, who had a son at the school, visited the camp and impressed on us that war with Germany must break out within two or three years, and that we must be prepared to take our part in it as leaders of the new forces which would assuredly be called into being." At an even earlier date, during his second term at school, the sons of businessmen would habitually "discuss hotly the threat, and even the necessity, of a trade war with the Reich. 'German' meant 'dirty German.'" Graves was peculiarly sensitive to this kind of talk, because he was himself half German. When this fact became known through having his name appear as R. Von R[anke] Graves on the school list, he insisted indignantly that he was Irish. Unfortunately, this claim was resented by an older and genuinely Irish boy who went out of his way to persecute Graves. This was topped off by his being subjected to a dose of the anti-Semitic feeling prevalent in his house, since "someone started the legend that I was not only German, but a German Jew." Small wonder that Graves was to confess later that all his life, from the time he went to Charterhouse until close to the end of the war, was a "forced rejection of the German in me."[25] A few months into the war, when Graves got to the Front, he was by chance assigned to a company mess in which four out of the five officers had either German mothers or naturalized German fathers. They were all aware that if they had not joined up when they did, things might have gone badly for them.

That Graves's experience was not isolated is confirmed by Stephen Spender, who along with his brother attended the University College School toward the end of the war. In a brief autobiographical account of his experiences there, entitled "Day Boy," Spender tells how the other pupils discovered that his mother's name was Schuster. "After that," he says, "they always called, and treated us, as Huns." And, in *In My Own Time* (1969), one of the volumes of his autobiography, John Lehmann remembers how during the war years he was terribly ashamed of his German ancestry. Nor is this surprising in the context of Horatio Bottomley's publication, during the first months of the war, in his mass-circulation *John Bull*, of weekly lists of "Germans who were treacherously changing their names from Knopp to Knox, from Baumann to Beaumont," maintaining firmly that "you cannot naturalize an unnatural beast—a human abortion—a hellish fiend. But you can exterminate it." Since the King of England himself was the grandson of a German and was destined soon also to change his name, one wonders what his feelings were on reading this item of news. And Bottomley himself undertook some major German name-changing himself; henceforth Germans would no longer be known as Germans, but as Germhuns.[26]

In the mind of the average Englishman, the German had come a long way.

From the amiable and rather coarse country cousin who was good at music and chemistry and liked his beer a little too well, he was about to be transformed into the barbarous Hun, a creature that would stop at absolutely nothing to gain its brutish ends. But before this national Dr. Jekyll is to be unmasked irrevocably as Mr. Hyde, it is worth pausing a moment to look at the case of a young Englishman who spent the six months preceding the outbreak of the war in Germany. More movingly than any other document of the period, the letters of Charles Hamilton Sorley evoke the curious love-hate relationship that existed between the English and the Germans in the early years of this century. Though conditioned like nearly all boys of his age and class to believe that Germans were superhuman in point of efficiency and subhuman in indelicacy of feeling, this young and gifted poet gradually came to realize that there were lazy and shiftless Germans as well as precise ones. One of his letters home recounts how the notoriously humorless Germans managed to poke fun at his supposed indifference to food. When he remarked one day at lunch that it was all the same to him what food he ate, so long as there was enough of it, he discovered his plate that evening heaped with quantities of bread and butter. Meanwhile, the others helped themselves to a number of tasty-looking dishes, which they did not seem inclined to share. It was not long before Sorley retracted his earlier remarks and helped himself to the good things on the table.

Going out for walks and hikes in the countryside around Schwerin in Mecklenburg, where he stayed for the first few months, Sorley thought the scenery flat and dull. But even this dullness began eventually to seem interesting, and one day, hearing a company of singing soldiers march past him on a lonely country road, he was filled with emotion—of all unavowable things, with patriotic emotion for Germany. (It must be to this passage, among others, that Sorley's father refers apologetically in his preface to the *Letters* of his son.) In fact, when Sorley started playing field hockey with the townspeople on Sunday mornings, among them two or three army officers, he discovered that they were human. "Now isn't that delightful?" he writes home after this experience, "Catch a beastly English officer making a public donkey of himself! I think it is the utter absence of self-consciousness that makes the Germans so much nicer than the English."[27] Talking with the local people, he came to recognize that the Germans felt they were being bullied by the warlike British and firmly convinced that "Edward VII spent his life in attempting to bring about a German war."

When Sorley left Schwerin for the more sophisticated University environment of Jena, he was disturbed by the rowdiness of the students there and by their overt, apparently homosexual expressions of affection. But he consoled himself with frequent visits to the theater in nearby Weimar, and even came to be reconciled to the massive Schiller and Goethe monument guarding its entrance. Late July and early August 1914 found him, in the company of an old schoolfriend, touring the Moselle valley, stopping every now and then to sample the vintage. The tide of history overwhelmed them in the guise of a German Shallow, a village constable who first proceeded to jail them and then release them under the impression that England and Germany were about to join in brotherly union to crush their arch-enemy, France.

Though he was no Shallow, a similar idea crossed the mind of F. H. Keeling who—by an almost Hardyesque little irony—had been wandering through the same German valley only days before Sorley. "I can't help thinking," he wrote in a letter on 30 July 1914, shortly after a hurried return to England, "we and the Germans will settle it somehow. I can't believe in the Russians and French politically or strategically." Here Keeling still thought of the "settlement" in primarily diplomatic rather than military terms, but even as late as August 2 he acknowledged feeling "a sort of secondary patriotism for Germany, and it seems to me madness that we should be fighting on the side of the Russian barbarians and the French, who have caused most of the wars of the last three centuries." When the "unbelievable" war actually broke out on 4 August, Keeling was ready to fight for his country, but he nevertheless respected "the confidence—magnificent confidence—of Germany daring the whole ring of nations all around her."[28] In his suspicion that England was joining in the wrong war against the wrong enemy and with the wrong allies, Keeling (and, to a lesser degree, Sorley) was echoing privately what was being proclaimed publicly in the pages of the *Manchester Guardian* and the *Daily News*, both organs of the Liberal Party. The story of how the Liberal Party—with its strong Little England orientation and traditional antipathy toward foreign embroilments—was drawn into war against Germany by its own Liberal Prime Minister and Foreign Minister, a war that was to lead (as A. G. Gardiner, the editor of the *Daily News*, foresaw) to the eventual destruction of the Liberal Party itself, has been told in great detail in Irene Cooper Willis's *England's Holy War* (1928) and elsewhere.[29] It is a story that might well be subtitled "The Death of the German Cousin," for it represents very nearly the last instance in English history and English letters when Germany and German culture were conceived of in positive terms by an important body of English public opinion. On 3 August 1914 *The Manchester Guardian* stated editorially in unmistakable tones: "Let us be quite clear about this. If we are jockeyed into fighting it will be for a cause supremely disreputable." And in the same issue, in the manifesto of the neutralist Provisional Committee signed, among others, by the editor of the *Guardian*, C. P. Scott, the war is seen only as serving to make Russia supreme in Europe. "Germany, on the other hand," the Manifesto goes on to say, "is a nation of sixty-five million, wedged in between hostile states, highly civilized, with a culture that has contributed enormously in the past to Western civilisation, racially allied to ourselves and with moral ideals largely resembling our own, possessing a commercial and industrial life that is dependent on an orderly and stable Europe. Our two peoples have maintained unbroken peace since their earliest history."

On the day when the Government issued its ultimatum to Germany, the lead editorial in the *Manchester Guardian* contained the following words: "If and when England joins in the war it will be too late to discuss its policy. Meanwhile we hold it to be a patriotic duty for all good citizens to oppose to the utmost the participation of this country in the greatest crime of our time." Sorley and Keeling, it is clear, were not alone in thinking and feeling as they did; but like the noninterventionist segment of the Liberal Party, they were politically powerless.

Once Sorley and Keeling reached England, both immediately enlisted. They lacked the enthusiasm of most of their contemporaries, thinking it outrageous that English philistines should call the Germans "Huns," and regarding all talk of a just war as mere self-deception. Though prepared to fight for England as having the better cause, Sorley considered the war "as one between sisters, between Martha and Mary, the efficient and intolerant against the casual and sympathetic. Each side has a virtue for which it is fighting, and each that virtue's supplementary vice." After the war, he hoped, it might be possible to purge those two virtues of their vices, and reach a real understanding between the warring nations. This is also the idea that underlies what is probably his best-known poem, the sonnet "To Germany":

> You are blind like us. Your hurt no man designed,
> And no man claimed the conquest of your land.
> But gropers both through fields of thought confined
> We stumble and we do not understand.
> You only saw your future highly planned,
> And we, the tapering paths of our own mind,
> And in each other's dearest ways we stand,
> And hiss and hate. And the blind fight the blind.
>
> When it is peace, then we may view again
> With new-won eyes each others' truer form
> And wonder. Grown more loving-kind and warm
> We'll grasp firm hands and laugh at the old pain,
> When it is peace. But until peace, the storm,
> The darkness and the thunder and rain.[30]

Sorley did not live long enough to be disillusioned. In the closing months of 1915, Charles Hamilton Sorley sent home the last of his wry, perceptive letters from the front. And less than a year later, Keeling wrote the last of his.

The most fitting epitaph, perhaps, for these two proponents of Anglo-

German amity and victims of Anglo-German enmity, is Thomas Hardy's "The Pity of It," written in April 1915:

> I walked in loamy Wessex lands, afar
> From rail-track and from highway, and I heard
> In field and farmstead many an ancient word
> Of local lineage like "Thu bist," "Er war,"
> "Ich woll," "Er sholl," and by-talk similar,
> Nigh as they speak who in this month's moon gird
> At England's very loins, thereunto spurred
> By gangs whose glory threats and slaughters are.
>
> Then seemed a Heart crying: "Whosoever they be
> At root and bottom of this, who flung this flame
> Between kin folk tongued even as are we,"
> Sinister, ugly, lurid, be their fame;
> May their familiars grow to shun their name,
> And their breed perish everlastingly.[31]

One of the immediate and most embarrassing psychological consequences of the war with Germany was what to do with the burdensome "cousinhood" so frequently cited in the preceding century. One or two practical measures could be undertaken almost at once: the House of Hanover could be quickly remodeled into the House of Windsor; the Kaiser—as much a grandson of Queen Victoria as George V—could be personally repudiated by having his banner of Knight of the Noble Order of the Garter removed from the walls of St. George's Chapel in Windsor;[32] and Prince Louis Alexander von Battenberg could be made to relinquish his office of First Sea-Lord, resign his German titles, and become first Lord Mountbatten. But for the rest it was not so easy. When the whole matter was not simply swept under the rug, an attempt was made to "prove" that the disreputable German connection was merely another delusion, attributable, as J. M. Robertson wrote in *The Germans* (1916), to the fallacious "English tendency to glorify alike Germans and Anglo-Saxons on the score of racial virtues claimed as common to both."[33]

It was fortunate that the Prussians were not part of the family. They were, as G. K. Chesterton pithily described them in *The Crimes of England* (1916), "descended from mongrel Slavonic savages"[34] —a term that, however soothing to angry English hearts, was not likely to please their Russian allies. Moreover, this view still left the English saddled with a great mass of German relations for whose deplorable behavior they could in some sense be held responsible. In this respect, Gilbert's brother Cecil attacked the business in a more straightforward and effective fashion. To begin with, it was obvious to him that in the nineteenth century all history had been "ransacked and distorted to support this view of our relationship"—namely, that the Germans were our "cousins." Most commonly, in Cecil Chesterton's view, this distortion was carried out by exaggerating extravagantly "the most obscure and largely legendary part of our history . . . when, as we conjecture, a certain (probably small) number of North Sea pirates and revolted German mercenaries achieved a measure of political power and perhaps a certain infusion of new blood in the deserted province of Britain." Just what they infused their blood into, if the province was deserted, is not clear. But what is abundantly clear is that Englishmen were sadly deluded "to prefer this dingy and unattractive origin" to the glorious and highly civilized heritage of the Roman Empire.[35] Other authorities on this subject found still more novel ways of disposing of their German cousins. Writing to his friend Henry Newbolt in August 1914, the poet Maurice Hewlett found relief in the latest anthropological researches. The English, he decided, were not really Germanic at all in origin. No, in point of fact they were Iberian or Mediterranean. It was the descendants of this race who chiefly made up the sturdy British Expeditionary Force now bearing the brunt of the Teutonic attack. "Our steady Iberians," Hewlett exclaimed as he thought of their struggle. "Thank God we are hardly Teutons at all. I always guessed as much." Professor Walter Raleigh's investigations into this question led him to nearly identical conclusions, namely, that the notion of a racial kinship between the Germans and the English was based on bad history and doubtful theory. For after all the English were a very mixed race, "with enormous infusions of Celtic and Roman blood." Why, this was practically self-evident, once one had been made aware that "the Roman sculpture gallery at Naples is full of English faces." Moreover, as any German secret agent could have informed the Kaiser—and there was no doubt that England had been infested for many years with German spies and agents—"no English hat fits any German head." How then, we may well ask, could they be cousins?[36]

Amid this curiously heated discussion, few bothered to remember the well-established tradition in British prewar thought on the subject, which foresaw conflict precisely *because* England and Germany shared a common ancestry. For Nottidge Charles MacNamara, in *Origin and Character of the British People* (1900), such a conflict would be tragic because "the unity and integrity of the great Teutonic race, of which the Anglo-Saxons form so important an offshoot, is of paramount importance, for upon this union the progress and the freedom of the human family depend." Unfortunately, however, this unity was gravely threatened by the "special weakness" of the "race": "The pure Teuton is warlike and aggressive, his patriotism turns towards a chief; under his chosen leader he will fight to the death. And so from early Sanskrit times up to the present, history teaches us how constantly Teutonic tribes and nations have destroyed one another." In this instance, however, the source of war was more likely to be Germany than Britain, since the British Teutons had mixed with the aboriginal Iberian and Mongolian population, a fusion that "probably renders the character of Englishmen rather more plastic than if they belonged to a pure race." Homer Lea's *The Day of the Saxon* (1912) is less preoccupied with Teutons and more with the "Saxon Race" (from which he regretfully excludes the United States), but he too foresees a conflict because of the similar goals pursued by these two peoples: "The convergence of the Teutonic and Saxon races to that ultimate point of contact which is war does not belong to those ephemeral causes that now agitate the British mind . . . but is the exemplification of laws which have governed, from the beginning of human association, the rise and decline of nations."[37]

J. A. Cramb, on the other hand, is less concerned in *Germany and England* (1914) with the supposedly inexorable laws of history than he is with visions out of Germanic mythology. For him, because of their mutual Germanic origin, a war between Germany and England would be a heroic war, something almost to be looked forward to. "And if the dire event of a war with Germany—if it *is* a dire event—should ever occur," he writes in the concluding paragraph of his study, "there shall be seen upon this earth of ours a conflict which, beyond all others, will recall that description of the great Greek wars:

> Heroes in battle with heroes,
> And above them the wrathful gods.

And one can imagine the ancient, mighty deity of all the Teutonic kindred, throned above the clouds, looking serenely down upon that conflict, upon his favorite children, the English and the Germans, locked in a death-struggle, smiling upon the heroism of that struggle, the heroism of the children of Odin the War-god!"[38]

For others, the war between cousins was inevitable, and perhaps even desirable, for purely scientific reasons. According to the influential *Saturday Review* it was precisely the close ties between Germany and England which foredoomed them to a struggle to the death. "In racial character, in religious and scientific thought, in sentiments and aptitudes," Peter Chalmers Mitchell noted in "A Biological View of Our Foreign Policy," published by *The Saturday Review* on February 9th, 1896, "the Germans, by their re-semblances with the English, are marked out as our natural rivals. In all parts of the earth, in every pursuit, in commerce, in manufacturing, in exploiting other races, the English and the Germans jostle each other." A clash, it appeared, was inevitable; and not only inevitable, but, as every good social Darwinian could see, desirable too. "Were every German," the detached biologist observed, "to be wiped out tomorrow, there is no English trade, no English pursuit that would not immediately expand. Were every Englishman to be wiped out tomorrow, the Germans would gain in proportion. Here is the first great racial struggle of the future, here are two growing nations pressing against each other, man to man all over the world. One or the other has to go, one or the other will go."[39]

A year later, the editor of *The Saturday Review*, Frank Harris (subsequently to be suspected of pro-German sympathies), in an article "England and Germany" dished up the same arguments in an even spicier form. The two nations, in his view, were "great, irreconcilable, opposing forces," England characterized by a "long history of successful aggression, with her marvellous conviction that in pursuing her own interests she is spreading light among nations dwelling in darkness," whereas Germany, though "bone of the same bone, blood of the same blood," has a "lesser will-force, but, perhaps . . . a keener intelligence." Given the dilemma that both are competing against each other in every corner of the globe, Harris reaches the same conclusion Mitchell did, with the same equanimity, but with less of a biological and more of a commerical emphasis. "If Germany were extinguished tomorrow," Harris confidently predicts, "the day after tomorrow there is not an Englishman in the world who would not be the richer." Moreover, and more important, Harris adds, anticipating Admiral Fisher by nearly a decade, it is in fact at present possible for England to execute this item of business "without tremendous risk and without doubt of the issue." Within "a few days" Germany's fleet would either be at the bottom of the sea or else in tow toward British ports. The German North Sea and Baltic harbors, and the Kiel Canal, "would lie under the guns of England, waiting, until the indemnity were settled." Unfortunately for the British—and for the Germans—when the war he had foreseen so clearly came to pass, matters were not so simple, and Harris's few days turned into long and bitter years.[40]

2

Joseph Conrad's Diabolic and Angelic Germans

> *There was a vast amount of red—good to see at any time,
> because one knows that some real work is done there, a
> deuce lot of blue, a little green, smears of orange, and, on the
> East Coast, a purple patch, to show where the jolly pioneers
> of progress drank the jolly lager beer.*
> *The map of Africa in 1900.*
> *Joseph Conrad, "Heart of Darkness"*
>
> *Hopes of bagging Fritz high.*
> *Joseph Conrad. (8 November 1916, at sea)*

Conrad's direct links with Germany were few and at no period in his life did he show much inclination to make them more numerous. As a boy he had traveled through Saxony on the way to take the waters in Wartenberg, Bohemia; and later, as a young man in his twenties, he made at least two fairly long transits through Germany on his way either to Poland or Bohemia, as well as a brief tour of the upper Danube, Munich, and the lower Rhine. Of his impressions he left virtually no record, except to note that his Austro-Bavarian-Swiss tour of 1873 was "the last year in which I have had a jolly holiday," and to add that on one of the other trips, in a hurry to change trains in Berlin, he forgot the uncompleted manuscript of *Almayer's Folly* in a restaurant, from which "a worthy and intelligent *Kofferträger* rescued it."[1]

This nameless porter is one of two decent Germans to appear anywhere in Conrad's work. For the rest, Conrad's Germans are either mediocrities or else nasty, brutish, and fat. For Conrad, as for most Poles of his generation, Germany was a feared and hated enemy, second only to Russia in its malignant hunger to feed on the dismembered and defenseless body of Poland. Though tsarist Russia was unquestionably the chief antagonist, Germany was the more insidious because the more intelligent and apparently civilized enemy. As early as 1905, Conrad made public his view in an essay entitled "Autocracy and the War" (the reference, of course, is to the

Russo-Japanese War) that "Germany has been the evil counsellor of Russia on all the questions of her Polish problem."[2] What Germany proposed, it seems, Russia disposed.

Even later, in the heat of a war that threatened to engulf and Germanize the Franco-British culture that above all else he held dear—and that caught Conrad and his immediate family vacationing in Austrian Poland and nearly extended their visit forcibly for the duration of the war—Conrad gave vent to a hatred that he had been fostering for decades. "Germany is the part of the earth's surface," he wrote in all seriousness and, presumably, sincerity in the memoir of his 1914 stay in Poland, "of which I know the least."[3]

It is therefore not surprising that Conrad should think of spiritual deserts when writing of Germany. "I had never lingered," he observes in 1915, forgetting entirely the jolly holiday still vivid in his memory only a few years before, "in that land which, on the whole, is so singularly barren of memorable manifestations of generous sympathies and magnanimous impulses. An ineradicable, invincible, provincialism of envy and vanity clings to the forms of its thought like a frowsy garment." (Just how a frowsy garment can be ineradicable and invincible Conrad does not explain.) But although he recalls no pleasurable vacations, he does remember that, as a boy, he had turned his eyes away from Germany "instinctively, as from a threatening phantom."[4]

Not only his eyes, however, but also, apparently, his tongue and his mind. One of the principal reasons why he did not qualify to attend the Gymnasium in Cracow (then located in Austrian Poland) was that he did not know enough German. And although his familiarity with German as a language and even as a literature was, to judge by the fairly frequent quotations and allusions throughout his writings, not inconsiderable, the three languages of his boyhood and maturity were, of course, Polish, French, and English—especially, one might say, French. Even so, there is a little evidence that suggests that Conrad did have some degree of speaking knowledge of German. In his wife's account of their return to England by way of Austria and (neutral) Italy, Conrad is described as suddenly launching into German at the Austrian border guard, a language, his wife notes, that "he had not spoken since he was a tiny boy."[5]

In a *Personal Record,* Conrad himself argues that it would have been possible for him to enter the Austrian naval cadet training school at Pola if he had been willing to expend "six months' extra grinding at German."[6] But then even Austria, though distinctly preferable to either Russia or Germany, was too much an enemy of Poland, as well as perhaps too insignificant a naval power, to satisfy a young Polish patriot and sea dreamer.

Conrad's direct links with Germany, there is no doubt, were few and rarely avowed. But his indirect links were close and more numerous. One of his most intimate friends of the early English years and someone with whom, according to Norman Sherry, Conrad frequently stayed when in London in the 1880s and 1890s, and to whom he owed considerable sums of money, was Adolf P. Krieger, a German-American. Conrad later used Krieger as the model for Verloc in *The Secret Agent,* but only, so Sherry claims, after he had repaid in full what he owed.[7] An even more important person in Conrad's life and work was Ford Madox Ford, with whom Conrad was in the closest literary and personal contact over quite a number of years, to the point of collaborating with him on several novels and short stories (e.g., *The Inheritors, Romance,* "Tomorrow," and *The Nature of the Crime,* and perhaps parts of others). Ford's real name was Hueffer, a name he retained until the World War made German surnames distinctly undesirable. Ford, whose complex and ultimately tragicomic feelings for his ancestral fatherland are treated in a later chapter, is not always the most reliable witness of his dealings with Conrad—or anyone else, for that matter. Still, even Jocelyn Baines, not the least skeptical critic of Ford's habit of magnifying his own importance, suggests that the closeness between Ford and Conrad may have arisen out of a sense that both were outsiders.[8] But if so, Ford's personal intimacy with Conrad did not lead the latter to revise any of his views about the generally unpleasant nature of Germans.

Four German characters figure prominently in Conrad's fiction, not counting characters like Adolf Verloc and Karl Yundt in *The Secret Agent,* whose nationality is never specified but whose names suggest that they are meant to be taken as Germans.[9] These are Gustav "So-and-So," Master of the ill-fated *Patna* in *Lord Jim;* Wilhelm Schomberg, the Bangkok-Singapore hotelier from Alsace who figures in a small way in *Lord Jim* and in the novella "Falk" (1903) and more significantly in *Victory* (1915); Stein, who plays a central role in *Lord Jim;* and Captain Hermann in "Falk." Of these four, two are outright villains—Schomberg and the German Captain—and another a more or less contemptible trimmer; only Stein is portrayed in a wholly positive way.

The really important thing to notice about Conrad's bad Germans is that they are not grandly bad, magnificently evil. They are soft, flabby types who lack the lean, hard, defiant and, so to speak, heroic qualities of Conrad's great villains like the "Gentlemen" Brown and Jones. Under different circumstances, Brown and Jones might well have developed into Tuan Jim or Baron Heyst; they at least have the right cachet. With Schomberg or the German Captain, no such evolution is imaginable under any circumstances. They are two-pfennig villains, full of sound and beer, signifying flatulence. Karl Yundt is such another.

Wilhelm Schomberg is Conrad's most extended portrait of the type. The fact that Conrad returned to him repeatedly suggests that he must have haunted his imagination. Although in the "Note to the First Edition" of *Victory* Conrad repudiates any notion that Schomberg is intended to represent the archetypal German, it is not difficult to demonstrate that, in effect, he does. The language of the disclaimer itself indicates how half-hearted (if not downright ironic) it is. "I don't pretend to say that this is the entire Teutonic psychology;" he writes, "but it is indubitably the psychology of a Teuton. My object in mentioning him here is to bring out the fact that, far from being the incarnation of recent animosities, he is the creature of my old, deep-seated and, as it were, impartial conviction."[10]

How impartial, as it were, that conviction really is emerges very quickly, just as quickly, in fact, as Schomberg himself puts in his appearance. These are the words with which he is greeted: "Big, manly in a portly style, and profusely bearded, with a glass of beer in his thick paw" (p. 25); a few paragraphs later: "Schomberg couldn't forget Heyst. The keen, manly Teutonic creature was a good hater" (p. 26); and again, after a few more paragraphs: "The innkeeper was not mercenary. Teutonic temperament seldom is. But he put on a sinister expression to tell us that Heyst had not paid perhaps three visits altogether to his 'establishment.' This was Heyst's crime, for which Schomberg wished him nothing less than a long and tormented existence. Observe the Teutonic sense of proportion and nice forgiving temper" (pp. 26–27). And observe too the Conradian sense of impartiality— how carefully he distinguishes between Schomberg and all those other Teutons. Thus prepared, the reader is hardly surprised when he discovers the manly Teuton bullying his cowed wife or cringing and whining before Jones and his companions, or lusting after a poor defenseless (English) maiden, or maliciously arranging the murder of the saintly Heyst. Viewed impartially, what else is to be expected?

Aside from being a nice example of Hun-baiting, this description of Schomberg is noteworthy because it seems intended consciously to confirm Conrad's view that the essential national characteristic of Germans is their grotesqueness. In another section of the same note, Conrad observes that, although he had used Schomberg twice before, only "in this instance, [do] his deeper passions come into play, and thus his grotesque psychology is completed at last" (p. viii). Precisely what Conrad means by *grotesque* here is not altogether clear, though it would be easy enough to draw one's conclusions from his descriptions of Schomberg. The need for any guessing is, however, rendered superfluous by Conrad's brief, explicit treatment of the subject in his 1905 essay "Autocracy and the War" and by two further references in another essay, contemporaneous with *Victory,* "Poland Revisited" (1915).

The passage from the former essay, though a little lengthy, is worth quoting here in its entirety because only then can one fully savor the weighty irony of Conrad's rhetoric:

The war of 1870, brought about by the third Napoleon's half-generous, half-selfish adoption of the principle of nationalities, was the first war characterized by a special intensity of hate, by a new note in the tune of an old song for which we may thank the Teutonic thoroughness. Was it not that excellent bourgeoise, Princess Bismarck (to keep only to great examples), who was so righteously anxious to see men, women, and children—emphatically the children, too—of the abominable French nation massacred off the face of the earth? This illustration of the new war-temper is artlessly revealed in the prattle of the amiable Busch, the Chancellor's pet 'reptile' of the Press. And this was supposed to be a war for an idea! Too much, however, should not be made of that good wife's and mother's sentiments any more than of the good First Emperor William's tears, shed so abundantly after every battle, by letter, telegram, and otherwise, during the course of the same war, before a dumb and shamefaced continent. *These were merely the expressions of the simplicity of a nation which more than any other has a tendency to run into the grotesque.* There is worse to come.[11] (My italics)

Here, in discursive form, we have much the same ingredients that go to make up the fictional Schomberg: thorough, irrational, and brutal hatred; pathetic, self-pitying public display of emotion; and simple, naive preoccupation with the self to the exclusion of any awareness of what impression that self is making on others. Power in the hands of a childishly cruel and paradoxically clever simpleton: for Conrad, that translates into the German or (as he prefers to put it) "Teutonic" grotesque. The same certainly applies to his views regarding "that race planted in the middle of Europe, assuming in grotesque vanity the attitude of Europeans among effete Asiatics and barbarous niggers," who swagger in their presumption of superiority beyond all moral bounds; or to the "truculent bearing, touched with the racial grotesqueness, in the men of the *Landwehr* corps, that passed through Cracow to reinforce the Austrian army in Eastern Galicia"—both descriptions of the Germans in Conrad's essay "Poland Revisited."[12]

The portrayal of *Schiff-führer* Hermann—or Ship-conductor Hermann as the Marlow-like narrator translates it—in "Falk" is also grotesque, though not quite in the same way as Schomberg. Hermann, for one thing, is neither a bully nor a womanizer, though in some ways the silent figure of his niece suggests the Lena of *Victory* just as the shy Norwegian Falk evokes the reticent Swede Heyst. Like Schomberg, however—that is, like the Schomberg of *Victory* and only to a much lesser extent the Schomberg of this tale—Hermann is given to bouts of false emotionalism, is easily cowed by a superior personality (like Falk's), has no notion whatever of the ridiculous figure he cuts, and is, in short, as the narrator puts it, "a simple and astute Teuton."[13] Though he has sailed the very waters that have proved so formidable an adversary to many a Conradian sea-dog, he is a docile landlubber-type with "the simple, heavy appearance of a well-to-do farmer, combined with the good-natured shrewdness of a small shopkeeper" (p. 7). The same is true, for that matter, of his wife as well as the children, whom quasi-Marlow encounters on deck playing with a wooden doll, "exercising and developing their racial sentimentalism by the means of that dummy" (p. 22). More grotesque even than these sea-going burghers is the ship they inhabit. Though officially hailing from Bremen, this vessel can only have sailed straight out of "Hansel and Gretel," equipped as it is with a bow that resembles a primitive wooden plough and a stern that looks like a miller's wagon, and with little greenish glazed panes in the cabin ports, decked with tiny white curtains and overflowing with flowers. As for the poop, that is hardly visible, since Hermann's wife has swaddled it with her ample washing. It is hardly surprising, therefore, that this sort of an amiable, cowardly *Pantoffelheld* should utterly fail to take the true measure of a man like Falk or even of the narrator himself.

If Schomberg is an instance of the pathetic Teutonic grotesque, Hermann represents the comically grotesque German. Both are contemptible, but in different ways and to different degrees. Schomberg is like a cur who, after barking loudly, turns tail at the first threat of real opposition. He is man's worst friend. Hermann, on the other hand, is a dimwitted ox, gelded and harmless and comic in his transparent attempts at guile. He is, as the narrator puts it with a self-avowedly peculiar emphasis, "a friend" (p. 6). Hermann's name, of course, only adds to the grotesquely comic effect, echoing as it does that Hermann (or Arminius) who annihilated Augustus's legions in 9 A.D. in the German forests, thereby giving encouragement to the Teutonic hordes to follow. What this particular Hermann is able to exterminate, however, is confined to the contents of a bottle of beer. So too with Schomberg, whose name, as every educated British reader of Conrad must have realized, alluded directly to Frederick Hermann Schomberg (1615–90), who in 1688 became First Duke of Schomberg as a reward for his services as the Commanding Officer of William of Orange's army and who later died leading the British forces at the Battle of the Boyne. Here once again Conrad's latter-day German is a feeble and ironic echo of his martial prototype. (There is also a possibility that Conrad may have wished his readers to catch a further reference to Sir Robert Hermann Schomburgk (1804–65), the German-born explorer of British Guiana, author of *Views in the Interior of Guiana* (1841)—which Conrad probably knew, if only to sketch the background of Costaguana in *Nostromo*—and creator of the so-called *Schomburgkline* fixing the boundary between Brazil and Venezuela.)

What Conrad may mean to suggest by all this is that some Germans are remarkably successful in insinuating themselves into British graces but are, for that very reason, not to be trusted. Significantly, Conrad's Schomberg speaks the language of his adopted Empire perfectly, without a trace of the

Milwaukeesque English that characterizes the speech of the Captain of the *Patna*, of Stein, and—so we are told—of Hermann (though in *Victory* Schomberg progressively interlards his English with German phrases). The same impulse may have led Conrad to make Schomberg an Alsatian, a Teuton who left his fatherland after the war of 1870 in order to hoist his false colors elsewhere.

This capacity of belonging to all places and to no place at all is also noticeable in Gustav "So-and-So," who is a New South Wales German when we first encounter him and who announces, shortly before his disappearance, that he "vill an Amerian citizen begome."[14] According to the omniscient narrator of the opening section of *Lord Jim*, Gustav was "very anxious to curse publicly his native country, but . . . apparently on the strength of Bismarck's victorious policy, brutalized all those he was not afraid of, and wore a 'blood-and-iron' air, combined with a purple nose and a red moustache" (p. 10). Marlow, who remembers him from a brief encounter some nine months prior to the *Patna* incident, confirms this verdict of the "jolly skipper" in almost the same words (p. 30). Even more than Schomberg or Hermann, he exemplifies the grotesque, though he alone approximates that conception of the grotesque which, in the words of Walter Kayser, is "*der Versuch, das Dämonische in der Welt zu bannen und zu beschwören.*"[15]

Schomberg and Hermann, grotesquely bestial though they may be, still remain sufficiently normal to be accepted as human. Not so the Captain of the *Patna*. He is the Prussian beast unmasked, contemptuous of all those "illusions" which, as this novel is at such pains to show, go to make up civilized man and heedful only of the instinct of self-preservation. His first recorded words, spoken as he watches a crowd of eight-hundred docile pilgrims boarding his vessel, are: "Look at dese cattle" (p. 11), a remark meant to boomerang upon himself.

But even cattle are usually too fine for the Captain. Hermann is cattle, but the Captain is quintessentially a swine. When he appears on deck shortly before the disaster, dressed only in pajamas and an open robe, his soft and greasy flesh strikes Jim as obscene, "as though he had sweated out his fat in his sleep" (p. 17). Indeed, in a kind of brutish epiphany he is revealed to Jim as "the incarnation of everything vile and base that lurks in the world we have" (p. 17). And as if Conrad were fearful that his reader might still not grasp his point, a moment later the Captain is made to appear as a "clumsy effigy of a man cut out of a block of fat" (p. 18). There can be no doubt that he is subhuman, a grotesquely—in the original sense of the word—human pig that asserts its existence by means of its enormous bulk and primitive grunts.

The Captain's bestiality is again insisted on during and after his interview with the British shipping-master, Elliot. Though he blusters at first, when he is actually about to be confronted with Elliot, he is seized with second thoughts "and some sort of animal instinct made him hang back and snort like an angry bullock" (p.32). Elliot, not averse to calling a brute a brute, greets him with a series of loudly voiced epithets of which, Marlow notes, "hound was the very mildest . . . that reached me through the open window" (p. 34). That this particular epithet should be singled out for notice is, however, peculiarly appropriate, because it is Jim's (mistaken) assumption that Marlow has called him a "cur" that soon thereafter brings about their acquaintance.

Then, despite his vast bulk—in fact, at the very moment when that bulk seems to expand impossibly—the Captain simply vanishes. "He seemed to be swollen to an unnatural size by some awful disease," the spectatorial Marlow observes, "by the mysterious action of an unknown poison." With a resolute waddle he makes his way to a waiting gharry "and began to jerk at the door-handle with such a blind brutality of impatience that I expected to see the whole concern overturned on its side, pony and all. . . . The little machine shook and rocked tumultuously, and the crimson nape of that cowered neck, the size of those straining thighs, the immense heaving of that dingy, striped green-and-orange back, the whole burrowing effort of that gaudy and sordid mass troubled one's sense of probability with a droll and fearsome effect, like one of those *grotesque* [my italics] and distinct visions that scare and fascinate one in a fever." And then the "snorting pony snatched him into 'ewigkeit' in the twinkling of an eye, and I never saw him again; and, what's more, I don't know of anybody that ever had a glimpse of him after he departed from my knowledge. . . . He departed, disappeared, vanished, absconded; and absurdly enough it looked as though he had taken that gharry with him, for never again did I come across a sorrel pony with a slit ear and a lackadaisical Tamil driver afflicted by a sore foot. The Pacific is indeed big; but whether he found a place for a display of his talents in it or not, the fact remains he had flown into space like a witch on a broomstick" (pp. 39–40).

The Captain is, it seems, not merely subhuman, but also superhuman, a minor and especially disgusting agent of Beelzebub, sent on a mission of plaguing a sorely tried and Job-like Jim. That, in fact, is just how Jim does view him when he gives Marlow his account of how the ship was abandoned; and Marlow, with a few reservations, tends to agree with him. Besides, how else to explain the utter disappearance of a being whose massive material existence could hardly be overlooked? A monstrous grotesquerie of such proportions could only be, as Marlow himself suggests at the close of the passage just quoted, the work of diabolic forces. So here at last we have it plain and apparently simple: the grotesque Germans have gone to the devil.

But, of course, the truth is not so simple, as nothing is simple in this most complex of all of Conrad's complex fictions. For juxtaposed almost directly with this most grotesque of Conrad's Germans is a character who, while undeniably German, is nevertheless the sanest and wisest figure in the whole book—perhaps even, if we are to believe Frederick Karl, in the whole of the Conradian corpus.[16] What is one to make of that? An answer that suggests itself immediately is that Conrad is here adopting the old saw that all Germans fall into two unequally divided categories, the good and the bad (or the grotesque and the sublime), a cliché that by the turn of the century was already firmly established and that is directly traceable to the success of Prussia in the War of 1870 and to the consequent unification of Germany under Prussian domination. The old peaceful Germany of "Dichter und Denker," according to the usual argument, was overwhelmed by a new and militarily aggressive Germany ruthlessly pursuing a doctrine of blood and iron.[17] There is some evidence in *Lord Jim* to support this hypothesis. Stein left Germany, forcibly and hurriedly, after the abortive Revolution of 1848, whereas Gustav seems to be the product of post-1870 Imperial Germany, despite his vociferous deprecation of it. Stein is a man of science and art, as his collection of lepidoptera and his familiarity with Goethe and Shakespeare indicate; the Captain is a brute, whose only argument is superior force or a loud voice. Finally, Stein is a Bavarian, a traditional ally of France and Austria and a traditional enemy of Prussia, whereas the Captain is definitely North German and quite possibly Prussian.

It is difficult to believe that Conrad, careful and conscious craftsman that he was, did not introduce these contrasts deliberately. Conrad, one is led to conclude, was using the German Captain and Stein to make a point about a Germany that, in 1900, Englishmen might still be tempted to confuse with that older and finer Germany that, Conrad knew, was either moribund or had ceased to exist altogether. But, granting this, there still remains much implied in the contrast that is not satisfactorily accounted for by this kind of purely political explanation. There remains, most strikingly, the whole demonically grotesque dimension of the Captain and the fact of his mysterious disappearance.

The fact is that Stein, though by no means grotesque himself,[18] is just as demonic as his vile countryman and counterpart. He is as much a representative of a benevolent deity, if he is not that deity himself, as the Captain is of an evil fiend. While others die, those whom he loves as well as those whom he hates, Stein miraculously survives. Whereas the Captain gains enormously in mass until the very moment he vanishes, Stein diminishes materially to a point where, in the crucial conversation with Marlow, he is only a disembodied voice wandering among his obscurely illumined cases.

Lest this appear a little far-fetched, it might be well to remember the very first words with which Marlow begins telling "us" the story of Jim.

"Oh yes. I attended the inquiry," he would say, "and to this day I haven't left off wondering why I went. I am willing to believe each of us has a guardian angel, if you fellows will concede to me that each of us has a familiar devil as well. I want you to own up, because I don't like to feel exceptional in any way, and I know I have him—the devil, I mean. I haven't seen him, of course, but I go upon circumstantial evidence. He is there right enough, and, being malicious, he lets me in for that kind of thing. What kind of thing, you ask? Why, the inquiry thing, the yellow-dog thing—you wouldn't think a mangy native tyke would be allowed to trip up people in the verandah of a magistrate's court, would you?— the kind of thing that by devious, unexpected, truly diabolical ways causes me to run up against men with soft spots, with hard spots, with hidden plague spots, by Jove!" (P. 28)

Is this simply to be dismissed as Marlow's imagination running away with itself? I do not think so. Marlow, for one thing, denies having an imagination, and for another, the disappearance of the German Captain is "demonstrably" diabolical. Marlow, it would seem, in speaking of guardian angels is referring to his own function in guarding Jim; and that means, I think, that the German Captain must be Jim's familiar devil, an identification that seems implicit in the oblique allusion to him as a cur. The Captain, significantly, clears off the moment Marlow comes on the scene.

The implications of the situation sketched by Marlow inevitably suggest Faust, and specifically Goethe's version. Here, as in Faust, there is a struggle between the forces of good and evil for the possession of a soul that seems almost surely damned, but that in the end is miraculously saved. Jim, to be sure, lacks the intellectual and spiritual depth of Faust, but he is just as determined to strive eternally against everything that stands in the way of what he conceives to be his destiny. The parallel is not exact in all except a few particulars, but in the general case it is striking. The cur, for example, echoes the diabolical poodle of the first part of Faust; and Jim, like Faust, must accept the cur as his own familiar, must carry him over the threshold of his own spirit, as it were, before the evil influence can take effect. That, I believe, is the principal reason why Marlow is so profoundly shocked by Jim's readiness to believe that he might have been called a cur. "There had never been a man so mercilessly shown up," Marlow says, "by his own natural impulse" (p. 63). *Never* is not a word that the usually moderate Marlow uses lightly.

Striking, too, is the resemblance of the second part of *Lord Jim*, the Patusan section, to the second part of *Faust*. Jim's wanderings correspond roughly to Faust's as a kind of voyage to the outskirts of hell and Patusan itself matches quite closely the final stage of Faust's activity. Both protagonists find peace in remote parts of the world, by working for the welfare of others and establishing a socially just community for which they are willing to sacrifice themselves; and both are paradoxically led by evil tempters into destroying the very people whom they set out to save. And both, I think, are nevertheless saved themselves.

Again, let it be repeated, the parallels are not always precise. Jewel is a poor substitute for Gretchen, abandoned though she is by her lover; and Jim is admittedly a poor intellectual replacement for Faust.[19] Nevertheless, Conrad seems to insist on the parallel to the point of even implying that Stein is a kind of Goethe of the Malay Archipelago. Like Goethe, Stein has a passion for universal knowledge, for classification and collection; like Goethe, he combines action with contemplation; and, like Goethe, he is the intimate friend and helper of a petty prince.[20]

The identification rises to the surface twice in the long conversation Stein has with Marlow: first, as Stein describes that moment in his life when real and ideal, desire and fulfillment fused most perfectly, when at one stroke he foiled his enemies and captured a rare and beautiful butterfly. As in his mind he seizes the insect once again, Stein quotes from the dramatic works of the "boet":

> So halt ich's endlich denn in meinen Händen
> Und nenn' es in gewissem Sinne mein.

The "boet," of course, is Goethe, and the lines are from *Torquato Tasso*.[21]

The second, and from the point of view of understanding Jim's character, more important instance takes place as Stein diagnoses Jim's malady and prescribes for it. The whole passage is couched in medical language, as Marlow himself is quite aware, with Stein being the specialist in spiritual maladies: "He had diagnosed the case for me, and at first I was quite startled to find how simple it was; and indeed our conference resembled so much a medical consultation . . . that it seemed natural to ask—'What's good for it?' " (p. 183).

Stein's verdict is rampant "romanticism"—something that leads this reader, at least, to think at once of Goethe's famous dictum, also couched in medical terms, that *"das Romantische ist das Kranke; das Klassische ist das Gesunde."* The cure is—what? Astonishingly, it is more of the same, in the way that poison sometimes functions as an antidote. Stein's prescription is for Jim to take the waters, to immerse himself in the destructive element of his oceanic dream. "That," according to this soul doctor, "was the way. To follow the dream, and again to follow the dream—and so—*ewig—usque ad finem* . . ." (p. 185). Here, surely, we have the identical ethical recipe that informs *Faust*. To follow the dream eternally and to the very end: what is that if not *ewig streben*? And like the restless, romantic Faust, that is precisely what the restless, romantic Jim does; achieving thereby in the end—paradoxically—a momentary glimpse of idyllic and classic peace. Stein, who admits to suffering from the "disease" himself and who has also achieved a measure of classic repose, dispenses advice that is also Goethe's advice: to keep treading water regardless of the fact that there is no land in sight.

Jim, if this argument holds water, is a kind of nonintellectual Faust, or unpoetical Tasso, whose dreams of glory seem at first to lead directly to perdition, but in the end are revealed as the harbingers of a far greater redemption. The other side of Jim's simplicity is Marlow's complexity; and on one level, at least, Marlow needs to be seen as merely another manifestation of Jim (and vice versa). How else to account for Marlow's extraordinary and, even to himself, not wholly explicable interest in Jim? Significantly, Marlow has no first name, Jim no surname. Both are seamen; both belong to the same social class; both have been in bad scrapes; both finally accept the central ethical doctrine implied by the recurrent phrase *one of us*. That doctrine itself suggests an ultimate unity; to be "one of us" is, after all, to be part of the whole, a member of the community of good men. "It is certain," so runs the epigraph from the romantic German Novalis that Conrad affixed to the first edition of *Lord Jim*, "my conviction gains infinitely, the moment another soul will believe in it."

For an Anglo-Pole who knew *Tasso* well enough to be able to quote from it in the original—choosing what are by no means the best known lines—for such a writer the name "Stein" *must* have had Goethean overtones, if only because in one of the principal characters of the play Goethe had drawn an ideal portrait of a woman he loved, Charlotte von Stein.[22] And just as in *Tasso* the Princess, alias Charlotte von Stein, serves as the standard whereby others are to be judged (as well as being Tasso's principal guardian angel), so too here does Stein. In their famous interchange in act 2, scene 1, in which Tasso laments the vanished bliss of a Golden Age of universal love and summarizes the code by which he lives—"*Erlaubt ist, was gefällt*"—the Princess replies that the Golden Age lives on in the community of the good, that it was never otherwise, and that in lieu of his doctrine of aesthetic-romantic license, the key to correct action lies in classic decorum: "*Erlaubt ist, was sich ziemt.*"[23] Tasso's lust for an ideal, imaginary world makes him disregard the Princess's advice, makes him forget the rules of the game of civilized life, thereby bringing disaster down upon himself; and yet, of course, the very intensity of his desire is what makes Tasso the great poet he is. It is what delivers Jerusalem in his poetic imagination, but destroys Jerusalem in his daily life. At the end, he is left alone with his worldly alter ego, Antonio, who will presumably undertake to educate Tasso in the science of "was sich ziemt" just as Marlow, the practical, self-avowedly unromantic man of the world, seeks to do with Jim. Tasso's last speech and the final lines of the play show him immersed in the destructive element, suffering shipwreck but clinging to the hope of salvation through Antonio:

> Zerbrochen ist das Steuer, und es kracht
> Das Schiff an allen Seiten. Berstend reisst
> Der Boden unter meinen Füssen auf!
> Ich fasse Dich mit beiden Armen an!

So klammert sich der Schiffer endlich noch
Am Felsen fest, an dem er scheitern sollte.[24]

While Stein's link with Tasso through his namesake, Charlotte von Stein, seems indisputable, it is also distinctly possible that Conrad means to allude as well to Baron Heinrich Friedrich vom Stein (1757–1831), the great Prussian political reformer and liberator of the serfs. Significantly, Stein—unlike the historical prototypes of Hermann and Schomberg—was not principally a military figure and, while an Anglophile and even related by marriage to the English royal house, remained very much a German patriot who stayed in Germany and devoted his ample energies to liberalizing Prussia and attempting to achieve, by peaceful means, the unification of the German kingdoms and principalities.

Aside from these allusions, however, there is probably also a conscious irony in Conrad's choice of "Stein"—which in German means "stone"—for a character who advises us to immerse ourselves in the destructive element of the sea. Stones, we surely do not need to be told, plummet at once to the bottom. What does Conrad mean by this? He means, I think, to suggest that there is an irony behind this irony, that, like the *Patna* which, all indications to the contrary, simply will not sink, Stein miraculously stays above water; so, for that matter, does Jim, at least *usque ad finem*. And, ironically, Stein, who bears so hard a name, is soft to Jim, whereas the blubbery Captain is hard (though, in spite of his fat, he cannot keep afloat spiritually). Stein is hard where it is good to be hard; he has no soft spots of decay.

Stein's hardness is also symbolic of his refusal to compromise his dream. His dream, in fact, *is* his existence, just as Marlow's dream is equatable with his existence or Jim's. Unlike the German captain, Stein does not vanish; on the contrary, virtually the last words of the novel are words spoken by Stein, and the very last ones describe Stein pointing toward his cases of butterflies (emblems of the dream). "What is it," Stein had earlier asked Marlow, "that for you and me makes [Jim]—exist?" (p. 186). The answer, though never pronounced explicitly, is unmistakably Jim's and their shared dream. The same answer might be given for Faust and even for Tasso.

It is Stein, the German, who points the way to that answer; Stein who, like an aged Goethe, seems to dwell on Olympian heights, uttering the delphic words that begin to fuse the fragments of our mundane existence into an imagined whole. Though profoundly demonic, he is at the farthest possible remove from his grotesque countryman, the Captain of the *Patna*. Like another famous Conrad character who bears a German name, Kurtz, he has seen the "horror," but, unlike him, he has survived it and passed beyond to gain a glimpse of a distant serenity. And, fittingly, the angel of stone and the devil of fat are made of the same German stuff.

3

E. M. Forster's Rainbow Bridge

Her position is impregnable. She is neither pro-German nor anti-German, because the great men who built her up all died before this world-trouble began, and have become our spiritual trustees.

E. M. Forster on culture in "The Functions
of Literature in War-time" (1915)

Though Forster is an archetypically English novelist, the subject and settings of his novels are often non-English. The most obvious instance, is, of course, *A Passage to India,* but both *Where Angels Fear to Tread* and *A Room With a View* take place partly outside of England and concern themselves, like *A Passage to India,* with the impact of another culture on English values, conventions, self-conceptions, and self-deceptions. Of his completed novels, only two—*The Longest Journey* and *Maurice*—are English in a narrowly defined sense, and even of these the latter deals with an England that, at the time Forster wrote the novel, was not openly acknowledged to exist. There are, then, the "Italian" novels, the "Indian" novel, the "English" novels—and there is *Howards End. Howards End* is, in Forster's novelistic canon and from this nationalistic point of view, unique. Its action is set almost entirely in England; but its subject and its cast of characters are not entirely English. Like the Indian and Italian novels, it deals—admittedly, among other things—with the confrontation of two mutually and paradoxically sympathetic and antithetical cultures, those of England and Germany. And like the English novels, it deals with that confrontation in a milieu that is almost wholly English. Hence it is perhaps too extreme to call *Howards End* Forster's "German" novel, but it is certainly both reasonable and revealing to call it his "Anglo-German" novel. After all, three of the chief characters—and the two protagonists, Helen and Margaret Schlegel—are half-German, bear a very recognizably German name, are extremely conscious of their German ancestry and heritage, and are frequently associated with visits to and from Germany and their German relations.

Undoubtedly part of the reason for these German elements in *Howards End* is to be found in Forster's biography. For about a year—from 1905 to 1906—Forster lived in Nassenheide in Germany, where he acted as tutor to the children of Elizabeth von Arnim (at that time well known in England as the author of *Elizabeth and Her German Garden*, 1898). Forster admitted this biographical connection himself when, in an essay written over half a century later, he stated that in *Howards End* he had "brought in the Oder Berge and other Pomeranian recollections."[1] But what he did not say was that he had brought in not only his strong, positive feelings for the German landscape—important as those were—but other, even more significant experiences and attitudes as well. Living at Nassenheide, in a household that was as English as it was German, must have suggested to Forster at least some of the situation that he was to depict later in *Howards End.* The three girls he tutored there were, like Margaret, Helen, and Tibby, the children of a German father and an English mother, even though in the novel it is the father's influence that is stressed rather than the mother's, whereas at Nassenheide it was unquestionably Elizabeth who was the dominant personality.[2] But then what Forster did with his experience of Germany in this work of fiction—as with his experience of Italy and India in other works of fiction—was not to render it literally but to shape it to the purposes of his art. Besides, Elizabeth's strong English influence on her children in Germany does have its counterpart in Father Schlegel's strong German influence on his children in England. In both cases, German and English culture and people have mingled and married, or, to borrow Forster's famous word, they have connected.

How very aware Forster was at Nassenheide of the fusion of the two cultures that he encountered there, and of the conflict of loyalties that his young charges faced as a consequence, is revealed by the topic he set for one of their essays: "If there were a war between England and Germany, which would you want to win?" The answer he received from one of the girls to this ominous question was characteristically Forsterian: "If there was a war between England and Germany, I shouldn't care which won: I should run away as fast as I could."[3] Something of this attitude finds its way into *Howards End* when Margaret, at thirteen, concludes that the conflicting chauvinist arguments of her German cousin and her English aunt cancel each other out: "To me one of two things is very clear," she tells her father; "either God does not know his own mind about England and Germany, or else these do not know the mind of God."[4]

And, aside from any personal contact with Germany or Germans, Forster—or any educated Englishman, for that matter—could not help but have been aware during the opening decade of this century of the intense commercial and military rivalry between England and Germany. These were the years of the great naval race, when the English press reported officers in

German messes drinking to "Der Tag," the day when Germany would finally challenge English supremacy at sea; the years of the Entente Cordiale with France (and later with Russia), a policy of reconciliation with old enemies and rivals doomed to produce a Malentendu Fatal with the new rival and enemy; the years when a series of invasion fantasies and spy scares (by Wells, Conan Doyle, LeQueux, and others) threw the English public into hysteria at the prospect of Prussian hordes overrunning English civilization as the Huns and Goths had once overrun the Roman. The great Wilcoxian poet of Anglo-German enmity, Rudyard Kipling—in so many ways the very opposite of Forster—was among the first to recognize this new trend of feeling and policy when, in "The Rowers" (1902), he denounced any attempt to form an alliance with Germany:

> In sight of peace—from the Narrow Seas
> O'er half the world to run—
> With a cheated crew, to league anew
> With the Goth and the shameless Hun!

This mood of rivalry and impending war infects *Howards End* at various points, most often when the Wilcoxes put in an appearance. In conversation with Margaret, Henry Wilcox explains to her the rationale of sending his son to Africa in the following terms: "Someone's got to go. . . . England will never keep her trade overseas unless she is prepared to make sacrifices. Unless we get firm in West Africa, Ger—untold complications may follow" (H 131). And later, while dining with Henry and some other members of his family at Simpson's on the Strand (described as "no more Old English than the works of Kipling"), Margaret overhears scraps of the talk of the surrounding Wilcoxian men of property and their hangers-on. " 'Right you are! I'll cable out to Uganda this evening,' came from the table behind. 'Their Emperor wants war; well, let him have it,' was the opinion of a clergyman" (H 153). For Forster it was precisely this kind of Kiplingesque talk, full of the sense of nationalist resentment and rivalry, that was dangerous. Those who consider a war inevitable, those who remark that "England and Germany are bound to fight" are those who help bring about the war, because, as Forster's narrator observes, that remark "renders war a little more likely each time that it is made, and is therefore made all the more readily by the gutter press of either nation" (H 63).

How right Forster was can be seen from A. G. Gardiner's editorial attack in the liberal *Daily News* (5 December 1914) on Northcliffe's warmongering, conservative *Daily Mail:* "You say that we prophesied Peace, but we worked for Peace, just as you prophesied War and worked for War. We lost and you won." In fact, it may have been "gutter press" considerations such as this that led Forster to delete a passage that he had originally intended for the scene of Margaret's lunch party in honor of Ruth Wilcox, a passage that would have matched (on the intellectual side) the later lowbrow one at Simpson's on the Strand:

> "Where's your sister?" asked one of the guests.
> "In Germany. She has gone back for Christmas with our cousin, and would you believe it, the weather there is perfectly glorious."
> "I don't believe in Germany," he replied. "It is outside the Roman Empire. C'est une [*sic*] pays barbare . . ."
> "Still they had brilliant sunshine."
> "Oh but does that *count?*" said another.[5]

Forster's attitude here is characteristically liberal. Despite occasional subsequent expressions of socialist sympathy, he is fundamentally an Edwardian Liberal, which means that he is against foreign engagements and embroilments, for free movement and free trade, against Great Britain and for Little England. In this context of the beginnings of a paranoic attitude toward Germany in the English public mind, it seems odd, however, that Forster's relatively disinterested point of view and even, at times, overt sympathy for Germany were not much remarked upon in contemporaneous reviews of the novel. In fact, only two reviewers were at all moved to remark upon the German aspects of *Howards End.* One, in the *Morning Post,* saw the novel as culminating in the Wilcoxes' putting a good face on the "triumph of the hated German family"; and the other, in the *Western Mail* (Cardiff), was rather puzzled at the Schlegels' being half German since they had "few German characteristics that we can see."[6] Such disregard on the part of reviewers should not be quite so surprising, however, since in this respect it has been matched by the similar disregard of the critics.

Forster, then, fused private experience and public opinion in creating the Germans and half-Germans of *Howards End.* But how extensive and how profound was Forster's knowledge actually of the Germany he lived in and read and wrote about? Did he really know more—though he clearly cared more—about German culture than the average Edwardian intellectual? What, for instance, did he know about German literature? These are difficult questions to answer, because the evidence bearing on them is not extensive and what there is is sometimes contradictory. Certainly Forster does not hesitate to speak very authoritatively and, presumably, knowledgeably, about the whole range of German culture. "Germany, like ourselves," he writes in *Nordic Twilight* (1940), "has had a great national culture. . . . She was supreme in music, eminent in philosophy, weak (like ourselves) in the visual arts, gifted in literature." In a different version of the same work, "Three Anti-Nazi Broadcasts," later published in *Two Cheers for Democracy* (1951), Forster gives the same estimate of German music, philosophy, and the visual arts, but revalues German literature upward and makes her "highly gifted though not supremely gifted in literature."[7] In both works he also specifically cites Goethe as one of the great examples of tolerance, probably influenced in doing so by his friend and mentor G. L. Dickinson's great admiration for that German writer.[8] These statements, whether we agree with them or not, would seem to presuppose considerable familiarity with German culture: for if they do not, we are left with the conclusion that "honest" Morgan Forster is here parading in plumage that does not belong to him. Is he doing that? Is he putting on airs? Well, probably to some extent he is; but then who else might there be with the requisite knowledge (and courage) for this kind of vast cultural comparison? And besides, as Forster is very well aware, in these pieces he is producing propaganda, and propaganda inevitably leads to broad comparisons—usually more invidious than these— in which ratings and other elements of prestige thinking play an important role. No, the problem with these broad estimates of German cultural achievement is simply that they are too broad, and that it is impossible for that reason to arrive at any valid conclusion about the extent of the knowledge on which they are based. Even so, it is interesting and perhaps suggestive that Forster changed his estimate of the relative importance of German literature, something that may indicate that he had, in fact, devoted some serious thought to this subject.

Before we attempt to make any educated guesses—whether neutral, for, or against—it is necessary to consider the evidence of another sweeping Forsterian pronouncement on Germany. This pronouncement comes at the conclusion of Forster's "Recollections of Nassenheide" (1959) and seems to represent a disclaimer of any intimate knowledge of German culture in favor of an intimate experience of German landscape: "It is curious that Germany, a country which I do not know well or instinctively embrace, should twice have seduced me through her countryside. I have described the first occasion [in Pomerania, May 1905]. The second was half a century later when I stayed in a remote hamlet in Franconia [in 1954] . . . The tragedy of England is that she is too small to become a modern state and yet to retain her freshness. The freshness has to go . . . Germany is anyhow larger, and thanks to her superior size she may preserve the rural heritage that smaller national units have had to scrap—the heritage which I used to see from my own doorstep in Hertfordshire when I was a child, and which has failed to outlast me."[9]

Here it is, or appears to be, the landscape—the spirit of the place—that has "seduced" Forster's heart, and not German culture that has "conquered" his mind. And yet here again one's impression may be incorrect or at least incomplete; for the second epiphanical experience to which Forster refers took place while he was attending the Bayreuth Festival in 1954, a cultural event of some magnitude and—what may be even more important—of a very "German" nature. Wagner exercised a great influence on Forster, and especially, as we shall see, on *Howards End;* and in his account of his visit to the festival, "Revolution at Bayreuth" (1954), Forster makes very clear his admiration for the German composer who, above all others, was associated with the Nazis. "In present circles Wagner is taboo," he writes, "and when I said I was going to Bayreuth I encountered such remarks as 'I am afraid I am for Mozart,' a slight pause being made between the *Mo* and the *zart* which had the subtle effect of a reprimand. Why an outsider like myself and why other outsiders should not be both for Wagner and Mozart I do not know. We are not composers. We have no creative obligations. And I believe that the coming generation, when left to itself, does like them both, and that consequently Wagner will endure. If he does not the human race loses." That Forster not only admired Wagner but knew his work very well becomes obvious in the course of the essay, as, for instance, in his censure of Wolfgang and Wieland Wagner for failing to observe strictly their grandfather's instructions to have Wotan wear a hat while speaking to Siegfried.[10]

What else is there that might convince us that Forster had a real understanding of German culture, aside from music? Well, there is his essay "Gide and George" (1943), with its explicit preference for that "very different Germany" of 1868 into which George was born. There is *Aspects of the Novel* (1927) in which English, American, French, and Russian novels receive detailed discussion, but the only German-language work that gets any attention at all is *The Swiss Family Robinson.* And there is *Howards End.* Aside from brief references in the manuscript to (Wilhelm) Busch and Goethe that he later deleted, Forster cites the following German writers, painters, and composers by name in *Howards End:* Hegel, Kant, Beethoven, Brahms, Mendelssohn, Wagner, Böcklin, and Nietzsche. Unnamed, but quoted, is Novalis; and named—but only indirectly—is August Wilhelm von Schlegel as well as perhaps his brother, Friedrich Wilhelm von Schlegel. This is a fairly extensive array of German cultural figures and, as we shall see, they are presented to us in such a way as to suggest that Forster knew something about them besides their names. The reference to Beethoven occurs, of course, in the context of one of the most celebrated descriptions of music in English literature, and both Brahms and Mendelssohn are used to show how much less great they are than Beethoven, as well as to suggest that they are nevertheless superior to the last composer on the program, Elgar. To some extent this is Wagner's function as well, though he is not so obviously Beethoven's inferior as the others. Along with Debussy, he is seen by Margaret as the chief originator of the new music—the "real villain" who "has done more than any man in the nineteenth century towards the muddling of the arts" but is nevertheless one of those "terrible geniuses . . . who stir up all the wells of thought at once. For a moment it's splendid. Such a splash as never was. But afterwards—such a lot of mud . . ." (H 39). Wagner is clearly important and Margaret's verdict is not, I think, to be understood as final.

As to Hegel and Kant, they are viewed as representatives of a Germany anterior to Bismarck's, a Germany of "Dichter und Denker" rather than of Blood and Iron.[11] They are associated with Father Ernst Schlegel. "If one classed him [Schlegel] at all," Forster's narrator tells us, "it would be as the countryman of Hegel and Kant, as the idealist, inclined to be dreamy, whose Imperialism was the Imperialism of the air" (H 28). Nietzsche, on the other hand, is seen by Helen as belonging to a new, nonidealistic trend in philosophy, espousing a "night-mare theory" about supermen who have no identities (H 234)—in other words, he is the philosopher of the Wilcoxes rather than of the Schlegels. As for Böcklin, he embodies "that interest in the universal which the average Teuton possesses and the average Englishman does not. It was, however illogically, the good, the beautiful, the true, as opposed to the respectable, the pretty, the adequate. It was a landscape of Böcklin's beside a landscape of Leader's, strident and ill-considered, but quivering into supernatural life" (H 170–71). He is an "idealist" painter, in other words, who paints as Hegel and Kant philosophize or Beethoven and Wagner compose. Böcklin—and by extension (Forster's extension) all of German culture—is the poetry, whereas England, in the persons of Elgar and Leader, is the prose. This, to be sure, is not, one should hasten to add, the whole truth about England and Germany as Forster sees it, but it is a genuine part of that truth.

There remain Novalis and Schlegel (or the Schlegels) to be accounted for. The former appears only very briefly in connection with Leonard Bast's first visit to Wickham Place, and is used in such a way as to suggest a spiritual kinship between Bast and the Schlegels. The quotation runs as follows: " 'My conviction,' says the mystic, 'gains infinitely the moment another soul will believe in it' " (H 124). Here again Forster provides a German idealistic backdrop for his characters, though this time rather more subtly, since he does not reveal the identity or nationality of the "mystic." What he does not reveal either but what he may have had in mind by introducing Novalis in this particular context is a linking of Leonard Bast with the protagonist of Novalis's novel, *Heinrich von Ofterdingen*, a rather confused young man who nevertheless pursues single-mindedly the "blue flower," the quest for the ideal. And what was almost certainly in Forster's mind here was to seek to associate Leonard and the Schlegel sisters with the historical connection and collaboration between Novalis and the Schlegel brothers.[12]

That Forster was quite aware of the significance of the name he chose for his main characters is evident from a notation in the manuscript of *Howards End* to the effect that Father Schlegel was "a distant relation of the great critic."[13] Just why Forster deleted this useful piece of information when he published the novel is not clear, but he may have felt that the connection was obvious anyway—as it is—and that there are dangers in making things too explicit (as in the case of Novalis). But why choose Schlegel out of a host of other possibilities? There are a number of reasons for this, one of them almost certainly connected with Forster's stay at Nassenheide. The name of his employers there—von Arnim—must have been one that he came to know a good deal about: it is also the name of one of the most famous German Romantic writers, Ludwig Achim von Arnim, best known for his poetical anthology (together with Klemens Brentano), *Des Knaben Wunderhorn*, containing some of the most celebrated folk poetry in the German language and a favorite source for German lieder composers from Schubert to Mahler. It is also the name of Bettina von Arnim (Ludwig's wife and Brentano's sister), whose association and correspondence with Goethe made her probably the outstanding woman writer of the Romantic movement. If Forster was aware of the von Armin background—and it is difficult to believe that he was not—then surely one reason why he chose the name Schlegel is because he could not choose the name Arnim.

If anything, Schlegel is an even better-known Romantic name than Arnim. It is also, significantly, a name that—like Arnim—is associated almost as much with women as it is with men. Both wives of the Schlegel brothers, Dorothea Mendelssohn Schlegel and Karoline Michaelis Schlegel (later Schelling), were writers in their own right, and, like Margaret and Helen, were women very much concerned with the leading social-intellectual issues of the day, among them radical changes in the relations of the sexes. Admittedly, it would be too much to assert that Forster had all of these associations in mind when he chose the Schlegel name; but even so these associations *are* suggestive and *may* have been intended. One association, however, does seem more sure than the others: the association with August Wilhelm von Schlegel's translation of Shakespeare into German. It was this translation, made in collaboration with Ludwig Tieck, that helped transform Shakespeare into "German Shakespeare," and which no doubt suggested to Forster that here—as with his own Schlegels—there was a case of successful cross-cultural "connection." (There is even a mildly ironic mention, by Margaret, of Shakespeare as a "German" in *Howards End.*) It is possible, too, since it is to Schlegel's reputation as a critic that the manuscript notation refers, that Forster may also have been aware of and was alluding to Schlegel's considerable influence on English Romantic critical theory, especially Coleridge's—another instance of connection.

This, then, is Father Schlegel's and his children's background: they are the biological and spiritual descendants of Romantic, idealist Germany, a Germany that, at the time the events of the novel take place, no longer exists. It had been overwhelmed by the political and expansionist aims of a militaristic Prussia. At first, so Forster's narrator tells us, Schlegel had shared in these aims and had even "fought like blazes" to achieve them, "against Denmark, Austria, France." "But he had fought without visualizing the results of victory. A hint of the truth broke on him after Sedan, when he saw the dyed moustaches of Napoleon going grey; another when he entered Paris and saw the smashed windows of the Tuileries." He had fought, it seems, without taking into account personal relations (especially those with the French Emperor) or the possible destruction of important cultural monuments. So Father Schlegel changed his mind—and his nationality: "He abstained from the fruits of victory, and nationalized himself in England." He secured a position in a provincial English university, married a wealthy English-woman, and retired to London, where he devoted the rest of his life to contemplation, reading, the education of his children, and the "hope that the clouds of materialism obscuring the Fatherland would part in time, and the mild intellectual light re-emerge" (H 29).

As one may appreciate from this brief account, Father Schlegel is some-thing of a stuffed symbol and his history a rather unlikely one. He is, very much as the Anglo-American cliché has it, the "Good German" who prefers the Reich of the spirit to that of the Kaiser. He is also an awkward and to some extent contradictory person, though Forster seems to want us to sympathize with him. His famous remark to his visiting German nephew (the "Bad German") about the vulgarity of thinking in terms of quantity rather than quality reflects very much Forster's own view. "It is the vice of the vulgar mind," Father Schlegel says, "to be thrilled by bigness, to think that a thousand square miles are a thousand times more wonderful than one square mile, and that a million square miles are the same as heaven" (H 29). Included, of course, in this indictment are English vulgarians as well as German, but even so what remains unexplained is—given this point of view—the logic of Father Schlegel's decision to leave the "big" German Empire in 1871 for the even "bigger" British Empire.[14] One cannot really escape the conclusion that at some conscious or unconscious level Forster is convinced that, vulgar though they may be, British-administered square miles are more virtuous than German. In this sense there is something fundamentally false about Father Schlegel, something that is reminiscent of the attitude that Forster's narrator attributes to his grocer, who, "when I complain of the quality of his sultanas" replies "in one breath that they are the best sultanas, and how can I expect the best sultanas at that price?" (H 182). Here also, it would appear, Forster wants to have his sultanas and eat them too.

Even so and in spite of Forster's evident participation in thinking about Germany and Germans in clichés, it must be said that his treatment of the subject is extraordinarily sensitive in comparison with any other work of fiction of the Edwardian period and virtually with any other major novel of this century. Unfortunately, his attempt to build a "rainbow bridge" between England and Germany, to connect the two cultures and nations, was doomed to failure. It was a noble attempt, but rainbow bridges will not bear the weight of gigantic Dreadnought races, Morocco crises, Ententes Cordiales, and ultimatums. They will not bear it any more than hay—even "such a crop of hay as never" (H 343)—will sustain civilized life at Howards End. It is nice that there are people who think so, but that does not change matters. And Forster knew that too: both Margaret and Henry, even after divesting themselves of most of their wealth, still retain a tidy sum safely invested in 3% consols.

Besides, retirement to Howards End and the cultivation of hay and Anglo-German amity there might have seemed just barely possible and desirable in 1910. Four years later it was very unlikely indeed. Had Forster been so inclined he might have written a very interesting, as well as depressing, sequel about the Schlegel-Wilcoxes' life during the Great War. One imagines, for instance, what it would have been like for Margaret and Helen to have had a neighbor like Kipling's Mary Postgate.

This, then, would appear to be the extent of the German aspects of *Howards End,* aspects that are surely important enough in themselves to warrant our calling it Forster's "Anglo-German" novel. But to stop here— that is, to stop with the enumeration and analysis of the overt German connections—would be to miss another whole dimension of the novel, a dimension that Forster has kept relatively hidden from us. Beneath the surface, that dimension exercises an enormous influence on the novel, all the more so because it is beneath the surface, because it constitutes the soil upon which the more conscious and exoteric elements of the novel grow. This subsurface layer is the mythological layer; and in this novel that layer is primarily Germanic.

All of Forster's novels rest solidly on a foundation of myth. In the earlier works this foundation is invariably classical, as befits Forster's training at Cambridge, with Pan and dryads and such-like creatures putting in more or less recognizable and obligatory appearances. In *The Longest Journey,* however, Forster begins to shift away from classical mythology, though he still remains heavily indebted to it; but his use there of the Figsbury Rings and their pre-Roman Druidic associations, along with his original intention (later abandoned) to give the character who was eventually to become Stephen Wonham the name of Siegfried, suggests experiments with other kinds of mythological material.[15] Forster's symbolic employment of the Figsbury Rings is, of course, reminiscent of Hardy's climactic scene at Stonehenge in *Tess of the D'Ubervilles,* and Siegfried at once evokes for us—as it must have for Forster—Wagner's great operatic tetralogy, *The Ring of the Nibelung.* Finally, in his last novel, *A Passage to India,* Forster moved farthest away from the classical mythology of his early novels in order to base his story on a body of non-Western myth.

Forster was very much aware of the important interrelations of myth and fantasy in fiction. In *Aspects of the Novel* he devotes one chapter ("Fantasy") and parts of another ("Prophecy") to a discussion of those interrelations. The distinction he draws in the former chapter between fantasy and prophecy in fact very neatly describes the difference between his use of classical material early in his career and his use of mythology generally in his later work. Fantasy and prophecy, he writes, "are alike in having gods, and unlike in the gods they have. There is in both the sense of mythology which differentiates them from other aspects of our subject . . . on behalf of fantasy let us now invoke all beings who inhabit the lower air, the shallow water and the smaller hills, all Fauns and Dryads and slips of the memory, all that is medieval this side of the grave. When we come to prophecy, we shall utter no invocation, but it will have been to whatever transcends them, to the deities of India, Greece, Scandinavia and Judaea, to all that is medieval beyond the grave and to Lucifer son of the morning. By their mythologies we shall distinguish these two sorts of novels."[16] Though in his later chapter on prophecy Forster makes more specific the kind of novel he means when he uses that term—chiefly the novels of Dostoevski, Melville, Lawrence, and Emily Brontë—and though clearly none of Forster's own books, even *Howards End* or *A Passage to India*, quite fits in with that company, there is unquestionably a prophetic element in *Howards End*, and that element is connected with the mythological substructure of the novel.

There are various points in the novel when, as might be expected, this mythological substructure exercises an almost tangible influence. I am not speaking here of quasi-epiphanic moments such as Leonard Bast's on the North Downs at night or Margaret's encounter with Miss Avery at Howards End. I mean, rather, those larger building blocks of the novel: the fifth chapter with its programmatic description of Beethoven's symphony, or the opening of the twenty-second chapter, with the famous purple passage about the rainbow bridge and about connection. These are certainly two of the most important passages in the whole novel—providing as they do essential guides for its interpretation—and they are, as we shall see, both profoundly infused with Germanic mythological elements. There are other instances as well, as in the six Danish hills or tumuli from which Hilton derives its name and to which the Howard name itself appears to refer, made up as it is of "how," meaning a local hill, mount of tumulus (from the Old Norse *haugr*), and "ward," meaning watching, guarding, or custody (from the Old English *ward*).[17] But such instances, important and suggestive as they are, are subordinate to the two major mythological passages already cited.

I shall take up the rainbow-bridge passage first. It occurs after Henry Wilcox and Margaret Schlegel have become engaged and Henry has made his first, shamefaced gesture of physical love: "Margaret greeted her lord with peculiar tenderness on the morrow. Mature as he was, she might yet be able to help him to the building of the rainbow bridge that should connect the prose in us with the passion. Without it we are meaningless fragments, half monks, half beasts, unconnected arches that have never joined together into a man. With it love is born, and alights on the highest curve, glowing against the grey, sober against the fire. Happy the man who sees from either aspect the glory of these outspread wings. The roads of his soul lie clear, and he and his friends shall find easy going" (H 186). This is one of the most remarkable—and most remarked upon—passages in *Howards End*. It describes in resonant, metaphoric terms, the process that two paragraphs later Forster will sum up even more enigmatically in the command "Only Connect!", the command that also forms the epigraph to the novel.

This rainbow bridge, as any student of Germanic mythology will recognize at once, is *Bifröst,* the bridge that flames in three colors and connects Asgard, the home of the gods, with Midgard, the home of men. It is guarded by Heimdall (sometimes called the father of men), who, at *Ragnarök*—the fated day—will sound his trumpet to warn the gods of the approach of the giants and their allies. On that day the giants will cross the rainbow bridge to Asgard and will destroy that bridge, along with Asgard and the gods, though they too will perish in the process. Even so, despite this nearly universal destruction, the world will survive and a new race of gods will be born, for the great ash tree—the world tree, Yggdrasil—will not share entirely in the destruction, but will put forth new shoots of life.[18]

Was Forster really aware of all this when he made the reference to the rainbow bridge in *Howards End?* Is all this mythology out of the Eddas not too esoteric for someone like Forster? I do not think so. To begin with, Forster's lifelong feeling for and connection with the countryside must inevitably have led him to a feeling for and a curiosity about its gods. It certainly did so in the early stories and novels, with the dryads and satyrs and sacred groves. It is unlikely that Forster would have reacted differently when he first encountered and was deeply moved by the German landscape. In fact, in one of the two diary entries quoted in his "Recollections of Nassenheide," he makes this association of German landscape with Germanic gods virtually explicit. On 28 May 1905, Forster, his pupils, and some of the other staff made a day's tour out to the Oder Berge. "The hills had a mountain stream running down them," he writes, "although they were only 300 feet high. The woods were full of bicyclists' paths. We had a second lunch. . . . Then through woods of spindly oaks to Falkendorf, where I saw two most beautiful things: bathers running naked under sun-pierced foliage, and a most enormous beech, standing in the village like a god."[19] These nude bathers and that ancient tree take Forster back into the pagan Germanic past, just as the great wych-elm growing next to Howards End does.

But if Forster is making use of Germanic mythology in *Howards End,* where is he getting his information from? From a number of sources possibly: from the opening lecture, perhaps, of Carlyle's *On Heroes, Hero-worship, and the Heroic in History* (1840); from Sir George Dasent's translation of *The Younger Edda* (1842), with its specific mention of the rainbow bridge; from the *Corpus Poeticum Boreale* (1883), which contains both the original texts and English translations; or from Jacob Grimm's monumental four-volume study of Teutonic Mythology, translated into English by J. S. Stallybrass (1883–88).[20] None of these works, except possibly for the *Corpus Poeticum Boreale,* was at all obscure and some of the information in them would have been part of the essential intellectual equipment of any educated person at the end of the nineteenth century—a century, after all, in which post-Darwinian anthropology was eager to trace back the ancestry and beliefs of the English people to their remotest Germanic origins.

All of this is possible and some of it is likely. What is certain is that Forster must have known a great deal about Germanic mythology from listening to Wagner's *Ring* cycle. As I have already observed, Forster admired Wagner's work and knew it intimately. In "Revolution at Bayreuth" he gives an account of the first performance of the *Ring,* which he saw in Dresden in 1904 or 1905. After fifty years he still had the original programs in his possession and still was able to provide details of the staging. In that staging—or, at any rate, in Wagner's own directions for it—the rainbow bridge plays an important part. This is how the libretto from scene 4 of *The Rhine Gold,* the first opera in the cycle, reads, in Frederick Jameson's 1897 translation:

> DONNER　　Brother, to me!
> 　　　　　　Shew them the way to the bridge!
> 　　　　　　*Froh* has also disappeared in the clouds.
> Suddenly the clouds disperse; *Donner* and *Froh* become visible: from their feet a rainbow bridge stretches with blinding radiance across the valley to the castle which now glows in the light of the setting sun. . .
> *Froh.*　　The bridge leads you homeward,
> 　　　　　light yet firm to your feet:
> 　　　　　now tread undaunted
> 　　　　　its terrorless path![21]

Wotan and the other gods speechlessly contemplate the glorious sight: and the curtain falls as they cross the rainbow bridge into Valhalla. The giants have been appeased: they have accepted the gold and the ring of power and given up their claim to Freia. Love, in short, has triumphed, at least temporarily, over gold, and the gods have "won," just as they have at the end of *Howards End.*

It is Wagner, too—and behind him, Germanic mythology—who rather ironically provides the key to Helen's perception of the significance of Beethoven's Fifth Symphony. Helen thinks of the conflicting themes of that symphony as representing the struggle of the gods and the goblins: ". . . the music started with a goblin walking quietly over the universe, from end to end. Others followed him. They were not aggressive creatures; it was that that made them so terrible to Helen. They merely observed in passing that there was no such thing as splendour or heroism in the world. . . .Helen could not contradict them, for, once at all events, she had felt the same, and had seen the reliable walls of youth collapse. Panic and emptiness! . . . Beethoven took hold of the goblins and made them do what he wanted. He appeared in person . . . he blew his mouth and they were scattered! Gust of splendour, gods and demi-gods contending with vast swords, colour and fragrance broadcast on the field of battle, magnificent victory, magnificent death! Oh, it all burst before the girl, and she even stretched out her gloved hands as if it was tangible. Any fate was titanic; any contest desirable; conqueror and conquered would alike be applauded by the angels of the utmost stars. . . . The goblins really had been there. They might return— and they did. It was as if the splendour of life might boil over and waste to steam and froth. In its dissolution one heard the terrible, ominous note, and a goblin, with increased malignity, walked over the universe from end to end. Panic and emptiness! Panic and emptiness! Even the flaming ramparts of the world might fall." But the ramparts, in the end, do not fall in flames. They are saved. Beethoven brings back the gods and scatters the goblins once again. Even so the struggle between them continues. Beethoven will not hide that fact under an easy optimism, "and that is why one can trust Beethoven when he says other things" (H 33–34).

Though ostensibly about Beethoven, this famous description is really based on Wagner's *Ring* cycle. Virtually all of the main Wagnerian elements are there: the gods, of course, and the goblins—a term that might include dwarfs as well as giants; the splendor of heroic battle in which gods and demigods participate, as do Siegmund and Siegfried; the magnificent victory and equally glorious death, impartially applauded by those angels of the utmost skies who behave not like Christians but like Valkyries; and the ominous suggestion of impending doom, of the collapse in flames of the universal ramparts, of the destruction of Valhalla and the twilight of the gods. This Wagnerian interpretaton of Beethoven's symphony has implications for the novel that reach out far beyond the chapter in which it occurs. Indeed, the struggle of gods and goblins provides the pattern for the struggle between the Schlegels and the Wilcoxes.

And it provides the pattern too for the ultimate resolution of that struggle. Helen, like Freia, is not given over to the Wilcoxian giants, even though they are, if not the builders, then certainly the preservers of Howards End/ Asgard. Helen, the embodiment of youth and beauty, is "saved." But instead Margaret takes her place, the Margaret who is like Fricka: older, less impetuous, conscious of the necessity for honoring contracts and preserving intact social institutions like marriage. Margaret knows too that the "giants," despite their industry and wealth, cannot survive without the life-sustaining sense of beauty of the gods, anymore than the gods can without the work of the giants. Only through the fusion of the divine and the autochthonous, of the primary—as Forster puts it—with the secondary virtues, can Howards End avoid the destruction that awaits either the giants alone (London with its satanic mills and imperialist hollow men) or the gods alone (rural decay). It is love, as Forster tells us, that must settle on the highest curve of the rainbow bridge: love that binds giants and gods. Those who forswear love, as Alberich and later Fafnir do in *The Rhine Gold*, or Charles Wilcox in *Howards End*, may gain material power, along with the curse that lies upon that power. Those, on the other hand, who forswear power in favor of love, will, like Leonard Bast, be saved, in spirit if not in body.

Wagner and Germanic mythology also prove helpful in the interpretation of other parts of *Howards End*. The story, as told in the *Prose* or *Younger Edda*, of the creation of the first man and woman by Odin and Hoenir, may have a connection with Ruth Howard Wilcox and the great wych-elm. The name of the first woman was *Embla* (elm) and that of the first man *Asc* (ash), the latter clearly linking mankind with the World Tree, Yggdrasil, also an ash. Mrs. Wilcox is closely associated with the wych-elm in *Howards End*, the tree that, as Forster once admitted, stands for England. She alone knows of the pigs' teeth embedded in the bark of the tree and of their healing properties; she alone fully understands the significance of Howards End. In this respect she resembles the Volva or Wise Woman of the first part of the *Poetic* or Elder Edda who, at Odin's request, describes the main outlines of the Germanic world and foretells its destruction. Volva is also clearly related to Erda ("Mother Earth"), whom Wotan summons at the beginning of act 3 of *Siegfried* and who refuses to tell him what she knows, because she knows he is doomed and that his fate cannot be altered. Like Mrs. Wilcox, Volva knows a great deal about the World Tree and about Odin's eye (wisdom) and Heimdall's horn (intuition?) that lie hidden beneath it; and like Mrs. Wilcox—who "foretells" Margaret's eventual inheritance of Howards End— she prophesies the destruction of Asgard/Valhalla and the present race of gods, as well as the birth of the new. And like Erda, Mrs. Wilcox is a goddess of the earth, full of knowledge but reluctant to impart it, except to those who can understand her language.

From Wagner, too, comes at least some of the mystery associated with Father Schlegel's sword. Margaret finds it, to her surprise, unsheathed and hanging "naked" among the books and furniture that Miss Avery has unpacked at Howards End. At the end of the scene, after Margaret has tried in vain to make Miss Avery understand the folly of her action, this odd and rather demonic woman turns to criticize Ruth Wilcox for having married the man she did:

"Whom should she have married?"
"A soldier!" exclaimed the woman. "Some real soldier."
Margaret was silent. It was a criticism of Henry's
character far more trenchant than any of her own. (H 275)

Nothing further is made of this remark; it drops like a stone beneath the surface of the novel, never to reappear. But, on a mythological level, it continues to reverberate. This is precisely the criticism that Siegmund levels at Sieglinde—and Sieglinde at herself—for having married Hunding, doing so in the context of another father's (Wotan's) naked sword, "Notung." It is Siegmund, the real soldier and hero, who pulls out this magical sword that has been embedded in the trunk of the tree, and thereby reveals his heroic stature. He is the true husband of Sieglinde, not the prosaic, Wilcoxian "corporation man" Hunding. It is from his loins that Siegfried, the greatest hero of all, will be born, not from Hunding's.[22]

It is the specifically "German" sword of the Schlegels that brings about Leonard's death at the hands of Charles Wilcox at the close of *Howards End,* but not before Leonard—the ironically and yet not-so-ironically lionhearted Leonard—has sired a male child that will one day inherit Howards End. Like Siegfried, he is the victim of a treacherous attack by someone who cares more for gold than he does for love, and who, as he commits the murder, claims to be upholding honor and respectability.

All this is not to say that Forster is here slavishly following Wagner's lead, or even carefully inserting Wagnerian and/or Germanic mythological elements into his novel. It is merely to say that these elements are there and that, to some undefinable degree, Forster knew they were there and wanted them to be there. It is quite clear, let me say again, that these elements are not present in an unambiguous, untransformed state. Forster has used them to suit the purposes of his own art: the twilight of the gods is, for instance, averted in *Howards End*; but unquestionably those elements do add to Forster's art: they enrich it and they deepen it. They connect the sometimes mundane people and events of this novel with one of the archetypal stories of Western man; and by means of that connection they join, by the rainbow bridge of inspiration, the prosaic earth with the heaven of poetry.

4

The Loves of English Women and German Men

*If there is ever to be any real understanding for this cousin of
ours, we shall have to forget that he is a cousin, and then we
shall have to untie our bundles of manufactured prejudices
concerning him and start afresh.*
      I. A. R. Wylie, Eight Years in Germany *(1914)*

In much of the British literary response to the Great War, there runs a
persistent contrast between opposing pairs of national characteristics. British
spontaneity is set against German rigidity; love opposed to duty; pacifism to
militarism; the careless "muddling" of the amateur to the meticulous planning of the professional; vitalism to mechanism; sensitivity to force; gentleness to brutality; civilization to barbarism. Some of these polarities
predate 1914, though inevitably the war served to intensify them.

Without trying to determine the degree of truth in these sets of contrasting
pairs—German writers tended to think in terms of German vitality versus
British exhaustion, or need versus satiety—one senses nevertheless that there
is, from a psychological point of view, something profoundly suggestive
about them. For it is clear that many of these supposedly characteristic
German traits are habitually associated with masculinity, just as the British
traits are usually conceived of as female. The rigidity of the German nation is
matched by the flexible softness of the British; the brutal militarism of the
former by the gentle civility of the latter; German boastfulness by British
modesty; ruthless logic by intuitive spontaneity; the aggressive thrust of the
Germans by the outraged defense of the British.

Seen in this light, even the invasion fantasies take on a new meaning: that
of an unsuspecting, innocent woman overwhelmed by the desires of a ruffian
whose aim is to penetrate and desecrate her inmost self. At times this sense of
male/female opposition seems almost to rise to the surface, though it rarely
becomes entirely explicit. It comes closest to consciousness in the "Rape of
Belgium," as the German invasion of Belgium was almost immediately
dubbed in the British press.

77

"Rape" unmistakably evokes a specifically sexual context, and the atrocity stories that soon arose out of the German invasion are often pornographic, describing in detail group rapes and sadistic mutilation of female sexual organs. Cartoons, posters, and other pictorial representations (as, for instance, in *Punch*) that deal with Belgium in the opening months of the war tend to portray Belgium as a prostrate or humiliated—but defiant—woman, straddled by a huge German soldier in a spiked helmet, erect and with legs outspread. For that matter, similar symbolic depictions of Britain rarely exhibit the male national totem (John Bull) but reveal a distinct preference for female Britannia, shown usually confronting a bullying male German figure who bears a marked resemblance to the Kaiser.

The most striking and memorable wartime embodiment of this archetypal British conception of Germany is Nurse Cavell. Her case will be examined in greater detail in a later chapter (along with the impact of German atrocities on the British mind in general), but for the moment it is enough to note that her execution in 1915 fitted perfectly into a pattern that had already been deeply rooted in the psyche of many British people. Here was an innocent, defenseless woman, devoted to peace and charitable activity, who had been martyred by the male German bully. The fact that she was executed in Belgium made the association with rape even more vivid and inevitable. In Nurse Cavell the British found reality and symbol fused and fixed.

The origin of this stereotypical conception of Germany is to be found almost certainly in the Franco-Prussian war. Prior to 1870, the most prevalent male characteristic of the Germans, as far as the British were concerned, seems to have been a taste for beer. For the rest, Germans were associated with the more "feminine" activities of music, romantic poetry, picturesque landscape, and unintelligible idealistic speculation. Queen Victoria's German consort, Prince Albert, is typical for this earlier conception.

With 1870, the German female virtues diminish or vanish altogether—or, as in Forster's *Howards End*, emigrate to England. Now begins the reign of the masculine, militaristic German bully. At first this bully is personified in the British public mind by Bismarck, the "Iron" Chancellor, often depicted in uniform, with his expansive, outthrust chest suggestive of the fat German who increases his girth by gobbling up other countries. The relationship to Bismarck of the unhappy Crown Princess of Prussia, Victoria's daughter and William II's mother, is characteristic of this phase of British perception of Germany, just as Victoria and Albert were of the earlier: a spirited, sensitive, and spontaneous woman oppressed by a grim and wily mustachioed military man.

It is an interesting and, I think, significant fact, in this context, that much of the British fiction of this period specifically dealing with Germany was written by women. Elizabeth (Beauchamp) von Arnim springs to mind immediately. Her *Elizabeth and Her German Garden* (1898) became something of a best-seller. This discursive book seems amiable enough, though a distinguished and by no means Germanophilic contemporary British critic finds it anti-German and "quite a scorcher in its unabashed bitchiness and arrogance."[1] In fact, the book scarcely portrays Germany at all, since much of its time is taken up with the elaborate revelation of Elizabeth von Arnim's insatiable "sensibility." And like her German surroundings, her German husband (whom she calls "The Man of Wrath") remains very much in the background, a shadowy figure whose primary function is to account for her presence in Germany rather than anywhere else. More remarkable than her book, however, is Elizabeth von Arnim's subsequent change of feelings toward Germany, for in this respect she serves as a kind of model for other British women writers about that country. In 1915, five years after her husband's death, she returned to England to become the wife of Frank Russell (Bertrand's older brother) and publicly rejected her ties with her sometime home. "Elizabeth," so Bertrand Russell observed that year of his new sister-in-law, "expressed regret at the fact that her five German nephews in the war are all still alive."[2] And two years later, in her novel *Christine*, she told the story of a young British girl bullied and maltreated by barbarous Germans, a story that, ostensibly about her daughter, she had by this time persuaded herself was her own.

Elizabeth von Arnim, as the wife of a well-to-do Prussian aristocrat with extensive holdings in Pomerania, experienced a Germany rather similar to the life led in wealthy English country houses; hence the title of her book, with its evocation of "English" gardens and an earlier English Elizabeth. The Germany she surveyed was primarily rural and *de haut en bas*. Not so, however, with most of the other British women writers about Germany. Though their class origins were not always noticeably different—Katherine Mansfield, for instance, was Elizabeth's cousin—their stays in Germany were either as guests in pensions, like Mansfield, or as governesses or "companions" in German boarding schools, like I. A. R. Wylie, Dorothy Richardson, and, apparently, Sybil Spottiswoode.[3]

Spottiswoode's *Her Husband's Country* and Wylie's *Dividing Waters* both appeared in the same year, 1911, and are remarkably alike in subject matter and approach. Both novels deal with a marriage between an English girl and a German officer, a marriage that for reasons of national character either turns out to be a failure or narrowly avoids failure. These novels are virtually forgotten today, but both—and especially Wylie's—deserve to be remembered not only as symptomatic of contemporaneous attitudes toward Germany, but as genuine, if minor, works of art. They manage to transcend the familiar genre of romantic fiction to which they belong through the sense of urgency that informs them, by their perception that behind the day-to-day reality that they depict, with its crises of the individual heart and the misunderstandings of individual minds, there lurks a vaster and more ominous shadow of impending international conflict.

Spottiswoode's heroine, Patience Thaile, an attractive, open-minded young woman of marriageable age, decides to leave her rural middle-class home in order to visit friends in Pomerania. There she meets a young German officer, Helmuth Rabenstedt, who courts her ardently and with whom she gradually drifts into love. Though handsome and even dashing, Rabenstedt shows early signs of developing into an archetypal German. He likes his beer and wine altogether too well. So, the narrator informs us, "the prophetic eye might have seen in the square jaw a future likelihood of double chins, and a general danger of unwieldy corpulence."[4] In every thin German, as it were—to turn Orwell's famous remark around—there is a fat German struggling to get out.

Patience is particularly attracted to Rabenstedt's confident impulsiveness, his lack of reserve, his open display of emotion, "one of the advantages of the Teuton temperament" (65), so unlike the reticent British. She dislikes, however, the vulgarity of German society; the subservient women who are either in the kitchen or else catering to the men; the lack of "smartness" in dress and the absence of any real understanding of the "elegance" so essential to English life.

Still, despite her doubts and the impoverished Rabenstedt's reluctance to marry unless Patience can assure him of an adequate income, they finally get married. For the first time Patience sees her new husband out of uniform, and the sight comes as a shock. She finds him attired in one of those "ill-cut and grotesque garments which constitute the usual attire of the ruck of Germans who have not come under the influence of English tailordom" (216). On their honeymoon in the Black Forest, Helmut ceases to shave regularly and, as Patience is dismayed to discover, he is not accustomed to keeping his body altogether clean. He does not appreciate either—nor, for that matter, do the other German guests—her need to dress for dinner. His eating habits, and those of his fellow Germans at the hotel, leave much to be desired. An aptly named Professor Grossmann sets the tone in this respect, as well as in the stupid anti-English remarks he makes.

Patience struggles to be loyal to her husband, but with increasing difficulty. Unhappy and alone in the woods one day, she chances to meet two English people, the mother and brother, as it turns out, of her sometime reticent, tall, spare, and athletic English admirer, Captain Cunningham Roper, V.C., D.S.O. The lady, small and slim, and the young man, impeccably dressed in a light flannel suit and panama hat, present a startling contrast to her obese husband and his German compatriots. "This soft-voiced old lady," she notes wistfully, "was so trim and *soignée* and the young man at her side so redolent of fresh air and water" (237). Inevitably the conversation drifts to the inevitably coming war, which the son sees as arising not out of hostility between Germans and English ("though this increases every year"), but from "the larger factor of the evolution of the two nations" (237), alluding apparently to Chalmers Mitchell and Frank Harris. The mother admits that the English find the Germans offensive, but recognizes that the feeling may be mutual. If this is so, objects the son, "then why do they [the Germans] intrude upon our preserves? Why do they go to hotels which are frequented exclusively by English people? I am sure I have never known Englishmen to go to an entirely German hotel or pension" (240).

After this meeting, despite heroic efforts, Patience never feels quite the same about her German husband, especially since this "huge creature" interprets his love for her as "an overwhelming animal passion" and shares the "national belief" that everything between a man and a woman must be "of an entirely sexual nature" (376). He insists on imposing his bulky self upon her "slender throat" and "sensitive lips" (379–80).

Fortunately, however, Patience's German nightmare comes to a sudden end. Her German infant dies and her German husband is thrown from a German horse and killed. She returns to England to marry the slim, well-tailored, and well-heeled Captain Roper who, in the meantime, has purchased Colne House, her former parental home. In these happy, familiar surroundings, Patience is able to reflect more calmly and objectively on her German experience. She grows aware that "her great mistake had been in not realizing from the first the radical and fundamental differences between the two nationalities" (400); and that she had erred also in seeing life with Rabenstedt only from her own point of view, without being able to appreciate his. "All along," Spottiswoode informs us in conclusion, "she had been grossly unjust in punishing the individual for the faults and characteristics of his nation" (411).

I. A. R. Wylie's *Dividing Waters* is considerably more sophisticated than Spottiswoode's novel. Where Spottiswoode unquestioningly and apparently unconsciously accepts the innate superiority of British elegance over German vulgarity, even to the point of allowing—without the least trace of irony—one of her English characters to comment on Germans "intruding" on "our preserves" in Germany—is it possible to imagine a German making an equivalent remark in an English context?—where Spottiswoode is at best naive and at worst the spokesman for the ethics of elegance and the philosophy of clothes, Wylie at least perceives and concedes the existence of actual Germans rather than simply the stereotyped Germans of the British yellow press.[5]

Dividing Waters tells the story of the growth of a young woman's mind. Nora Ingestre, of Delford in rural England, is the daughter of a Vicar who might easily have stepped out of the pages of *The Way of All Flesh:* a narrow Victorian hypocrite and prig. Nora's mother, though seriously ill with an unspecified disease—one suspects the real disease is her husband—is completely different: a kind of Mrs. Wilcox who quietly sees beneath the surface of things in a deeply religious way that does not find expression in official rites. Her mother urges Nora to leave home to visit an old German acquaintance of hers in Karlsburg (Karlsruhe). "With a lot of fat, greasy, gobbling Germans?" asks Nora in astonishment (15). To which her mother replies that she has begun "to think that God cannot have reserved all the virtues for us English" (16–17).

Unconvinced, Nora nevertheless decides to go. Once in Germany, her train compartment inevitably begins to fill up with Germans. Though not yet twenty and alone in a foreign country for the first time, Nora remains unperturbed; even the presence of the whole Imperial family would not have put her out of countenance, for she was "sustained by a calm and inborn knowledge of her racial superiority." This sense of innate superiority remains unshaken when she observes how poorly Germans dress and what dreadful boots they wear.

It is music that first begins to draw Nora out of her insular shell—the music of Wagner. After seeing *Die Walküre*, she writes home to her mother that she now understands things she never understood before. This understanding is materially assisted by Nora's growing romantic involvement with the nephew of her hostess, a young German officer named Wolff von Arnim. With him she goes riding—and he rescues her when her horse bolts; with him she plays piano duets—and he compliments her by saying she does not play like an Englishwoman.

They are engaged, much to the chagrin of her father and her brother, Miles. When Wolff arrives in Delford for the wedding, he is dressed in civilian clothes that are all too obviously ready-made. Miles mocks the inadequate tailoring of the German "bounder," but for Nora Wolff's face, at least, remains the same. After their marriage, they move to a fourth-floor apartment in Berlin, where Wolff has been assigned to work for the General Staff. The apartment is small and filled with ugly furniture, but Nora disguises these facts—and her growing unhappiness—in glowing letters to her family.

Nora patiently endures her lot, but only until her brother arrives for a visit. Then she suddenly sees everything through his "English" eyes and is mortified: her vulgar, inelegant surroundings, her smug husband, satisfied with his army friends and with his cheap wine and sausage.

After Miles's arrival and her chance meeting with a sometime English neighbor and suitor, Captain Robert Arnold, it is downhill all the way. Miles sponges on Wolff and intrigues behind his back; Nora consoles herself with Arnold in increasingly indiscreet ways. She even begins to see in her husband a potential enemy of England. Arnold tells her that "these beggars are beginning to suspect us of fear or incompetence, and the sooner they are disillusioned the better" (268), and Miles echoes these sentiments more bluntly with a warning that "the beggars want more than is good for them, and we've got to keep them in their places. That's the gist of the matter. It has to come sooner or later" (307). Under such pressure Nora, near the breaking point, bursts out to Wolff that she loathes and detests his country and his people, that she is English to the core and was "mad, mad, mad to believe I could ever be anything else" (301).

Not long thereafter a diplomatic crisis breaks out between Britain and Germany—Wylie may be alluding to the Morocco crisis of 1906—and Nora encounters overt anti-English feeling for the first time in the Berlin streets. Her impulsive reaction makes it unmistakably clear where her true loyalties lie: not with her husband's country but with England. "You fools," she tells the Germans, "you poor fools, who dare to rise against US—US, the elect of God among the nations" (336).

Now there is no turning back. Together with Arnold, she boards a train for England, leaving Wolff behind to fight a duel in Miles's behalf, a duel Miles was too cowardly to fight for himself. Miles rewards Wolff by also leaving for England, but not before rifling his desk and absconding with some important secret documents belonging to the General Staff. Wolff, gravely wounded, awaits death and disgrace alone, believing that it was Nora who took the documents.

Back in Delford, in the company of Miles and the Tory Squirearchy, Nora begins to have second thoughts. Her dying mother urges her to return, to build a bridge between her own country and the country of her adoption—shades of E. M. Forster. She begins to realize that in England she is surrounded by selfishness and muddling, that life with Wolff, whatever its faults and disappointments, had at least had a kind of nobility, inspired as it was "by a great idea worthy of the sacrifices it demanded." Walking out into the English countryside, Nora encounters the tall, familiar figure of Arnold coming toward her out of the mists—but now, like herself, a chastened figure. "We can't see," he tells her, "that the world has changed, that we have to face a race that has all our virtues in their youth and strength—all our tenacity, all our bull-dog purpose, all our old Stoicism . . ." (365).

Repentant, filled with a new resolve and a resurgence of her old love for Wolff, Nora returns to Berlin, ready to start building her bridge of nations. She takes with her the papers Miles had stolen, whose return will at least restore Wolff's honor, as her renewed love promises to restore his health.

Like Spottiswoode's *Her Husband's Country,* Wylie's *Dividing Waters* is obviously a romantic melodrama; but then it is arguable that the relationship between England and Germany at this time possessed many of the ingredients of melodrama: hatred as well as love; admiration and contempt; envy and—at least in Wylie's case—a willingness to concede some trace of nobility in the soul of the villain. But Wylie's novel often manages to rise above the level of melodrama, like Forster's *Howards End,* on the wings of irony. That she lacks Forster's deftness of ironic touch, as well as his rich symbolic texture, is undeniable and unfortunate; it keeps her novel from joining the ranks of the immortals. But in its very mortality it manifests an urgency, a topicality, a sense of what "ordinary" English men and women thought and did in a way that Forster's novel does not. If Forster has a fault, it is that he is not vulgar enough.

Neither Forster's nor Wylie's bridge to Germany was to survive 1914. In the case of Forster the flood tides of war washed it away; in Wylie's case, she dismantled it herself. In her autobiography, *My Life with George* (1940)— "George" is her better, "creative" self—Wylie tells the story of how she came to change her mind about Germany but, unlike Nora, never to change it again.

She tells how she came to Germany at nineteen, leaving behind a domestic Australian/British hell, ready to find a foreign paradise; of how she entered that paradise to the music of Wagner, plunging herself ecstatically on the average of three times a week "into the boiling lava of his turgid Teutonism." She lived in Germany for eight years and wrote three books about it, "lying" books at whose memory George "cowers." Her weaknesses of mind and character predisposed her to the "German virus." Being "naturally flamboyant and responsive to uniforms, military bands and large, imposing gestures," possessing "a romantic and sentimental streak which involves inevitably a streak of cruelty," and feeling "temporarily exhausted and tired of struggle so that I welcomed authority," Wylie became "a typical young Nazi" before the First World War.[6]

It was only when she returned to Britain that she began to realize what true civilization was. Invited to Scotland by a wealthy British boarder at her German school, she received her first taste of true elegance. She was stunned by the splendor of British upper-class dressing for dinner and shamed by the inadequacy of her own solitary frock laid out by the servant (136). There was nothing like this in Germany, even though, as she noted in *The Germans* (1909), "the occasional lack of polish is beginning to be a thing of the past, and will disappear altogether when the German has acquired riches enough, and has had time and experience enough to apply them to his physical and material culture."[7] But such a Germany lay in the future—and when a later Wylie looked back on the Germany she herself had experienced, she found that her years there had been "crippling and retarding. They forced my impressionable mind into a hard small mold. They kept me from friendship and understanding with my own people."[8] For Wylie, in the end, then— quite unlike her fictional Ibsenite Nora, or even her own former self that had once hoped for "an *entente cordiale* with our cousin,"[9] there was to be no more bridge to Germany. The gulf was unbridgeable. Germans and British might share a "racial affinity," but unalterable geographic facts made Germans suspicious and fanatical, just as they made their happier cousins tolerant and self-assured.[10]

Unlike Spottiswoode and Wylie, Katherine Mansfield never spent much time in Germany. In 1909 she lived for a few months in Bavaria, first in a nunnery and later in a pension at Woerishofen, where her mother had advised her to go after separating from her husband, George Bowden, and becoming pregnant by another man. The pregnancy ended in miscarriage, but while in Germany Mansfield met a number of impoverished intellectuals and artists—a situation later evoked by D. H. Lawrence in the closing "Tyrolean" section of *Women in Love* (1920), where Mansfield is the original of Gudrun. Gudrun leaves Tyrol for Dresden, has a child, and is absorbed into a bohemian existence, whereas in actuality Mansfield returned to England without a child to lead a bohemian artistic life in the company of A. R. Orage, Beatrice Hastings, and John Middleton Murry. While at Woerishofen, however, Mansfield and her friends planned, according to one of her biographers, Sylvia Berkman, "literary journals, they talked of translating Miss Mansfield's stories. Association with these men reawakened her own creative zest. She began to write the sketches of German life later collected and published as *In a German Pension*."[11]

Though Mansfield spent only a relatively short time in Germany, she was neither wholly ignorant of the German language nor entirely unsympathetic to Germany. At Queen's College a few years earlier she had fallen under the influence of her German professor, Walter Rippmann, a remarkably sophisticated teacher who singled Mansfield out as one of the students invited to the literary *soirées* at his home, where "he introduced a select and envied group to the heady wine of the decadents."[12] Rippmann may very well be the original model for the initially extraordinarily civilized but in the end bestially dirty old German in "The Little Governess," the only Mansfield story with a German background not included in *In a German Pension*.

For a time Mansfield was sufficiently charmed by things German that— perhaps in imitation of her cousin Elizabeth—she would sign some of her letters "Kath Schönfeld," a literal translation of her surname, Beauchamp. A few of the entries in her *Journal* dating from the Woerishofen period are written in intelligible, though far from perfect, German. So Mansfield would seem to have been fairly well qualified to provide an English audience with an insight into the German character.

And provide it she does, with a vegeance, so that her insights are more in the nature of incitements: a kind of catalogue of German follies and villainies, a pension of German fools. The searing irony of these stories never includes the narrator or the English, and their overt hostility to Germans is so blatant that it is difficult to believe critics like John Carswell who argue that Mansfield's anti-German feeling is purely accidental, a result of her "deft, detached observation," which "as it happened, put Germans in a bad

light. From Katherine's point of view this was the merest of acci-
dents. . . ."[13] An accident, from whatever point of view, it was not; but it
was certainly a case of hit and run.

Mansfield's collection opens with a story called "Germans at Meat,"
describing a group of porcine Germans swilling down their breakfast while
commenting on the large breakfasts of the English. Meanwhile, the Herr
Rat—*Rat* means councillor in German but Mansfield is here playing on the
English meaning as well—stares at the Mansfield-like narrator "with an
expression which suggested a thousand premeditated invasions."[14] A moment later she manages only by adroitly changing the subject to forestall a
vulgar North German salesman's relating in grotesque detail the effects of
sauerkraut on his digestive tract. Then, in the afternoon, the Germans—
"their mouths full of cherry stones" from eating too much cake—are as-
tonished that the narrator should not know what her husband's favorite kind
of meat is.

The next story demonstrates graphically that German aristocrats are no
less gross and vulgar than the German middle classes. The narrator's attention is drawn to the Baron because he never speaks to anyone and always eats
alone at a separate table. Inevitably, she wonders why. Soon the mystery is
cleared up when the Baron informs her that he needs to devote his full
attention to food.

> "I sit alone that I may eat more," said the Baron, poring into the
> dusk; "my stomach requires a great deal of food. I order double
> portions and eat them in peace."
> Which sounded finely Baronial.
> "And what do you do all day?"
> "I imbibe nourishment in my room," he replied, in a voice that closed
> the conversation.

The next few stories deal with the loves of the Germans, though these too
are intimately bound up with the grosser bodily functions. In one story, a
romantic student is overheard by the narrator telling his beloved of his
"severe nasal catarrh" which necessitated, during the previous night, the use
of three different handkerchiefs. Another story, about a wedding, recounts
how a group of noisy Germans enjoy themselves in a "stench of beer and
perspiration." To illustrate the Germans' behavior on such formal occasions,
the mother of the bride takes a deep swig out of a beer mug and then "spat on
the floor and savagely wiped her mouth on her sleeve."

And, of course, there is the inevitable Herr Professor. His life is made up
of feeding and lusting grossly, much like Professor Grossmann in Spottiswoode's *Her Husband's Country*, who may very well have served as a
model for Mansfield. While eating a batch of cherries and spitting out the

stones, the Professor recounts "a very interesting experiment" that he once carried out with a colleague at his university: "We bit into four pounds of the best cherries and did not find one specimen without a worm."

In the evening, there is singing—that is, German "Kultur." Naturally, that too is gross: "The Frau Oberlehrer tripped on the platform followed by a very young gentleman, who blew his nose twice before he hurled his handkerchief into the bosom of the piano." The evening concludes with the Herr Professor and his soulful Fräulein heading for the woods.

These were the stories that made Mansfield's reputation when they were first published in A. R. Orage's *New Age,* where they would be sure to catch the attention of an avant-garde audience. Published in book form a little later, the stories were also successful with a more general public, a success attributable almost certainly as much to Mansfield's subject matter as to intrinsic merit. According to her husband, Middleton Murry, *In a German Pension* "was immediately recognized. It passed quickly into three editions, when its sale was disastrously interrupted by the sudden bankruptcy of her publisher."[15] Mansfield was never to return to drawing blood from German subjects; and to her credit it should added that during the war she refused to allow the republication of the book for propaganda purposes.

Dorothy Richardson, despite being a decade or more older than the other women writers considered here (except for Violet Hunt), did not publish her first "German" book until 1915. *Pointed Roofs,* however, bears few traces of the war because it had been virtually finished in 1913. It forms the first part of Richardson's multi-volume fictional autobiography, *Pilgrimage,* and is, technically speaking, a *tour de force,* using stream of consciousness and abrupt transitions and juxtapositions, as well as a limited point of view. It is a kind of *Portrait of the Artist as a Young Woman,* completed and published at almost the same time as Joyce's novel, but with Germany instead of Ireland as its setting.

Miriam Henderson, Richardson's heroine and fictional alter ego, is seventeen when she decides to leave her impoverished but respectable English family. Though she loves her sisters and suffers from homesickness in Germany, she finds intolerable her family's obsessive need to keep up social and sartorial appearances. Even while accompanying Miriam to Holland, her father persists in playing the "rôle of the English gentleman."[16] Hence she feels that she would "rather stay abroad on any terms—away from England—English people." Like Spottiswoode's and Wylie's heroines, trouble at home predisposes Miriam to tolerance for the strange ways of abroad. Her position as a kind of junior English mistress at Fräulein Pfaff's small boarding school in Hanover is not overly demanding. She has time to listen to music and to practice playing the piano herself. As in Wylie's novel, the Germans play differently. Even the German schoolgirls have it, this other thing: "a quality she had only heard occasionally at concerts, and in the playing of one of the music teachers at school" (36). This quality may arise from the German readiness to express emotion and affection openly and unreservedly, though later, when she hears one of the English pupils at the school giving a recital at the piano, she decides the difference is really one of ego. The English girls, though technically perfect, "did not think only about the music, they thought about themselves too" (53). But Miriam is convinced—rightly so, as it turns out—that she too can play as the Germans do.

The inner life of the Germans attracts her; the outer life, less so. She has to endure having her hair washed with ordinary soap and water rather than the cantharides and rose water she is accustomed to. She is mortified at having to accompany the schoolgirls to the public baths, where she had never been before; and she wishes that "Fräulein [Pfaff] could know that there were two bathrooms in the house at Barnes . . . " (138). A visit to a German doctor reminds her of an earlier visit to an oculist in Harley Street; the shabby, over-furnished, German consultation room compares unfavorably. The English, she concludes, are certainly "more refined than the Germans" (122).

But unlike Spottiswoode's or Mansfield's or even Wylie's heroines, Miriam is not so sure that she prefers English refinement to German vulgarity. English refinement, as she knows from the experience of her own family, may be a cloak for English hypocrisy. Going to the English Church in Hanover, she is put off by the cold elegance of the parishioners, and decides that "certainly she did not belong to these 'refined' English—women or men" (94). The German religious services are preferable, where the singing and hymns are more natural and less "like a 'proclamation' or an order" (103). So for the time being she thinks it best to remain with the Germans. In one of the coffee shops in Hanover, Miriam watches the German women talking and laughing; she is repelled by the sight but at any rate, she reflects, "they did not pretend to be refined as Englishwomen did . . . they had the same horridness . . . but they were . . . jolly . . . they could shout if they liked" (126).

Not that Miriam decides one way or the other easily or finally, though in the end she does return to Britain after staying only six months in Germany. But she returns a changed person. At one point, Fräulein Pfaff tells Miriam that she has "something of the German" (170) in her; to this Miriam does not reply, but it seems clear that she agrees, and her agreement is not limited to the way she plays music. When, after a quarrel with the Fräulein, Miriam finally departs, feeling "English and free," she is nevertheless touched by the words of Millie, one of the English pupils whom she leaves behind. "To stay in Germany? You'd rather do that than anything?" Miriam asks. To which Millie answers: "I'd rather be in Germany than anything" (280–81).

Better than any other British writer of the period, except perhaps Charles Hamilton Sorley, Richardson catches the contrary moods of attraction and repulsion between the two countries, and leaves us with a sense that Britain and Germany are connected and divided by sets of uncomplementary vices and virtues.

More clearly than anyone else too, Richardson perceives that the conflict between Germany and England is one between "men" and "women." Though sexually attracted to the music teacher at the school, Miriam is in general repelled by German men. She finds their attitude toward women different from that of either French or British men; German men "despise women" (106). What is more, German women allow themselves to be despised. Though they are being educated in music and the arts at Fräulein Pfaff's finishing school, the fate that awaits them is only too clear: to marry, to cook, to sew, to bear children, to be good *hausfraus*. For Miriam such a fate is unimaginable. With German men Miriam *is* refined: she cannot bear the "fast, horrid," impudent young German students who seek to approach her companions during an excursion into the otherwise idyllic countryside. As to going with one of her pupils to visit her German home, Miriam sadly concludes that this would never do, for it would mean meeting German men. It would mean having to be angry at once, for German men "had all offended her at once. Something in their bearing and manner. . . . Blind and impudent . . ." (255).

So Miriam goes home alone, without the experience of a romantic involvement with a German man. It is impossible; there will be no "marrying a German professor" (9), as she had whimsically speculated before setting out for Germany. Germany, as Richardson was to remark later during a war "against the desire for regimentation and domination of anything whatsoever," Germany was a "masculine culture."[17] As such, it was really no place for a woman, whatever its other virtues, and especially not for a woman so deeply imbued with the feminine culture of Britain as was Dorothy Richardson.

One German, however, who did manage to make a success of his marriage to an Englishwoman was Franz Hüffer, the father of Ford Madox Hueffer, nowadays better known as Ford Madox Ford. Franz Hüffer, an intellectual and a gifted musician, made a reputation for himself in Britain as a music critic and amateur philosopher; and Ford's mother, Catherine, the daughter of the Pre-Raphaelite painter Ford Madox Brown, brought Hüffer into intimate contact with one of the leading circles of late nineteenth-century thinkers and artists. Ford was to make use of both heritages in his long and variegated career as editor, novelist, poet, raconteur, publicity agent, and man of letters.

Ford was half German. As such, according to German law, he was eligible for German citizenship himself, a legal fact of which he was quite well aware and of which he was eventually to avail himself. Technically, therefore, it seems fair to think of him, if only half-seriously, as a German.

The full story of Ford's quest for German citizenship and his efforts to gain a German divorce, which would allow him to marry Violet Hunt, will not be retold here. Those who are interested in this sometimes bizarre affair can turn to Ford's own radically fictionalized account in *Parade's End* (1921–28); or Violet Hunt's in *Those Flurried Years* (1926; American title, *I Have This to Say*); or Douglas Goldring's *South Lodge* (1942); or—the most objective and thorough of the lot—Arthur Mizener's *The Saddest Story* (1971).[18] What I propose to do here instead is rather to look at Ford's changing view of Germany and of his own German identity; and to place these in the context of Violet Hunt's experience of the man she was accustomed to calling Joseph Leopold.

Ford's German period lasted for about a decade, from 1903 to 1914, during which time he made frequent trips to Germany, with occasional visits to his plentiful, vaguely aristocratic, and definitely well-to-do relations there. This culminated in his naturalization as a German in 1911, at Giessen in the German state of Hessia. The primary reason for seeking German nationality did not lie in Ford's desire to repudiate his British background and upbringing; for him it seemed rather a means, perhaps the only means, to the end of ridding himself of his first wife, Elsie—who refused to grant him a divorce in England—and then to marry Violet Hunt. Oddly enough, however, Ford stopped his efforts to receive a legal divorce once he had secured his new national status. For reasons that still remain unclear, he and Violet simply announced that there had been a divorce and that they had subsequently married. This fiction, understandably, did not withstand the scrutiny of the British courts.

Of Ford's naturalization Douglas Goldring writes that Ford had second thoughts even before he went through with it: "As Ford was not only 'psychic,' in the sense that he had a good deal of intuition about forthcoming events, but was also well-informed and observant, it is probable that he guessed that war between Germany and the Entente was inevitable. If it broke out he would be faced with the prospect of fighting against France or being put up against the wall and shot."[19] It is true that in the first volume of *Parade's End*, Ford's alter ego, Christopher Tietjens (whose supposed real original is Ford's friend Marwood), is remarkably prescient, not to say omniscient, and in 1911 predicts a European war by the time of the "grouse-season" of 1914; but one may be permitted to doubt that the real Ford of 1911 enjoyed a similar clairvoyance.[20] In fact, there is very little trace of the inevitable warrior in Ford at this time. On the contrary, the two essays on "High Germany," published in *The Saturday Review* at the end of September and beginning of October 1911—immediately after Ford's naturalization—are fairly glowing with optimism and pro-Germanism. And if there are any thoughts of war here, they are of a war placed in a far distant future when, for the good of the "Anglo-Saxons," the Prussians may one day consent to take over their mismanaged country.

The first part of "High Germany"—the title possesses not merely geographic but also moral significance—opens with fulsome praise for the Duchy of Hanover and its inhabitants, among whom, in the first person plural, Ford includes himself. "We," the Saxons (i.e., the Hanoverians, Westphalians, and Hessians), and our other Anglo-Saxon kindred, may be pretty good at producing heroes by the dozen in moments of crisis, but in between times we tend to be slack. The other day, Ford goes on to say, he heard an "excellent, energetic, and quite English lady" (Violet Hunt?) tell him that she wished "to heaven the Prussians would conquer this country and administer it. Then there would be an end of our disgusting slackness." This opinion, admittedly astonishing to "us," nevertheless from the perspective of contented, prosperous, and peaceful Hanover seems "inevitable": "Not today, not tomorrow, not in ten years, not in twenty, not in any time into which there will survive any of the passions or bitternesses of today, but in some time when the English won't care and the Prussians will. That is the real secret of it all."[21]

And if the Prussian does not come, who will? For in the end "we" will be ruled by one of three possible masters: "Prussian, Jew, or hungry tradesman." That is inevitable. "And for ourselves we say as we get up and go down the hill [outside Hanover]: 'Please God that it will be the Prussian.' He at least will administer; will enrich us and will leave us somewhere some barrows in the sun amongst which to be. Possibly He [sic] will even put up an Aussichtsthurm and a tea garden. At any rate he alone of those sleepless ones will not strip us naked to the breezes."[22] So much for Ford's worries in 1911 about an impending conflict between his two fatherlands in which he would be put up against a Prussian wall and shot.

The second installment of "High Germany" is subtitled "Utopia." Here Ford first describes the prerequisites, cultural, aesthetic, and social, that would be needed to make up a Utopian environment; the list is long and impressive. Ford admits, of course, that this list is fantastic and that "such a town is impossible. It is unthinkable." Yet in the very next sentence he adds that it is "from this town we are writing . . . now we live in Utopia."[23] The actual place from which Ford was writing these words was Giessen, according to Goldring a "wretched little University town" (96).

There can be little doubt that Ford's tongue was occasionally in his cheek while he was writing the two parts of "High Germany." There can be even less doubt, however, that they are also filled with the pride and prejudice of one of Germany's newest citizens. Ford very much liked having an Aunt Emma who was, or possibly was, a Countess; especially since the Countess had ideas of getting the family title revived in his favor. Had this actually happened, Ford would have passed into English literary history as the unlikely nobleman Joseph Leopold Ford Hermann Madox Hueffer, Baron von Aschendorf.

In his heyday as a German or would-be German, Ford liked to plume himself with the noble feathers of his ancestry. To Douglas Goldring he once proposed a journey to the Kaiser's court in order to secure his German Imperial Majesty's support for the *English Review*. The Baron von Aschendorf, it appeared, was privy to the Kaiser's artistic councils and his voice was heard there with respect.[24] In the end, however, natively British financial support was found and the prospect of the Kaiser's helping to launch Ezra Pound and a new era of English letters was banished forever.

When Ford wrote the preface to Violet Hunt's *The Desirable Alien* (1913), he referred to Germany as "my beloved country" and worried out loud about that country's being "threatened with immense Slav empires, kingdoms, and states." Germany was being encircled by enemies, barbaric on one side and virulently vengeful on the other. Ford confesses that "I should hate the thought that this proud people, full of free passions, should cease to bulk large in the comity of nations"; and he hates too the idea that German regimental standards may one day fall "into alien hands." He knows the French hate the Germans because of the provinces lost in 1870, so for the sake of peace he wishes that they would regain those provinces; but in compensation Germany should receive a "place in the sun" and Britain should "lose nothing either."[25] Just how this miracle of foreign policy was to be brought about, Ford was unable to say.

Ford's German period ended abruptly and ignominiously in the first days of August, 1914, when the worried German citizen scurried to consult his friend, C. F. G. Masterman, in whose company, together with Violet Hunt, he had toured the battlefield of Sedan three years earlier.[26] Ford wished to discover how things now stood with his British citizenship, and Masterman reassured him that he remained a British subject in good standing. Nevertheless Ford continued to be an object of suspicion. Afraid that Ford might be a German spy, the Chief Constable of West Sussex ordered him to leave the county, an order that was rescinded only through Masterman's influence.

Though at first still a little unsure of his political and national bearings—as late as August 8th, he was still blaming the French for starting the war[27]—Ford now began shedding his German identity. Violet Hunt started to put it about, according to Frieda Lawrence, that Ford/Hueffer was really of Russian origin; and David Garnett remembers that at this time Ford's ancestry had become Ruthenian.[28] In any case, Ford officially eliminated the middle name "Hermann" from his certificate of baptism, though he continued to retain the Hueffer until June 1919, when that too was dropped.[29] Through Masterman, Ford also became involved in the highly secret literary propaganda work organized under Masterman's direction in Wellington House. In September 1914, with the assistance of Richard Aldington, he started writing the first of the two books he did for Wellington House, *When Blood is Their Argument: An Analysis of Prussian Culture* (1915), which first appeared serially in the American magazine *The Outlook*. Gone were the halcyon days of idyllic Saxon-Hessian-Westphalian-English cousinhood in the Prussian tea garden beneath the Prussian *Aussichtsthurm*. Gone too were the memories of the newly proud German citizen touring the grassy slopes of the site of the great Prussian victory at Sedan.

Now it was resistance to the death against the hobnailed boot of the Prussian bully. Now it was "the damned fact" that "in 1870 Liberal opinion in England upon the whole supported Prussia"—even the damnable, though unavowed fact that his own grandfather, Ford Madox Brown, had done so—not to mention Franz Hüffer.[30] Not that it was impossible to understand why Prussia embraced "the materialistic view of civilisation." After all, as the notoriously well-nourished Ford put it, "you must, I suppose, eat before you can talk of the higher things"; but that was no reason why other (and better-fed) countries should have admired and sought to imitate "a set of semi-starving, semi-Tartar peasants on horseback, dwelling east of the Elbe."[31] One wonders what Ford's newly discovered Russian or Ruthenian connections thought of this observation, dwelling, as they did, even farther east of the Elbe than did the despised Prussians. But then, according to Ford's other book of wartime propaganda, *Between St. Denis and St. George* (1915), his ancestry was really French, since the South Germans from whom he was descended were "really and historically" the same people as the Franks.[32]

Perhaps Ford's two propaganda books should be properly viewed as a last, rather heavy-handed joke of that fat German, Hueffer. It is difficult to take them any more seriously than his earlier paeans to High Germany. Peter Buitenhuis, however, in his remarkable essay on "Writers at War" (1976), fails to see anything funny in them. He takes Ford severely to task for his hypocrisy in "waving the banner of Victorian prudery over Germany," piously censuring, for example, "the bitter and terrifying lyrics of the most modern German poets, and the incredibly filthy—the absolutely incredibly filthy—productions of the German variety stage."[33] Even so, Buitenhuis finds *When Blood is Their Argument* to be sweetness and light in comparison to *Between St. Denis and St. George*. He quotes a passage from the latter work in which Ford declares, apparently oblivious of the fears for Germany's continued existence expressed in the preface to *The Desirable Alien* only a year earlier, that he wished "Germany did not exist, and I hope it will not exist much longer." According to Buitenhuis, the greatest harm Ford did in his second propaganda book, however, was its lying attempt to discredit the peace movement in Britain by attacking its principal "Anglo-Prussian Apologists": Russell, Brailsford, Ponsonby, Brockway, Angell, and Shaw.[34]

There is no doubt that Ford cuts a pathetic figure in these propagandistic performances; but somehow, like a real-life Anglo-German Falstaff, it is difficult to lose one's sympathy for him altogether: the reversal from lyrical pro-Germanism to virulent anti-Germanism is so sudden and absolute that it takes one's breath away. Such effrontery demands admiration; and one can therefore almost in a double-think sort of way, understand how Douglas Goldring could write some twenty-five years later that *When Blood is Their Argument* is "an historical study of the first importance, fully documented and annotated, and as an example of the writer's prose style ranks among his highest achievements. Both books are as valuable today as when they first appeared, and they are probably the only two, out of the mass of propaganda literature put out between 1914 and 1919, which deserve to survive. They ought to be reprinted in a series of classics, and their study made obligatory for any candidate aspiring to enter the Foreign office or Diplomatic Corps" (117). And Ford himself remarked many years after the war in his autobiographical *Return to Yesterday* (1932) that after rereading the "great bulk" of propagandistic writing he had produced during the war, he found it the "mildest in tone" and "probably the most instructive that was written for the Allies." He "saw nothing in it that I should now wish to alter."[35]

With all this, it may come as something of a surprise that Ford's best-known and most critically acclaimed novel, *The Good Soldier* (1915), has almost nothing to say about the Germans, either good or bad, although the novel is largely set in Germany, in a small spa, Bad Nauheim, not far from Ford's Giessen. But then, this may be because the novel is narrated by a naive or maybe not so naive American, Dowell, who in this respect, at least, lives up to his name. There is one scene, however, set in M—(Marburg), in which the background momentarily merges into the foreground. Marburg is the place where Luther, Zwingli, and the Duke of Hessia met to agree on Protestant doctrine—they failed—and therefore may be viewed as one of the chief points of departure for "their" bloody arguments.[36] For the rest, however, Germans appear in the shadowy capacities of servants or public officials, making sure that all is in proper order to receive their annual visitors, the handsome Edward Ashburnham, sometime Colonel of the Indian Army, and his ravishing wife, Leonora. In this respect the Germans of Ford's novel resemble Camus's Arabs: they are largely absent from their own country.

The Good Soldier, despite its title and date of publication, has nothing to do with the Great War. But this is not true of Ford's massive novel in four parts, *Parade's End*, which is to some extent the literary fruit of Ford's own experience of the war. Insofar as this novel has a plot, it concerns Sylvia Tietjens's increasingly grotesque attempts to persecute and humiliate her husband, not because she hates him but because she loves him so much. Incidentally, the novel is also about the moral decay wrought or at least brought to the surface by the Great War, heralding the end of the old

England. From now on, as Tietjens melodramatically and elliptically pronounces in *No More Parades* (1925), there will be no more "Hope, no more Glory, no more parades for you and me any more. Nor for the country . . . nor for the world, I dare say . . . None . . . Gone . . . Na poo, finny! No . . . more . . . parades!"[37]

It is the end of an era, but the bloody argument that brought the world to this pass is no longer exclusively German. Indeed, the Germans in this novel, though of course always the enemy, are no longer semi-starving, semi-Tartar barbarians dwelling east of the Elbe. There is hatred for them still, but by the third part of the novel, *A Man Could Stand Up* (1926), this hatred is confined to the civilian population, for it has become "curious to consider how the hatred that one felt for the inhabitants of those regions [i.e., Germany] seemed to skip in a whole trajectory over the embattled ground. It was the civilian populations and their rulers that one hated with real hatred."[38] And by the end of the war, the upper-class Englishman Christopher Tietjens could no longer be bothered even with hating civilian Germans anymore; they were not really worthy of strong feeling. They are now simply "bores." When, in the immediate post-armistice period, the Germans are decimated by an influenza epidemic, Tietjens calmly reflects that "anyhow, Germans were the sort of people that influenza *would* bowl over."[39] Germany, as the author of *Between St. Denis and St. George* had once devoutly hoped, had ceased to exist.

Still, Tietjens's vast and imperturbably objective intelligence absorbs and dispenses information about the Germans as it does about virtually every other subject. Tietjens quotes Heine (162)—incorrectly, alas, though this error may be meant to be taken ironically.[40] Tietjens is disgusted by the novelist Mrs. Wannop (Mrs. Humphry Ward?), who, at the outbreak of war, falls to her knees, "from which she only with difficulty rose [note the peculiarly German construction of this sentence], shouted hoarse prayers to God, to let her, with her own hands, strangle, torture, and flay all of his skin, a being called the Kaiser." (288). As a gentleman, Tietjens would never comport himself in this fashion and he consequently refuses to have anything to do with Mrs. Wannop's literary elaboration of the supposed German corpse factories, "as being below the treatment of any decent pen." St. George and St. Denis suffer a decanonization as well. Tietjens denounces his own people as having "always been boodlers and robbers and reivers and pirates and cattle thieves, and so we've built up the great tradition that we love . . ." (295). He maintains that Britain should have stayed out of the war and grabbed "other people's" colonial possessions as the price for remaining neutral. As for France, well, he confidently but fortunately not infallibly predicts a war between the English and French by 1930.

This is the strange and often wonderful history of the German Ford/ Hueffer. But it is not the whole story. For German Ford brought into

German orbit at least one English woman of literary note and, eventually, notoriety, Violet Hunt. Not that Hunt was wholly ignorant of Germans or Germany before she met Ford. Like many children of the more cultivated upper class in late nineteenth-century England, she had had a German nursemaid. Milly came from Paderborn, "the home of folklore and superstition"; for a time she made Violet and her sisters "into such little Germans that it was found useless to give us an order or scold us in any other tongue." This lasted until Hunt was eight years old, when the more elegant French language took over, but her early recollections nevertheless predisposed her to sympathy for the fatherland of the Frog Prince.[41] Moreover, Germany was also the country to which Hunt's parents were accustomed to repair for their health and their holidays. "It has become difficult," Douglas Goldring remarks of this custom in *South Lodge,* "for the younger generations to credit the romantic affection with which their Victorian elders regarded the home of the Butcher Birds" (94).

When Hunt, therefore, began to take up with Ford, they had several points in common, aside from literary interests and ambitions: they were used to an environment of intellectual and artistic speculation, as well as a certain lack of conventionality, inherited from the Pre-Raphaelite ancestry they both shared; and they were also both inclined to look toward Germany as a place from which they could benefit and learn, though initially this was far more true of Ford.

They took their first trip together to Germany in September 1910, elaborately chaperoned by Ford's Aunt Emma in the best Victorian manner. They also spent some time during this visit in Bad Nauheim, time which Ford was later to put to literary use in *The Good Soldier* and in the first part of *Parade's End.* Hunt was also busy storing up literary impressions that she hoped to incorporate into *The Life and Letters of Hubert Herkomer.* This work, which never got much beyond the planning stage, was to tell the story of the German-born painter Sir Hubert von Herkomer who, in 1888, married the sister of his deceased second wife. Since such marriages were then illegal in Britain, the ceremony took place in Germany, whither Herkomer had returned briefly and resumed his former citizenship for the occasion. This elaborate and quite factual story appealed to Hunt for obvious reasons, though she may also have intended to blend in elements of the life of the Pre-Raphaelite painter Holman Hunt (*not* her father), who had also defied British law and shocked Victorian sensibilities by going to Holland to marry his sister-in-law.[42]

Though *Hubert Herkomer* never saw the light of day—neither did Violet Hueffer, for that matter—Violet Hunt did transform her German experience into a work that often drifts from truth into fiction. *The Desirable Alien* (1913) is ostensibly an impressionistic sort of travel book, a personal and rather chatty account of various aspects of German life and culture. But it is also a book written by a Violet Hunt who is the "bride" of the German Ford Madox Hueffer, who introduces her to his country, to his apparently German "Mutterchen" (mother), and to some of his three-hundred and sixteen other relatives in Muenster.

The Desirable Alien begins with a chapter describing how one becomes an alien—an alien, that is, in Britain. For, having "married" German Hueffer, Violet Hunt has now become German as well, a novel status to which, she informs us, she took "quite kindly" (3). Her upbringing, her German nurse, the tales of the Grimm brothers had in any case, according to her "husband's" preface to the book, predisposed her to look upon the Germans "with a friendly and indulgent eye, to find them instinct with all the old Germanic virtues of kindliness, hospitality, modesty, and sobriety" (ix). Hence, as Violet Hunt herself concludes, "my Germanhood was obviously fate" (5).

The journey down the Rhine, bringing the British bride to her new homeland, leaves her ecstatic. "We were all Germans," she exclaims of herself and her fellow passengers aboard the Rhine steamer, "the proud possessors of this unique waterway" (114). When she steps ashore, she is no longer a British subject. She enters as a German into a Germany to which the Kaiser—now her First War Lord—has brought happiness, a happiness that, if it never reaches the peaks of joy possible to the English or the French, also never plunges to the depths of misery or despair of those rival nationalities. For the Germans are a solid, good people, possessing a stable national mind that is preferable to the "tricksy, moody genius of the Englishman" or "the alert, erratic, passion-driven one of the Frenchman" (28–29). Hunt sees the "officers of my nationality . . . wearing the handsome uniform of Prussia" walking down the streets of "our principality," benevolently ruled by "my Grand Duke" (3). She even takes enthusiastically—in one of the longest chapters of the book—to the ubiquitous German beer gardens that in England are always treated "with a certain degree of tolerant moral deprecation" (65). She finds these places of healthy, decent refreshment quite unlike the vulgar pubs of Britain or the "swinish" *buvettes* of France. The spas too are full of elegance and the good life, despite being frequented by celebrity-hunting, *nouveaux riches* Americans. In reality, she says, they are quite different from descriptions of them in Thackeray's novels, who was anti-German anyway.

Everything, to be sure, is not perfect even in High Germany. Life is too regimented and there is poverty in the rural areas, though nothing approaching the abject wretchedness of the slums of urban Britain. There is a streak of bigotry in the Germans, as can be seen in the cruel way the Anabaptists were put to death long ago in Joseph Leopold's home town of Muenster. And most worrisome of all are the pervasive preparations for war, the continual noise of marching feet and military drills. Crossing the frontier from

Belgium into Germany—in the closing chapter of the book—she sees the piles of German railway track lying ready to be laid into Belgium when the next "combat" breaks out. It is a frightful omen, even for a desirable alien and even after Joseph Leopold's confident assurance that "there will be no war" (322).

When Joseph Leopold was proved wrong only a year later and the "combat" did break out, Hunt, like her "husband," quickly buried her now no-longer-desirable alien status in oblivion. Hunt's sometime First War Lord, the Kaiser, and her former sovereign, the Grand Duke, together with hordes of their officers in handsome Prussian uniforms, were now transformed into the evil masters of the German "Night Hag," the German zeppelins that, "drunk with hate," came nightly to drop their bombs on London. In *Zeppelin Nights* (1916), written jointly with Ford, Hunt recounts how "it was this pre-eminently German spectre which rode us all those summer months terrifying some of us beyond mental endurance; making us all, strong and weak, profoundly wretched and uneasy, filled with a restlessness that was worse than pain."[43]

The fear of this night *hag* drove any remaining sympathy for Germany out of Violet Hunt. By the time she came to write her autobiography ten years later, she looked back on her experience in Germany with intense dislike. "Germany had been my Canossa," she now reflected, "fatal to me. I had never liked Germans, never felt at home with them. I hated them in fact."[44] For Ford, however, the night *hag* was to have a more immediately adverse impact. In a review of *Zeppelin Nights* published in *The New Witness*, a Catholic journal edited by Cecil Chesterton, Ford was singled out for attack as someone who was peculiarly susceptible to being terrified by night *hags*, whereas ordinary Londoners reacted calmly and humorously—and definitely not fearfully—to the onslaught of the Zeppelins. Ford, in short, so the reviewer J. K. Prothero implied, was a coward. Since Ford "is not exactly of pure European extraction, and this book certainly tends to confirm such impression," his cowardice is not surprising; after all, "in certain parts of London, notably in the foreign quarters of Whitechapel—and by 'foreign' I mean those parts which are inhabited by non-Europeans—the fear of the 'German Night Hag' has created something of a panic. . . ."[45]

Ford, who was serving at the front by this time, was defended in a letter by J. M. Barrie who, while admitting that *Zeppelin Nights* was one of the worst potboilers ever published in London, saw this as providing no adequate reason for calling Ford a coward and a Jew. Ford, Barrie pointed out, was at the front, and, in any case, was not a Jew but a Catholic. To this, Prothero replied that because someone becomes a Catholic, that is no reason to suppose "he ceases to be a Jew."[46]

From this ugly and stupid little episode one can perhaps draw the conclusion that hatred and prejudice breed hatred and prejudice. In return for

Ford's wallowing in national stereotypes and anti-Semitism in "High Germany" and elsewhere, he received a dose of the same poison himself. The Kaiser's night hag, it seems, was not the only loathsome specter abroad. There were other, even uglier and more dangerous hags dwelling, not east of the Elbe, but in the heart and mind of Ford Madox Ford and many of his contemporaries.

5

The Mental Slum: H. G. Wells and Rudyard Kipling

*We shall finish the German eagle as the merciful lady killed
the chicken. It took her the whole afternoon, and then, you
will remember, the carcass had to be thrown away.*
   Rudyard Kipling, The Fringes of the Fleet *(1915)*

A mental slum, like a slum in a city, soon tends to grow monotonous. The
buildings assume a drab sameness and the individuals merge into a shabby,
demoralized, and somewhat threatening mass. So too with the thousands of
pages of explanation and justification, attack and counterattack, produced by
politicians, professors, journalists, historians, and propagandistic men and
women of every description, public and private, during the Great War. The
decay of intellectual and artistic life among those who supported the war was
so great that virtually everything they wrote was either stillborn or else, in
some peculiarly horrible way, congenitally maimed. With a very few notable
exceptions, only out of disillusion and opposition did works of art worthy of
the name emerge. This is principally true of the poets—of Wilfred Owen,
Siegfried Sassoon, Isaac Rosenberg, and Robert Graves—but in a quite
different way it is true also of a novelist like D. H. Lawrence or even of a
playwright like George Bernard Shaw. With the poets, almost all of whom
lived (and some of whom died) in the muddy subterranean slums of Flanders
and Northern France, it required an enormous effort of will to wrench
themselves out of mindlessness and into art; hence even their best work is
often marred by melodramatic touches. When one is living a melodrama, as
these poets were, it requires very great genius to escape it altogether.

Such genius was not given either to H. G. Wells or to Rudyard Kipling in
the fiction they wrote during the war. To differing but unmistakable degrees,
their work betrays the hand, as it were, of the slum landlord.[1]

The hero of Wells's *Mr. Britling Sees It Through* (1916) novel is, as his name
proclaims, a little British man, a kind of prototype of the middle-class
intellectual Liberal (though he writes for *The Times* rather than for the *Daily*

100

News, as Wells did). He is middle-aged, not unattractive, a "thinker" with something of an international reputation, a family man well into his second family, a bit of a philanderer who still remains "innocent," an unconventional country gentleman, and a spontaneous, kindly, perceptive soul. As the novel opens, we find him in the company of an amiable but slightly obtuse American "intellectual" entrepreneur, Direck, who wants to invite him to lecture in Massachusetts. It is through Direck's neutral eyes that we come to know and appreciate the leisurely life at "Matching's Easy," enjoy the informal and spirited games of field hockey, and realize, if not to put into words, just what it is that constitutes the spirit of English life.

It is early summer. The year is 1914. A time for love: between Direck and "Cissie" Corner, between Britling and his wife, Britling and his mistress, and (a little ironically) between Britling and Britling. There is dancing in the disused barn at night. Even the stiff, musical, humorless, slightly stupid German tutor, Herr Heinrich, is drawn into the magical aura of "Matching's Easy." But the shadows are falling upon this world, a world, as Wells was later to describe it in *The Outline of History* (1920), "of amazing and unattainable plenty."[2] Harmless as he is personally, fair-haired and polite, Herr Heinrich is the symbolical serpent in Paradise. That he is merely representative of evil rather than evil in himself, that he cannot help being what he is, is regrettable; but it in no way diminishes the threat that emanates from Germany. Germany is clean and stiff and organized and humorless and prematurely "old"; England, though possessed of an older culture, is "younger" because it is more spontaneous, less machinelike, and more organic. "The old system of life was organization," Britling observes. "That is where Germany is still the most ancient of European states. It's a reversion to a tribal cult. It's atavistic. . . ." Britling's son Teddy is good-looking, charming, careless, and easygoing; Herr Heinrich is plain, careful, and thorough—"one of the most fundamental contrasts in the world," as Britling says.[3]

It is this contrast that constitutes the real heart of the novel, though it frequently digresses to deal with other matters. The ostensible plot—Direck's courtship of Cissie, Britling's amatory entanglements—takes up much room, but is only incidental to the fundamental drama of the impact of an atavistic, primitive, and mechanical culture on a spontaneous, modern, organic one. Unlike works of propaganda, *Mr. Britling Sees It Through* portrays this conflict not without subtlety and a fair amount of appreciation for both points of view. When the threat of war suddenly interrupts the peace of "Matching's Easy" and Herr Heinrich returns hurriedly to Germany, when Belgium is invaded and an utterly unprepared England is drawn into battle, Britling's psyche undergoes a gradual but profound change. Direck, just back from a brief trip to the Continent, gives him the first reports of German atrocities. "They have been raping women," he says, "for disciplinary purposes on tables in the market-place of Liège. Yes, sir. It's a fact" (W 217). How characteristic this is of the Germans: rapes out of a sense of order and duty, not from a spontaneous passionate rage.

Nevertheless Britling remains partly skeptical. What finally convinces him after "some months" is a chance examination of a batch of German comic papers: "They were filled with caricatures of the Allies and more particularly of the English, and they displayed a force and quality of passion. Their amazing hate and their amazing filthiness alike overwhelmed Mr. Britling" (W 277). A people that could hate with such thoroughness and efficiency and find such vile caricatures of an enemy humorous must be a people that was capable of horrendous atrocities. But the Germans, who "perceived the indolence of the English and Russians . . . and perceived their disregard of science and system . . . could not perceive the longer reach of these greater races . . ." (W 302). Britling therefore comes to the conclusion that "the Germans were in some distinctive way evil, they were racially more envious, arrogant, and aggressive than the rest of mankind" (W 278).[4]

Subjected to the villainy of German hatred and the barbarism of German atrocities, Britling begins to succumb to hatred himself; and so does the rest of England. "Under that strain the dignity of England broke," Wells writes, "and revealed a malignity less focussed and intense than the German, but perhaps even more distressing. No paternal government had organized the British spirit for patriotic ends . . ." (W 289). When Britling's Aunt Wilshire is killed in a Zeppelin raid, he comes close to madness, indulging in an orgy of hate fantasies, fantasies that bear a striking resemblance to Wells's own in *The War in the Air* or *When the Sleeper Wakes* (1899): "He found great comfort in scheming vindictive destruction for countless Germans. He dreamt of swift armoured aeroplanes swooping down upon the flying air-ship, and sending it reeling earthward, the men screaming. He imagined a shattered Zeppelin staggering earthward in the fields behind the Dower House, and how he would himself run out with a spade and smite the Germans down. 'Quarter indeed! Kamerad! Take *that*, you foul murderer!' " (W 298). But these fantasies are insane and before long Britling realizes that himself. His reason reasserts itself and so does his memory. After all the British, he remembers, have not always had lily-white hands; they too have committed atrocities: in Tasmania, the Himalayas, and in China, if not in the Great War. He recognizes that there is always something, though perhaps only a little, to be said for the other side, that "always there was the element of a perceptible if inadequate justification." And the same would be true of him if—and here Wells alludes directly to the central event in Kipling's short story "Mary Postgate"—if "presently he were to maltreat a fallen German airman" (W 301–2).

In Kipling's mind, however, a great deal could be said for maltreating a fallen German airman, but very little could be said for the airman himself.

Nevertheless, "Mary Postgate" is probably the most remarkable story by a pro-war writer to come out of the war. Begun in March 1915, it deals with a lonely, middle-aged servant-companion's loyalty and revenge: loyalty to her invalid mistress and her mistress's boisterous nephew Wynn, and revenge for the death in an accidental plane crash of that nephew and for the killing of a small child in a nearby village. The murderers are the German nation in general and a German airman in particular who, gravely wounded, drops into the garden one rainy afternoon while Mary is burning Wynn's effects. The story climaxes with Mary's gloating at the German's slow and painful death: "An increasing rapture laid hold of her. She ceased to think. She gave herself up to feel. Her long pleasure was broken by a sound that she had waited for in agony several times in her life. She leaned forward and listened, smiling. There could be no mistake. She closed her eyes and drank it in. Once it ceased abruptly. 'Go on,' she murmured, half aloud. 'That isn't the end.' " When the end does come a moment later, she shivers from head to toe. " 'That's all right,' said she contentedly;" and then she trots off to indulge in a "luxurious hot bath before tea."[5]

What to make of this curiously cruel tale? Was it written by a man who could fairly be described, as Bonamy Dobrée described Kipling in 1929, as the symbol "not of hate, but a deep compassion; not indignant grandiosity and brute force, but humility and tenderness amounting to deep pity"?[6] Pity for whom, one wonders. Dobrée later elaborated his original analysis of Kipling into a full-length study, *Rudyard Kipling: Realist and Fabulist* (1967), but his subject is still the same humane, avuncular soul of nearly forty years earlier. Though he is aware of Kipling's deep-rooted conviction that the Germans, by their aggression and cruelty, had put themselves beyond the pale of the Law, Dobrée nevertheless asserts that " 'Mary Postgate' . . . is not a story embodying hatred of the Germans." Instead, it is merely a realistic tale, for after all, given Mary's feelings for Wynn and her emotional state as she is burning Wynn's effects, "one may wonder whether, if people would look into themselves . . . they could with certainty say they would have acted otherwise?" Or to take another instance of this "shocking realism": Mary does not consider "that, after all, Wynn was equipped to do the same thing; and Kipling could have pointed out to her that the German was only obeying *his* Law." Or the final shocker: Mary's rejuvenation at the end of the story is due to the release of "her suppressed emotions toward Wynn."[7] In other words, it is strongly implied that "Mary Postgate" is not a story about German atrocities—that is merely the incidental background— but about an essentially individual conflict, culminating in the sudden release of years of repressed hostility.

This kind of interpretation of the story is by no means unique to Dobrée. Kipling's authorized biographer, C. E. Carrington, declares flatly that this story is "entirely personal, a tale about frustrated passion and vicarious revenge, not about any particular campaign. It is concerned with the quality of ruthlessness, an extension of the sardonic verse, 'the female of the species is more deadly than the male.' "[8] To be sure, Carrington avoids Dobrée's implicit identification between Wynn and the German airman, placing the stress wholly on Kipling's misogyny. The real villain of the piece, it seems, is not the German, not Mary Postgate, but "das ewig Weibliche." The opposing, yet parallel, view to this is W. W. Robson's contention that "Mary Postgate," while admittedly containing some bitterness—attributable to "poignant personal reasons"[9]—is an attack neither on Germans nor on women. "What those who condemn Kipling would say," Robson argues, almost certainly referring to Boris Ford, "is that the author is quite aware of the moral incoherence of Mary, but exploits her as a vent for the release of emotions which a sahib himself cannot admit that he feels; women, as contradictory and inferior beings, can be allowed the indulgence which the author himself desires. But this amounts to attributing to Kipling—the Kipling of this story—the outlook of young Wynn. It ignores the careful art of the story in avoiding any sentimentalization of Mary or Wynn or the relationship between them. Above all, it ignores the essential identity—symbolic, of course, not literal—between the dying airman and Wynn. (He too, like Wynn, has fallen from his airplane.)"[10] Leaving aside for the moment that Wynn has not fallen from his airplane but crashed *in* it, one wonders what Robson finds so shocking about equating Wynn's point of view with Kipling's. This is nearly as curious as Dobrée's having Kipling hypothetically point out to Mary that the German has his Law, almost immediately after having demonstrated that for Kipling the Germans had no Law.

These two threads—the resentment of a bullied servant-companion and the innate sadism of the human female—of this interpretation are effectively joined in J. I. M. Stewart's essay on Kipling in *Eight Modern Writers*. Stewart, like Carrington and Dobrée, argues that "the horror and fear and hate in the story are occasioned by Mary, not by the wicked Germans." He then adds suggestively that this may not have been what Kipling thought he was doing. This interesting distinction between a conscious and an unconscious intention, one to which I shall revert later, may derive from Noel Annan's 1954 essay on Kipling, where Annan sees "Mary Postgate" as a great opportunity missed: a story in which art and irony (the unconscious?) are sacrificed to Kipling's rigid insistence on preaching that Germans are outside the law (the conscious).[11]

J. M. S. Tompkins, the most generally praised interpreter of Kipling's shorter fiction, provides a reading of "Mary Postgate" that, while quite as sympathetic to Kipling as any of the foregoing, offers some novelties. Her reading stresses the "normal" rather than the "abnormal" relations of Mary to Wynn and to the German airman. Mary's feelings toward Wynn, in her view, are not those of a resentful servant or a frustrated would-be lover; on the contrary, they are those of a grieving foster-mother. Mary's hatred of the German airman is not endorsed by Kipling; it is simply the predictable response of a woman who has been so tried by sorrow and horror that she lapses into temporary insanity. What we have here, Tompkins affirms, is a Kipling who means to demonstrate in drastic ways how cruelly the war can affect even the best of people.[12]

C. A. Bodelsen picks up this note and strikes it even louder. For him, "Mary Postgate" is "a very subtle story, where obviously a good deal must be read between the lines." In doing so, Bodelsen notes that the pleasure Mary takes in the dying German's agony carries sexual overtones and is therefore "sadism in the original sense of the word." But it is known that Kipling does not approve of sadism. Can it therefore be "really believable that Kipling should have gone on record like that with what would be almost a glorification of perversion?" Obviously not, from which it follows logically that Mary's and Kipling's attitudes are not to be confused. Like Tompkins, Bodelsen concludes that, in the final analysis, "Mary Postgate" is a cautionary tale of how, impelled by the horror of German warfare, "a kindly and respectable English spinster finds herself turned into a torturer."[13]

These are the main interpretations of "Mary Postgate" put forward by scholars in the last few decades. Let me stress that none of these analyses exceeds a few pages in length and the majority take up only a page or so. Bodelsen's, for instance, is relegated to a lengthy footnote. Indeed, in at least one scholarly study of Kipling's stories, Elliott Gilbert's *The Good Kipling, Studies in the Short Story* (1971), discussion of "Mary Postgate" and of the related "hate" stories is omitted altogether. Despite avowals to the contrary, it seems that the most effective way of dealing with the "bad Kipling" is to ignore his existence.

What to make of all this? Are Kipling's academic apologists justified in separating Mary from Rudyard, in denying allegations that Kipling is here vicariously but lovingly extracting the tooth that is owing him? The answer, I would respectfully submit, is no. No, because, if for no other reason, there are ample grounds to suspect that all the available evidence has not been brought to bear on the case of "Mary Postgate."

It is true, as stated earlier, that Bonamy Dobrée does concede that Kipling was not specially fond of the Germans. He quotes him as saying in a speech at Southport in June 1915 that "however the world pretends to divide itself, there are only two divisions in the world today—human beings and Germans"; and he quotes from *France at War* (1915) to the effect that "we are dealing with animals who have scientifically and philosophically removed themselves inconceivably outside civilisation."[14] But it is also true that Dobrée makes nothing whatever of these quotations, thereby suggesting that

Kipling's sociopolitical opinions had nothing whatever to do with his art. He does not even mention, for instance, that his quotation from *France at War* is taken from the mouth of a woman who, like Mary, has had experience of German atrocities.

Kipling was a vigorous and notorious Hun-hater.[15] Notice, for example, how he describes the Germans in *The Eyes of Asia* (1918), from the point of view of a couple of Indian officers fighting with their regiments on the Western Front. "The nature of the enemy," one of them writes home, "is to commit shame upon women and children, and to defile the shrines of his own faith with his own dung. It is done by him as a drill. We believed till then they were some sort of caste apart from the rest. We did not know they were outcasts. Now it is established by the evidence of our senses. They attack on all fours running like apes. They are specially careful of their faces. When death is certain to them they offer gifts and repeat the number of their children. They are very good single shots from cover."[16] Are we really to understand here, in the manner of Tompkins's interpretation of "Mary Postgate," that this is a lamentable case of battle fatigue? Or, as Dobrée might have had it, that this is a shockingly realistic account of what it was like to be an Indian officer at the front? Or should we distinguish, in the style of Bodelsen, between the views of Subidar Major Bishen Singh Saktawat and those of Rudyard Kipling?

As early as Christmas 1902, Kipling had heaped scorn on a British policy that sought "to league anew/with the Goth and the shameless Hun!" When the war broke out, he trotted his Huns out once more in "For All We Have and Are" (1914):

> For all we have and are,
> For all our children's fate,
> Stand up and take the war.
> The Hun is at the gate![17]

Does this long and dishonorable tradition of versified Hun-baiting seem to confirm the general critical view that in "Mary Postgate" the Huns are all Mary's rather than Kipling's?

To be sure, most of this evidence is extraneous. At best it can prove that Mary's hatred of the Germans was not alien to Kipling, and it can perhaps also reinforce the suspicion that Mary is, on one level at least, a mouthpiece for his hatred. But it can prove no more. What is not extraneous, however, and what can prove more is the poem "The Beginnings," which Kipling appended to "Mary Postgate" and whose theme makes it a (conscious?) counterpart to Ernst Lissauer's infamous "Hassgesang gegen England" (Hymn of Hate):

It was not part of their blood,
It came to them very late
With long arrears to make good,
When the English began to hate.

They were not easily moved,
They were icy willing to wait
Till every count should be proved
Ere the English began to hate.

Their voices were even and low,
Their eyes were level and straight
There was neither sign nor show,
When the English began to hate.

It was not preached to the crowd,
It was not taught by the State.
No man spoke it aloud,
When the English began to hate.

It was not suddenly bred,
It will not swiftly abate,
Through the chill years ahead,
When time shall count from the date
That the English began to hate.

This poem seems clearly intended to serve as a kind of moral signpost for the story. The stanza by stanza tracing of the development of England's hatred for Germany matches the gradual intensification of Mary's emotional response. As with the English in the poem, Mary is originally patient and good-natured, outwardly unemotional but inwardly full of deep and genuine feeling. These virtues have been tested and found true in years of devoted service to Miss Fowler, to the Village Nursing Committee and in caring for Wynn. Again, as in the poem, Mary does not give vent to noisy denunciations of the Germans, nor, for that matter, does she hear any. Her hatred arises individually and spontaneously and in reaction to what she herself has seen and suffered—Wynn's and the little girl's deaths—not to any propaganda, public or private. Mary, in short, hates just as Kipling tells us the English do; and as Wells, for good measure, does also.

From this it seems safe to conclude that "Mary Postgate" is a story designed to illustrate how the English, epitomized by the humble figure of Mary Postgate, came to feel hatred for the Germans. "English" here includes not just Mary, not just middle-aged women, not just servants, but all loyal English men and women, Kipling as well. But it does not mean, necessarily, that Kipling likes or approves of this hatred per se; neither, of course, does it mean the opposite. The ultimate responsibility, it is clear, for this hatred and for the war that is its immediate cause, rests squarely with the Germans. If they are allowed to die wretchedly, that is their fault alone. It is in this limited sense that Dobrée is right in arguing for the realism of "Mary Postgate": Kipling *is* depicting a hatred that actually exists. But Dobrée is surely wrong to suggest that Kipling is to be separated from that hatred. If Mary is English, then she is automatically privileged to hate, and if she is privileged to hate, then she cannot, obviously, be held responsible for the death of "it." Neither can Kipling.

As if all this were not clear enough, Kipling had already made a preliminary study of this subject in a somewhat earlier story, "Swept and Garnished" (written in October 1914). The title alludes to the Germans' reputation for fanatical cleanliness, a mania that does not extend, in Kipling's view, to their consciences. The setting for most of the story is the immaculately neat apartment of a slightly indisposed Frau Ebermann. The tone is set by her opening reaction to the news that the German army has won another victory, capturing multitudes of prisoners and guns. "Frau Ebermann purred," Kipling informs us, "one might almost say grunted, contentedly" (477).[18]

This woman is haunted by the ghosts of five Belgian children, all victims of German atrocities. There is some coyness about these ghosts on the part of the omniscient narrator: are they simply figments of her fever, that is, her diseased conscience? Or are they real? Though this ambiguity is never resolved, it becomes amply clear that, real or symbolic, these five children are only a tiny percentage of the "hundreds and hundreds and thousands and thousands" (484) of dead Belgian children who are making the circuit of Berlin homes to prove to these morally unclean people that everything cannot be swept and garnished. At the end of the story, they propose to make a little excursion to the Emperor's palace. Murder will out, as Chaucer concluded long ago in a tale not wholly dissimilar.

Though none of the critics has made the connection, it seems fairly clear that "Mary Postgate" is a reprise of "Swept and Garnished." Mary's removal and destruction of Wynn's things are also acts of cleanliness, but of moral, not merely physical cleanliness. Mary's sweeping and garnishing are spontaneous and emotional, whereas Frau Ebermann's are merely the products of rigid habit. In the English home, however, Miss Fowler is a genuine cripple who needs a helper, while Frau Ebermann is only a momentarily bedridden tyrant. Their reactions to the suffering of their nations' enemies, superficially similar, are at bottom radically different. Mary acts resolutely and with an easy conscience: she dispenses justice, the only kind of justice a barbarian can understand. She is against the airman and for the dead child. Frau Ebermann, on the other hand, is testy, irresolute, cowardly. Her conscience is filthy, she grunts contentedly at barbarous victories, she loves the soldier above all foster-motherly feeling. Not surprisingly therefore, Mary grows youthful at the end of her experience; Frau Ebermann ages.

There is a resemblance in technique between the two stories as well, namely, an unresolved hint that the events may be taking place only in the minds of the central characters. This is one of Kipling's favorite narrative devices, which, as we have seen, functions so prominently in "Swept and Garnished" that it might almost be called a ghost story. In "Mary Postgate" there is the same ambiguity, but it is so much less obvious that it has been usually disregarded. J. I. M. Stewart, one of the few who do touch on it, argues that "conceivably against Kipling's conscious intention, the German is not quite real—there is no final thought that the police or military must be called, the body disposed of."[19] According to Stewart, it follows from this ambivalence that Wynn is perhaps to be identified with the German airman.

Interesting as Stewart's hypothesis is, it contains some grave flaws. While it is certainly odd that neither the police nor the military are notified of the German airman, it is surely quite as odd that Mary does not mention him to Miss Fowler either, or for that matter does not tell her about the explosion in the village and the dead child. Surely there is no doubt about the reality of the dead child? There is, in fact, a quite simple explanation for Mary's apparently curious behavior; she is merely following Dr. Hennis's and Nurse Eden's instructions "not to say anthing—yet at least" (506), presumably to prevent a panic in the village. What there is a definite doubt about, however, is the cause of the child's death. Mary's explanation of a bomb is her explanation exclusively, confirmed neither by Nurse Eden nor by Dr. Hennis, and supported only by her suspicion that she heard the sound of propellors as she was walking past Vegg's Heath, Wynn's habitual landing field. In fact, Mary's explanation is contradicted outright by Dr. Hennis somewhat later when he tells her that "the accident at the 'Royal Oak' was due to Gerritt's stable tumbling down. It's been dangerous for a long time" (506). Mary remains skeptical and so presumbably should the reader, but nevertheless Hennis cannot be simply disregarded, for if Hennis is right, it follows that the German airman is either a figment of Mary's imagination or else not guilty of the child's death. Miss Tompkins's assertion that Hennis is intent on hushing up the truth is by no means self-evident in the context of the story; Nurse Eden shares Hennis's view and, for a time, even Mary is halfway persuaded. Besides, what conceivable personal interest could Hennis be serving by trying to cover up the truth? Are we to suppose that Hennis and Nurse Eden are in fact German spies? Hennis may be and probably is wrong, but his explanation cannot be simply dismissed out of hand.

Kipling deliberately cloaks the entire incident in ambiguity. No one at the actual scene either sees or hears a German Plane, nor any other plane for that matter. To be sure, as a point of historical fact, air attacks were sometimes made with the engines shut off, but it is nevertheless suspicious that an entire village should have been thus left ignorant of their presence.

What is the purpose of all this ambiguity? To suggest that German atrocities against children and civilians are the hallucinations of middle-aged spinsters? Surely not, since such atrocities form the substance of the earlier story, "Swept and Garnished," and since German bombing raids, beginning in January 1915, were obviously far too real to be ignored. Why then? To suggest that Wynn, like the German, might have killed children in the line of duty? No again, since not only is this possibility expressly denied in the story (Wynn is a "gentleman," the German is an "it"), but the British were at this time only using aircraft in combat areas. Was it then to express, as Stewart and others intimate, an even greater abhorrence of women than of Germans? Possibly, since Kipling's hatred of women ran notoriously deep and surfaced repeatedly in places like "Baa Baa, Black Sheep" and *The Light that Failed.* Nevertheless, this hypothesis is belied by the appendage of "The Beginnings" with its suprasexual hatred and by the fact that the description of the German airman evokes—with his head as pale as a baby's—the dead child as much as his uniform does Wynn.[20] Even more important, it is also belied by the fact that on Mary's return from the village, Miss Fowler tells of two planes having passed overhead half an hour earlier. The attack was real enough, apparently, and not a figment of a hysterical spinster's imagination—though even at this point a lingering doubt still remains.[21] Since their nationality is not specified, there is a possibility that the planes might have been British. Wynn's base, after all, is obviously within easy flying distance. This possibility is admittedly rather remote, especially in view of "The Edge of the Evening" (also in *Diversity of Creatures*), another story in which German airmen appear unexpectedly and are summarily dispatched.[22] But what then is the cause of this elaborate display of Bismarckian red herring?

Some part of the reason lies, I suspect, in Kipling's desire to emphasize the spiritual and not merely the physical damage of this particular war. This would account for the focus, in "Swept and Garnished" as well as in "Mary Postgate," on women and domestic surroundings. Even here, Kipling seems to be saying in the former case, can we see the root of the evil; and even unto here, in the other, does that evil penetrate. If Kipling had been merely an Ian Hay sort of writer, Wynn would have been the hero of his story, never an old maid like Mary. The very fact of Mary's drab appearance and existence suggests Kipling's conviction that England is engaged in a war in which the feelings and doings of ordinary people matter as they had never mattered before. And for this the Germans are to blame: for they kill not the armed warrior, but the child and the civilian.

Something of this is suggested by the juxtaposition of Mary's firing Wynn's personal effects—his books, his toys, and other memorabilia—in the "destructor" while watching the German die. Indeed, the German's death and the burning down of Wynn's funeral pyre ("sprinkled with sacrificial oil") occur simultaneously. But this emphatically does not mean that Wynn and the German are to be identified. On the contrary, it means that Wynn's death has, to some small degree at least, been paid for, even if only in the imagination. An eye for an eye, and a tooth for a tooth: that is the Law. And that is why the airman resembles not merely Wynn but also the dead child, that is why, in "Swept and Garnished," the children are waiting in Berlin until "our people" get there. Before the new-made angels can enter paradise, the new-made devils must be sentenced to hell. In Kipling's world, the wounds of grief can only be washed clean in the blood of one's enemy.

There are hints elsewhere that the story is to be read on this level of spiritual allegory. Wynn is perhaps to be viewed as a sacrificial Christ figure whose name presages ultimate victory; and Nurse Eden's name suggests the prelapsarian condition of rural England before the German Satan quite literally fell into it (and the child Edna's name is also, significantly, a near anagram for "Eden"). Even more pointedly, the airman falls into a *garden*, where he pleads for a mercy he himself is not prepared to give, and where instead of yielding to his wiles and seeming innocence, the virginal "Laty" Mary gives him death.

In the context of the story, Mary is undoubtedly good, no matter what later ages and critics have thought of her. It is only very superficially that Mary demonstrates the "truth" that the female of the species is deadlier than the male: she puts *paid* to a German, whereas Wynn never did. To argue such a position seriously, however, would necessarily entail arguing that Mary's inaction is more reprehensible than the German's action; for despite being an "it," the German is still a man. Moreover, Mary's relation to Wynn is wholly different from that of the "Aunty" figure to her charge in either "Baa, Baa, Black Sheep" or *The Light that Failed*, the two *loci classici* of Kipling's alleged hatred of women. Mary genuinely loves Wynn—the match that lights his pyre also burns "her heart to ashes" (436)—and she patiently submits to a great variety of indignities for his sake. If she resembles anyone in those two stories, it is the kind and gentle mother figure.

But why then choose a woman, and specifically a woman like Mary Postgate, and show her behaving in ways that Kipling must have realized might be thought of as unwomanlike, even when directed at Germans? The answer to this rather important question is to be found, I think, in Mary's concluding ruminations as she waits for the fire to burn out and for the German to die. "A man, at such a crisis," she thinks, "would be what Wynn called a 'sportsman'; would leave everything to fetch help, and would certainly bring It into the house" (440). But she, because she is a woman and not "a sportsman" does not (and, suggestively, the books she is burning—Henty, Marryat, et al. are full of the "sportsman's" ethic). This should not be taken to mean, however, that Mary is, in Kipling's view, acting reprehensibly. On the contrary, she—along with her fellow countrymen in "The Beginnings"— has come to realize, as Wynn could not, that it is impossible to be sportsmanlike with an enemy who specializes in hideously unsportsmanlike conduct. Hence the huge revolver and its dumdum bullets, which, according to Wynn, "were forbidden by the rules of war to be used against civilized enemies" (437). But then the Germans are *not* civilized; they are, as Kipling so unambiguously put it, "inconceivably outside civilization." The Law of the Jungle, as *The Jungle Books* testify, applies only to such animals as possess a Law.

There is an analogy here to Maupassant's famous story "Lit 29" that is worth exploring, if only briefly, because it makes a similar distinction between a man's and a woman's duty in fighting against a hated enemy. Maupassant's Captain Epivent, like Wynn, is a sportsman who fights fairly in the field; and his mistress, Irma, though in all other respects radically different from Mary, fights unfairly and to greater effect at home. Infected with syphilis by a Prussian officer during the war of 1870, she continues consciously to lure the lustful enemy into her bed, there to put him *hors de combat.* Her apparent shame is in reality a great virtue; her immorality one of France's greatest glories. So too with Mary, although in a rather less lurid fashion. "*But* it was a fact," Mary thinks to herself. "A woman who had missed these things [a husband and family] could still be useful—more useful than a man in many respects" (440). Women, while socially and perhaps biologically disqualified from actual participation in battle, can and must do their duty in other, less glamorous ways. They also serve, to sum it all up, who only stand—or lie—and hate.

"Mary Postgate," one can agree in conclusion, is a story that has been misunderstood, perhaps chiefly because of an unwillingness on the part of the dons to face up squarely to Kipling's unsightly moral underbelly. Hatred and vengefulness are not popular literary commodities nowadays and the attempt to play down their presence in Kipling is understandable. Still, these qualities were undeniably very much a part of his stock in trade, as "Mary Postgate," but not "Mary Postgate" alone, testifies. To deny that is to turn a bull into an ox. Like most writers who have achieved great and perhaps excessive popularity in their own lifetimes, Kipling is very much fixed in the prejudices of a particular time and place. He must be understood within those limits, or not at all.

When "Mary Postgate" was published, its hatred produced no disapproval, or even surprise. Other men than Kipling had been "guilty" of such intemperance. Winston Churchill, for example, fulminated repeatedly against German monsters and "baby-killers." Even the distinguished classical scholar Gilbert Murray looked forward to the starvation of German women and children.[23] Are we to conclude, then, that Churchill or Murray or even Kipling would have enjoyed watching the actual, step-by-step demise of some wounded German? Surely not. The abstract desire for the death of a hated enemy, even an elaborately executed daydream on this subject like "Mary Postgate" is quite distinct from the real thing. Siegfried Sassoon, who had rather more opportunity to witness such events, realized this fully. In the semi-fictional account of his wartime experience, *Memoirs of an Infantry Officer* (1930), he describes how virulently his civilian friends and relations hated the Germans, whereas he himself, who was daily exposed to their enmity, bore them no grudge. His Aunt Evelyn, for instance, felt that it was her patriotic duty to agree with her vicar's axiom that "every man who killed a German was performing a Christian act." Even so, Sassoon goes on to say, alluding more or less obviously to Kipling's story, "if Aunt Evelyn had found a wounded Prussian when she was on her way to the post office, she would undoubtedly have behaved with her natural humanity (combined with enthusiasm for administering first aid)."[24] That Mary Postgate does not do so is less a function of her own cruelty than of Kipling's ignorance. As C. E. Montague was to observe in *Disenchantment* (1922), "war hath no fury like a non-combatant."[25]

6

Wellington House and the Strange Death
of a Liberal Professor

*The diversities between our different nations are irrational;
each of them has the same right, or want of right, to its
peculiarities. A man who is just and reasonable must nowadays, so far as his imagination permits, share the patriotism
of the rivals and enemies of his country—a patriotism as
inevitable and pathetic as his own.*
George Santayana, Three Philosophical Poets *(1910)*

One of the first and most momentous literary consequences of the Great War
was a meeting on 1 September 1914 at Wellington House, the headquarters of
the National Insurance Commission in London. Here, at the instigation of
the chief of that commission, C. F. G. Masterman, met a group of the most
distinguished writers in Britain, including Barrie, Belloc, Bennett, Robert
Bridges, G. K. Chesterton, Conan Doyle, Galsworthy, Hardy, Masefield,
Gilbert Murray, and H. G. Wells. It was, as another one of those present, A.
C. Benson, noted in his diary, "an extraordinary gathering." Masterman,
"soft, worried, mild," was in the chair and elaborated for this august assem-
bly the "fatuous request" he had earlier made in the letter summoning them
to Wellington House, namely, that "the Government were concerned about
the extent of German propaganda in America and wanted a united effort
from British writers to counteract it."[1]

Most of the other authors at this meeting did not share Benson's view of its
fatuousness. On the contrary, as Peter Buitenhuis has shown in his remarkable study of Wellington House, "Writers at War" (1976), they were eager to
do their bit.[2] Quickly a "committee was formed, a manifesto drawn up, and
the more elderly, less adventurous authors began to do good work at
Wellington House, which soon became a busy centre of propaganda."[3]
Arnold Bennett, for example, eventually turned out over four hundred items

of literary propaganda and, toward the end of the war, was put in charge of the whole effort of waging war by literary means. No one else quite matched that record, though John Buchan came close—and was also appointed to head the literary propaganda section for a time—and a few others, like Ford Madox Ford, Belloc, Chesterton, and H. G. Wells wrote prolifically as well.

Bennett's work for Wellington House is mostly dreary, unimaginative stuff, the predictable fulminations of a distinguished literary hack. He is given his reward in Pound's "Hugh Selwyn Mauberley," where, in the person of Mr. Nixon, he disburses advice to the younger generation, in the cabin of his "cream-gilded yacht," on how to make money out of literature. The same is not true of Wells, some of whose fiction, as we have seen, was to have a major impact on the way the British thought of the war and of their enemies. Nor is it true of John Buchan, who, at the time the war broke out, was virtually unknown as a writer.

Buchan—together with H. N. Brailsford, who was to become one of the best-known pacifists during the war—had been a pupil of Gilbert Murray's at Glasgow in the nineties of the last century. Murray outlived his sometime Scottish student by more than a decade and a half; and in the preface he wrote for Buchan's posthumous *The Clearing House* (1946), he remembers Buchan with affection and comments admiringly on his remarkable "range both of knowledge and sympathy."[4] After Glasgow, Buchan—like Murray—went on to Oxford, where he established a brilliant record, winning the Newdigate Prize for English Verse, becoming President of the Union, and graduating with a First Class Honours degree.

Though the decade after leaving Oxford was not unproductive—he was admitted to the Bar, joined Milner's "Kindergarden," dabbled in history, fiction, journalism—Buchan's achievements did not really measure up to his early promise. He made a respectable living as a partner in and literary adviser to his Oxford friend Nelson's publishing house. If the Great War had not interrupted this comfortable routine, Buchan would be remembered today—if at all—as a very minor literary figure. Instead, his name looms large both politically, as the sometime head of the Department of Information (i.e., propaganda) during the war and as Lord Tweedsmuir, the Governor General of Canada; and literarily, as the author of some of the most successful and influential novels written during the war.

These latter are the so-called "Richard Hannay" stories, named after the hero and first-person narrator of these tales. There are three in all: *The Thirty-Nine Steps* (1914), *Greenmantle* (1916), and *Mr. Standfast* (1919). The first is unquestionably the most famous, partly because of the brilliant film Alfred Hitchcock was to make of it, but also because it catches exactly the mood of the early months of the war, the sense of an innocent, unsuspecting England engulfed by an evil German conspiracy. In the end, that conspiracy—the evil Black Stone—is foiled, owing to a good deal of luck but also to the determined courage and ingenuity of Hannay. The ring of German spies disguised as English gentlemen is broken and England is saved.

Buchan's novel is not really original. It is a fairly obvious retelling of Arthur Conan Doyle's final Sherlock Holmes story, "His Last Bow" (August 1914). As with *The Thirty-Nine Steps*, Doyle's story is set in Britain shortly before the outbreak of the war and involves a long-standing German plot to overwhelm Britain in a surprise attack. Doyle's spies, like Buchan's, disguise themselves as gentlemen and mingle on equal terms with the amiable and unsuspecting British. As the villain von Herling tells the villain von Bork: "And all the time this quiet country house of yours is the center of half the mischief in England, and the sporting squire the most astute Secret Service man in Europe." Holmes, of course, unmasks the plot in time, but like Hannay—who acknowledges that "in his foul way" his opponent "had been a patriot"—Holmes tells the captured von Bork: "After all, you have done your best for your country and I have done my best for mine, and what could be more natural?"[5]

This note of "sportsmanship," of the game of espionage, runs through all of the Hannay stories. Buchan's Germans only rarely degenerate into brutal Huns. The Germans are the enemy, of that there can be no question, but they are not altogether unredeemed; and while they are never gentlemen—indeed, their claim to gentlemanliness is explicitly disavowed in *Mr. Standfast*—they are often motivated by a kind of perverse idealism. On the one hand, the fat, militaristic, gorillalike German is frighteningly real: von Stumm in *Greenmantle* strikes Hannay as "the German of caricature, the real German, the fellow we were up against"; but at the same time, Stumm is balanced by the "good German" Gaudian, who is someone Hannay admits he could even have worked with himself, "for he belonged to my own totem."[6]

The most unusually sympathetic portrait of a German is that of the Kaiser in *Greenmantle*. Meeting him briefly at a railway station, Hannay hears the Kaiser make the expected excuses that he did not want the war and that England and Russia are to blame. Still, the Kaiser strikes Hannay as belonging to an altogether different species from Stumm and his kind, since he has "the power of laying himself alongside other men," a trait that in Germany, according to Hannay, is usually confined to Jews. But the Kaiser, "the chief of a nation of Stumms, paid the price in war for the gifts that had made him successful in peace. He had imagination and nerves, and the one was white hot and the others were quivering. I would not have been in his shoes for the throne of the Universe. . . ."[7]

By any measure this is extraordinary: to depict the Kaiser, in the middle of the war, as anything other than a mad, bloodthirsty beast run wild. It speaks well for Buchan's own imagination and nerves. And yet one is left wondering. . . . What is the point of these "good" or at least partly "good" Germans? Are they real, or any more real, than Buchan's "bad" Germans? (There is a similar problem with Buchan's good and bad pacifists in *Mr. Standfast.*) Is the "good" Kaiser to be taken seriously or is he simply a product of a literary strategy that will make us believe Hannay's other, less amiable views? Is Hannay a complex character, whose response to people and situations involves his whole personality and is therefore profound? Or are his understanding and sympathy simply a veneer, a kind of mask to make the inveterate Tory beneath more likable? So, for example, Hannay is able to realize the "crazy folly of the war" while spending Christmas Eve high in the Bavarian Alps in a cottage belonging to a poor German woman and her three children. "What good would it do Christian folks," he wonders in these surroundings, "to burn poor little huts like this and leave children's bodies by the wayside?"[8] This seems moving and sincere and decent. But on the other hand, in different surroundings, Hannay shows no qualms whatever in burning and bombarding Turkish cities—full of women and children.

Certainly, when Buchan writes of the Germans outside of a fictional context, he is a good deal less friendly. In his essay on "The German Mind" (1915), he explicitly denies Burke's assertion that one cannot draw up an indictment against a whole nation. At least three-quarters of the German people are guilty and mad; and the source of their madness—"the chief fount of the virus"—is German industry and high finance, together with "their obedient satellites, the University Professors"—who, according to Buchan, are often Jewish. And in his *History of the Great War,* Buchan presents a rather different version of the Kaiser than he does in *Greenmantle.* Here the German Emperor appears in the guise of "Mars as the travelling salesman," whose "vulgarity did not offend, because it was the vulgarity of modern Germany." The Kaiser is no longer a figure of flawed—and hence, tragic—nobility, but a mere clown, "an object for pity perhaps, rather than commiseration."[9]

Perhaps the strange gulf between Buchan's fictional Germans and his "real" ones is the result not of the difference of medium and audience. Perhaps it is really due to a difference between Buchan's conscious and his unconscious mind; or, to put it another way, a difference between Buchan the Wellington House propagandist and Buchan the individual human being. Perhaps the unofficial Buchan knew more and dared to say more than the official one ever imagined.

A similar but less striking dichotomy is evident in a far better-known Wellington House writer, Thomas Hardy. For the most part, Hardy was too much of a poet to allow his work to sink to the level of mere versified propaganda. At least two of his wartime poems, "The Pity of It" (1915) and "In Time of 'The Breaking of Nations' " (1916), rank with the greatest English poems written about the war. But not all of his verse reaches so high a level of intensity and sincerity. One poem, "England to Germany in 1914" (1914), is a direct reply to Ernst Lissauer's infamous "Hassgesang" ("Hymn of Hate"), and expresses Hardy's quite genuine and quite unpoetic puzzlement at why Germans should hate the English so violently:

> —Is it that Teuton genius flowers
> Only to breathe malignity
> Upon its friend of earlier hours?

Hardy concludes that the probable result of such malignity can only be that it will succeed in fouling the Germans' "ancient name" in future "and present sight."[10]

Hardy also wrote a number of "occasional" poems on Belgium, with muted references to German atrocities, as in "On the Belgian Expatriation" (1914), with its vision of "foes of mad mood" smashing Belgian carillons "to shards amid the gear / Of ravaged roof, and smouldering gable-end." The apex—or nadir—of Hardy's propagandistic verse, however, is unquestionably his poem in support of conscription, "A Call to National Service" (1917), with its exhortation to rise

> Up and be doing, all who have a hand
> To lift, a back to bend.[11]

The seventy-seven-year-old Hardy concludes this piece by asserting that if his age allowed, he would be up and doing at the front himself.

The work of Wellington House was a closely guarded secret.[12] Only a few of its records survive, so that its history can only be reconstructed, as Peter Buitenhuis has done, by means of what must be called literary archaeology. The aim of Wellington House was explicitly to influence American public opinion, by sending copies of propaganda books—not labeled as such, of course—by famous English writers to influential people in the United States. An elaborate network of "colleagues" and "friends" was set up who would take on the job of sending free copies of these works to America. Their principal purpose was to convince American readers that the Germans were a nation of barbarians and that it was therefore necessary to join or at least support the English effort to preserve the values of humanity and civilization. There can be no doubt that the Wellington House writers succeeded in this effort, even though, as Hilaire Belloc remarked to G. K. Chesteron in 1917, it was "necessary sometimes to lie damnably in the interests of the nation. . . ."[13]

According to Peter Buitenhuis, Wellington House in fact did its job too well. It encouraged writers like Buchan and Ford to lie too damnably and too successfully, so that a gullible public was tragically misled about the true nature of the war, as, for instance, in Buchan's hypocritical account of the Battle of the Somme, or in Ford's account of the supposedly treacherous activities of pacifist and other opponents of the war. Buitenhuis concludes, however, that the worst effect of the lying onslaught of Wellington House propaganda was to distort the aims and moral nature of the enemy so profoundly and irreparably—by turning him into a bestial Hun—that it became impossible to conclude a rational peace with Germany. The result was Versailles and all that.

Buitenhuis may be right. Certainly Wellington House is one of the most extraordinary instances in British history of the government management of literary production, and it anticipates in frightening ways Orwell's prophecy of even more absolute control in *Nineteen Eighty-Four*—a prophecy, by the way, partly based on a similar but much more open management of writers at the BBC during the Second World War. Still, one is left wondering if Wellington House *per se* made all that much difference. If there had been no Wellington House, with its apt and aptly named Masterman, would there have been appreciably less damnable lying on the part of British writers during the Great War? Perhaps. In hindsight it is difficult to tell. But the atmosphere of hatred and hysteria, especially during the early stages of the war, was so intense that it is difficult to believe that most of the writers who cooperated actively with Wellington House would have refrained from writing much the same sort of thing they actually did write. It is true that the administrative machinery of Wellington House helped to guarantee financing, publication, and wide distribution of the work of its writers, but it is also true that most of these writers were well enough known in any event to secure publication and a large audience for anything they cared to write. Perhaps a writer like Bennett would not have written so enormous a mass of propaganda, but it seems unrealistic to suppose that he would not have written any.

In the end, then, it seems fair to say that it was not Wellington House or official government interference with the pure sources of the literary imagination that poisoned the minds of British (and American) readers and prevented rational discussion about peace with Germany during the war. Wellington House is really more of a symptom than a cause. The poison was in the system, in the muddied literary imagination itself. Rudyard Kipling is a case in point. Though invited to attend the first "founding" meeting at Wellington House, Kipling was unable to attend. And later Masterman was glad that Kipling had not come, since he grew to believe that Kipling's brand of propaganda was so counterproductive as to be dangerous.[14] Still, Kipling had no difficulty in publishing his stories or histories of the war; on the contrary, the war helped greatly in reviving Kipling's sagging reputation and enlarging his readership.

Kipling is, of course, an extreme and highly predictable case. More interesting and more significant is the case of Gilbert Murray. Before the war, Murray's credentials as an intellectual and "man of reason" were impeccable. He very visibly and capably occupied the chair of Greek at Oxford; his opposition to war was so well known that his friend Shaw took him as the model for Cusins in *Major Barbara* (1905); and he was a leading member of the pacifist movement trying to keep Britain out of Continental entanglements. Shortly before the actual declaration of war, he signed the famous neutralist manifesto published in the *Guardian*.

It was, so Murray later claimed, listening to Sir Edward Grey's speech to the House of Commons on 3 August 1914 that finally made him change his mind.[15] And once convinced, Murray threw his very considerable energies and abilities wholeheartedly into supporting and justifying the cause of the Allies. This is how Murray told the story of his conversion. But whether in the case of a man like Murray, a single speech—no matter how brilliant, and Grey's speeches were never noted for their brilliance—can overthrow the convictions of a lifetime, may be doubted. One senses in Murray, as one does in other sometime dedicated opponents and subsequently dedicated supporters of the war, that he wanted to be convinced. His opposition had become a burden of which he hoped some honorable excuse might relieve him.

How thankful Murray was not to be standing alone in an unpopular cause emerges poignantly in his first publication in support of the war, *Thoughts on the War* (1914). Here we find the distinguished Oxford professor reborn amid an almost religious enthusiasm. The war has managed to do in only a few days what no amount of socialist agitation had ever achieved: a society in which all Englishmen, no matter of what class or political party, were brothers. Murray now became a "mate" to his fellow countrymen, and his fellow countrymen were "mates" to him. A war that had made this happen must be a good war.[16]

Murray's *Thoughts on the War* were just that, the first impressions of a man impelled to make his newfound convictions known. Almost immediately, however, Murray set about analyzing in detail and in scholarly fashion the whole course of British policy toward Germany in the decade preceding the war. The fruit of this labor, *The Foreign Policy of Sir Edward Grey, 1906–1915* (1915), is an examination of the British public conscience in the person of the Foreign Secretary, but it is also implicitly an examination—and exoneration—of Murray's own conscience. That conscience is pure. Britain was guiltless of any hostility toward Germany or of any intent to mislead Germany regarding British actions and motives in the event of war. Grey had labored manfully—almost angelically—to prevent war, and up to the very last moment before actual hostilities he had tried his utmost to bring Germany to reason and mediation.

The upright and honorable Grey became a symbol for Murray. Grey's behavior stood for the behavior of all Englishmen: modest, tolerant, and true, not given to being aggressive but, when pushed to the limit, prepared to fight. It was Grey's example, as well as his words, that now seemed to shine forth with an almost unearthly sanctity. Whatever the actual truth behind all this, one senses here that Murray is describing his own conversion from prewar skepticism to fervent pro-war patriotism.

The words Murray wrote about Arthur Heath, a colleague at Oxford and a recent casualty of the war, might equally well have been penned about himself: "He had at first, like all thoughtful Englishmen, a feeling of utter horror at the prospect of European war, and an uneasy suspicion that, however necessary it might be, now at the last moment for England to fight, surely our policy for many years back must have been somewhere dreadfully at fault. The White Paper was the first thing to reassure him; then came the study of earlier questions; and in the end he felt confidence in the wisdom and good faith of British diplomacy since 1904, and conceived in particular a great admiration of Sir Edward Grey."[17]

Not that Murray was ever altogether naive or that he sank to the level of a vulgar hun-hater. Though he rejoiced in the deaths of Germans, even of Germans he had known as students, he always retained the knowledge that such rejoicing was terrible. He knew also that an Allied victory over Germany might bring with it certain improvements in terms of national frontiers, but he also knew that any such gains would be more than matched by the terrible result that "in the heart of Europe, instead of a treacherous and grasping neighbour," there would be "a deadly enemy, living for revenge."[18]

This is why Murray had hoped from the very beginning that the war would conclude with a "generous settlement" for a defeated Germany.[19] During the war Murray never abandoned this hope, though he grew more and more convinced that Germany needed to be crushed. For the war was, according to Murray, fundamentally a war of ideas, not a war of prestige or territorial ambition. It was a war in which the universal triumph of one of two utterly opposed principles was to be decided: "Democracy or Despotism, Freedom or Compulsion, Consent or the Power of the Sword."[20]

Britain was basically decent; Germany, basically indecent. Germany was prepared to stop at nothing in the mad pursuit of its aims, not even at the most horrible kinds of atrocities. But not the British. "Now we do not act like that," Murray observes in *Ethical Problems of the War* (1915); "there is something or other in the English nature which will not allow it. We shall show anger and passion, but we are probably not capable of that organized cruelty, and I hope we shall never be."[21]

There was no really rational explanation for the conduct of the Germans in the war. Before the war the British had "liked them. Most of Europe rather liked and admired them." And, in fact, the Germans had not been "so wicked to start with"; it was only "afterwards they became devils."[22] But devils they had become; and it was now the task of every upstanding Englishman to exorcise them.

Once Grey had been beatified and the Germans diabolized, it became easier to recognize the hand of infernal powers in other quarters of the globe as well. Murray's essay on "The Dublin Insurrection" (1916) admits that the rising against the English was partly the work of a few "leading Sinn Feiners and sentimental Irish enthusiasts," but the chief responsibility for the "reign of terror" was to be placed squarely at the door of certain "wild Labour men, who had been disowned by the trade-unions," and their cohorts, "actual criminals." These maverick Labourites and fellow criminals, like their German friends, were not above using "explosive bullets" and committing "some acts of great cruelty," things the English would never do.[23]

Some surviving part of the prewar Murray must have realized that in committing to paper views of this sort he was—if not lying damnably in his country's behalf—at least engaging in a doubtful commerce of half-lies and half-truths. It is perhaps to this atmosphere of moral corruption—the atmosphere that he himself daily breathed in and out—that he refers to in "The Turmoil of War" (1917). "If we had known," he hypothesizes in that essay, "that, in addition to the awful waste of human life, in addition to the incalculable sum of suffering, in addition to the desperate impoverishment of Europe, the war was likely to bring upon us a certain lowering of the national ideals, and a time of bitter and perhaps sordid reaction; if we had known all this, should we still have declared war against the German Empire?" To this momentous question, Murray's simple answer was, "Yes."[24]

But it was no longer a resounding affirmative. Grave doubts had begun to shake at the foundations of Murray's belief in Britain's exclusive virtue. Now, in a single sentence, Murray was suddenly prepared to overthrow the whole structure he had so laboriously erected two years earlier in *The Foreign Policy of Sir Edward Grey*. As if teetering himself now at the edge of despair, Murray writes of the origins of the war that "it makes some difference in one's ultimate judgement, it saves one from a wild reaction against all organized human society as an accursed thing, if we realize that the war is not really the work of man's will. It is more a calamity to pity than a crime to curse."[25] Here Murray comes very close to the point of view expressed in a few famous words by another patriotic Englishman, Wilfred Owen: "The poetry is in the pity." Pity, not hatred—not even heroism—is the proper reaction to the war; and pity not only for the dead or those daily exposed to the risk of death, but pity also for ourselves.

Pity for himself and bewilderment at his government's foreign policy runs through Murray's *The Problem of Foreign Policy* (1921). Here Murray makes no bones about having supported his government during the war, but he nevertheless accuses the government, in the person of its Prime Minister, Lloyd George, of missing the most magnificent opportunity "in the whole course of modern history" to choose between "plain good or plain evil. And he chose, deliberately, evil."[26]

Lloyd George's infamous "hang the Kaiser" campaign—the so-called coupon election of 1918—left Murray incredulous. Now it was the turn of his fellow Englishmen to fall prey to the devil. "I did not realize," he confesses sadly, "that anyone could be, I will not say so wicked, but so curiously destitute of generous ambition, so incapable of thinking greatly." The Treaty of Versailles he termed a "monstrous breach of faith," and foresaw that in it the Allies had "sown the seeds of future war." Murray's hopes and the hopes of other English liberals for a "high-minded" and "scrupulously fair" peace had been cynically crushed.[27] And among these fellow liberals by this time was also Murray's sometime chief at Wellington House. "There is not one good cause," C. F. G. Masterman observes in *England After War* (1923), "which can be said to have been enriched by the murderous operations of this war. The territorial delimitations of Europe have not been settled. They poise desperately on a Treaty of Versailles which has no friends, and which is rapidly being torn to fragments. The economic stability of Europe has not been settled."[28] Was it for such an end that Masterman and his literary colleagues at Wellington House had labored—and lied damnably—for so long?

Who, aside from Lloyd George, was to blame for all this? The ultimate fault lay, according to Murray, in "the horrors of the propaganda of hate." Because of the pressure exercised by "mob-inspired journalists and journalist-inspired mobs," the Supreme Council of the Allies had felt compelled to break the word it had given when it signed the Fourteen Points of the Armistice. The result was "an utter and all-devouring peace of revenge, including the starvation and enslavement of half Europe for thirty or fifty or a hundred years. . . ."[29] There were no more "mates" here, alas, just rabid journalists and mad mobs—English journalists and English mobs.

But in fact not only the journalists and the mobs were to blame. Now too Murray was prepared to admit that during the war the government had been forced to commit actions that were "not exactly crimes" but that were nevertheless hideous. One such action was the starvation of the Poles. The Americans had offered to send food to Poland and the Germans had agreed that it would go exclusively to the Poles. Even so, the British government refused. "There was no choice," Murray writes of this decision. "But the man who had to sign that order may well have wished he had died before the need came to him."[30]

No less hideous but less excusable was the continued blockade of Germany after the Armistice. Though "not a technical breach of faith," the continuation of the blockade of food and other basic necessities after the

German surrender was, according to Murray, "one of the many acts of almost incredible inhumanity which have made the recent Great War conspicuous in the annals of mankind and shaken thoughtful men's faith in the reality of modern civilisation." So deeply was Murray's own faith shaken and his credulity strained that he was even prepared to confess that "the old German accusation that England entered the war in order to destroy a trade rival, utterly untrue at the time, seemed to receive some colour by the terms of the peace."[31]

In *The Ordeal of This Generation* (1929), Murray returns to many of the same issues and reaches similar conclusions. The war was nobody's fault in particular. It took place, not out of individual wickedness, but "because the international system was wrong." Moreover, the war was poisoned by hate and lies, especially on the part of noncombatants, because they had no other way of discharging their pent-up anger and vicarious suffering; they could only vent the intense internal pressures through words and emotions. Still, it is only with shame that Murray was able to think of "the organized system of mendacity which developed towards the end of the war."[32] And in an even later book, *Then and Now* (1935), Murray remembers the incredulous astonishment with which he first heard of the German atrocities, concluding that anyone who did such things must be mad; but "gradually we found, as the War went on, that no nation stood alone. One after another was added to the black list of the inhuman, and that insane streak still remains in the postwar world long after the actual War has ended."[33]

After the war, then, Murray came to the conclusion that the war had been mad; and after the war—even to a slight degree during the last stages of the war itself—Murray realized that the war was something at one and the same time intensely human and yet beyond human control. After the war, Murray looked back with horror, disappointment, and disgust at the vile qualities of human nature that the war had revealed. "Scratch a European," as Murray had once put it in a famous and almost Swiftian epigram, "and you will find a savage." After the war, the peace that settled upon Europe no longer seemed to justify his elevated esteem for the noble altruism of British foreign policy. After the war, Sir Edward Grey—and with him Gilbert Murray—came back down to earth.

There is something extraordinarily touching, something almost pathetic, in Murray's postwar bewilderment at what the war had wrought. It is like watching a man who has lost his faith and does not quite know if it will ever be possible for him to believe in anything again. But there is also something disingenuous in Murray's disillusion, a note of falseness that echoes—discordantly—his earlier clarion tones of patriotic illusion. For, as Murray must have known somewhere deep down in himself, it was not merely the mob-inspired journalists or the journalist-inspired mobs who were to blame for the poisonous atmosphere of the war. Some of the poison had emanated from minds as fine and distinguished as Murray's own; and the professorial poison, though more rarefied, had done its deadly work, too, in choking off the life-breath of peace.

Murray's postwar tragic awareness of the hell that is war—as in the supposedly necessary starvation of the Poles or the supposedly unnecessary starvation of the Germans—must be put in the context of his own earlier conviction that the starvation of the enemy, though unfortunate, was right and good. In *Thoughts on the War,* Murray had viewed with complete equanimity the prospect of what would, he hoped, happen to one of his former students at Oxford. Paul Maass, Murray observed, had sent him from Germany not long ago a photograph of his first baby, Ulf, and Murray and Maass had exchanged jokes about his wise appearance, his knowledge of Greek, and so on. "And now," Murray continues, "Maass is with his regiment, and we shall do our best to kill him, and after that to starve Ulf and Ulf's mother."[34]

The eminent Oxford Professor who desired so fervently to starve women and children was the same eminent Oxford professor who later branded the Irish rebellion the work of madmen and criminals and who proclaimed Sir Edward Grey a saint and the English a people constitutionally incapable of committing atrocities. The journalists who took the professor at his word, and the mobs who took the words of the journalists, cannot be held exclusively responsible for spreading intellectual and emotional poison. The really guilty poisoners were not in Fleet Street or Trafalgar Square; they were in Wellington House and Oxford.

Some members of the younger generation realized that. "No, it is not the war-records or our 'yellow' journalists," Douglas Goldring wrote in 1920, "that the youth of England will concern itself to examine, but the records of how those who before the outbreak of the War were accounted our leaders acquitted themselves. Can we trust them anymore?"[35] Goldring's accusation is here leveled principally at another great Wellington House author, H. G. Wells, but it is equally applicable to Murray. It was the corruption of the best that the young were worried about, not the corruption of the worst. Lilies that fester, after all, smell far worse than weeds. That journalists would twist the truth or mobs succumb to hysteria was a well-known fact long before the war. Even during the war, A. C. Benson—who, after the first meeting, kept himself largely out of the reach of Wellington House—noted that "if the nation was really the sort of people typified by the newspapers, they would not be worth perpetuating or fighting for."[36]

That it was, however, possible for someone who shared the initial enthusiasm for the war, even for someone who had agreed to write propaganda for the government, to change his mind in mid-course and mid-war, is evidenced by Jerome K. Jerome. This writer of popular stories and novels was sent to the United States by the British government to vilify the Germans.

But it was a job he could not stomach. He protested that "this attempt to make them out a nation of fiends seemed to me as silly as it was wicked." As a result of this protest, Jerome got into trouble with the press and "a select number of ladies and gentlemen did me the honour to send me threatening letters."[37]

Jerome eventually moved completely away from supporting the war to join a small group of similarly minded intellectuals who tried to work for a reasonable, negotiated peace. This group included at least one former Wellington House author, Israel Zangwill—who had struck Bennett at the first meeting as talking too much—as well as Ramsay MacDonald, Dean Inge, and E. D. Morel. The efforts of this group, of course, ended in failure. By this time the war had gone on too long and had become too bitter for anyone in power to listen to reason, even if someone could be found with the necessary courage and clarity of mind to speak reason. As Clive Bell discovered when, in 1915, he published a pamphlet entitled *Peace at Once*, the Lord Mayor of London ordered its immediate destruction.[38]

Jerome's change of mind during the war is a relatively isolated instance—among noncombatants, that is. For actual participants in the conflict, it was less unusual. A whole group of soldier poets—Sassoon, Graves, Rosenberg, Nichols, Graeme West, and, most of all, Owen—changed their minds. By a strange irony of literary history, this group has become known as the "War Poets," though their best poetry is directed against war. The voice of that poetry is not always sweetly reasonable. Sassoon's poems, especially, frequently break out into direct and open violence. But, then, at a time when the public fonts of reason had been polluted by propaganda, it is not surprising that the few remaining springs of truth should burst out with the blood of grief and pity.

7

Into Cleanness Leaping: Brooke, Eliot, Shaw, and Lawrence

In the most widely used contemporary anthology of modern poetry—the Norton *Anthology*, a volume of nearly fifteen hundred pages—one will find selections from the works of such early twentieth-century British poets as James Stephens, John Masefield, Edwin Muir, and Edith Sitwell; but one will search in vain for even a scrap of the poetry of Rupert Brooke. Brooke, it seems, is not an important poet.

Nevertheless, his poetry remains in print, even in paperback, and, to judge by the annual academic bibliographies, there is a modest but continuing interest in Brooke on the part of critics and scholars. As a figure on the fringes of Bloomsbury, as a friend or acquaintance of such greats as Strachey and Forster and Woolf and Frye (and Churchill), he pops up with some regularity in studies of these undiminished titans, as well as in more general works about the period when they lived and loved and wrote and, as in Brooke's case, died.

What is more, if the editors of the Norton *Anthology of Modern Poetry* have forgotten Brooke, they have remembered—in some cases, amply remembered—other poets whose careers were also bound up with the Great War: Wilfred Owen, of course, but also Siegfried Sassoon, Robert Graves, David Jones, and Herbert Read. Not that these poets should be omitted and forgotten. But then why omit and forget Brooke, who was certainly a more notable and influential poet than, say, Herbert Read?

The answer to this question is, I think, not far to seek. Part of it lies in the postwar attack on the Georgian poets, an attack led by such powerful voices as those of Ezra Pound and T. S. Eliot. The Georgians, and by association Brooke, since he was often thought of as their chief representative and greatest glory, the Georgians were just too old-fashioned and "lucent-siropy," too given to writing pretty-pretty poetry about natural scenery and birds—belated Romantics, in other words, remnants of a by-gone age rather than harbingers of a new. One of the ironies of this view is that Brooke discovered and imitated the metaphysicals at the same time Eliot did, that he was equally fascinated by the modern appreciation of vulgarity and ugliness, the juxtaposition of wispy illusion with gross reality—as, for instance, in a poem like "Channel Passage." Another irony is that Brooke was among the first to recognize Pound's promise as a poet, finding his poetry "blatant, full of foolish archaisms, obscure through awkward language not subtle thought, and formless"; yet at the same time original, vital, relieved by flashes of brilliance and the promise of greatness to come.[1] And the final irony is that Eliot actually admired Brooke and, as we shall see, drew on him and shaped some important aspects of his own poetry on Brooke's.

So that Brooke is neglected because he is not thought of as a modern poet and therefore has no place in an anthology of modern poetry, though a poet like Housman does.

That is part of the answer. The other part is that Brooke is the author of a brief but at one time inordinately famous sonnet sequence, "1914." These poems glorify the outbreak of the Great War; or, to put it even more bluntly, they glorify war plain and simple. An anthology conceived, collected, and published during the last phases of the Vietnam debacle could hardly endorse such a point of view.

This is not an occasion for easy mockery. Poetry can be a weapon, as some of the poets of the thirties believed; and because this is so, one must recognize that the weapon can sometimes be pointed the wrong way. The subject matter of literature *matters*, a view which I strongly share, for otherwise I would not have written this book. Still, if poetry is a weapon, it only seems sensible to try to familiarize ourselves with its parts, all of the parts, including those used by the enemy. To ignore a poet of the stature of Brooke is to risk turning the weapon on oneself.

When war broke out, Brooke lost little time in enlisting. Though something of a Bohemian, a fervent Fabian socialist, and a critic of bourgeois society, he loved England deeply. Any challenge to his country was a challenge to be met personally and selflessly. Although he had intimate connections at the highest levels of government—Edward Marsh and, through Edward Marsh, Churchill—and could probably have arranged for some important desk job or at least for a relatively safe sinecure behind the front lines, Brooke was ready and eager to risk himself. He was present at the German seizure of Antwerp early in the war—where he lost the field glasses Forster had given him—and, as everyone once knew, he died in April 1915 of an infection while en route to Churchill's planned invasion of Turkey at Gallipoli. Death came suddenly and unexpectedly to a man who, as a fellow poet put it, was "magnificently unprepared," though I suspect the adverb "deliberately" would have stated Brooke's psychological condition more accurately. He is buried on the Greek island of Scyros, a kind of latter-day Byron.

But before he died at the age of twenty-eight, Brooke had prepared his testament in "1914." The five sonnets that make up the sequence were unquestionably the best known and most intensely loved poems to come out of the conflict. Only after the war, and only after the poetry of Wilfred Owen began to make an impact, did their luster diminish, though, notwithstanding the Norton *Anthology*, that luster has never altogether dimmed.

The first sonnet, entitled "Peace," sets the tone for the rest, as well as for an as yet untested generation going to war with a smile on its lips. That Brooke was utterly sincere in expressing the intense emotions of this poem emerges unmistakably from a letter to Violet Asquith written at about the same time: "I've never been quite so happy in my life, I think. Not quite so *pervasively* happy . . .":

> Now, God be thanked who has matched us with His Hour,
> And caught our youth, and wakened us from sleeping,
> With hand made sure, clear eye, and sharpened power,
> To turn, as swimmers into cleanness leaping,
> Glad from a world grown old and cold and weary,
> Leave the sick hearts that honour could not move,
> And half-men, and their dirty songs and dreary,
> And all the little emptiness of love!
>
> Oh! we who have known shame, we have found release there,
> Where there's no ill, no grief, but sleep has mending,
> Naught broken save this body, lost but breath;
> Nothing to shake the laughing heart's long peace there
> But only agony, and that has ending;
> And the worst friend and enemy is but Death.[2]

The octave of this sonnet deals with peace as it is conventionally defined but not conventionally understood: it is peace, the absence of war. Such peace belongs to a world of moral decay and the neglect of honor, a world without real men, whose dreary and unclean songs waste themselves upon the trivial subject of sexual relations. It is an old and sinful world that is being smashed, not for the first time, by the hand of God, who does not like such worlds. His hour, specially planned and arranged, has arrived, an armageddon devoutly to be wished. A new world is about to be born: a world of the young, the newly awakened, with strong bodies and bright minds, leaping out of the filth of the "peaceful" and infernal past into the purificatory cleanliness of the divine present. It is the baptism of a new age: away from stasis and the formal acceptance of beliefs or the ritual repetition of deeds no longer filled with living substance; toward—in a daring leap heavenward—a dynamic existence vitalized by the risk of death and informed by a holy mission, toward a Love that is not merely love, not the petty amatory preoccupations of degenerates who have nothing better to do, but a Love that in its religious grandeur overwhelms all, even and especially one's own self.[3]

The sonnet's concluding sestet defines this new condition of peace, which is war. The shame and sinfulness of the past are washed away; reborn, like children, into the true peace of war, we find release or salvation, a paradisal state in which grief and unhappiness are accidental rather than systemic, and therefore temporary. In imitation of Christ, we offer up our bodies to be broken or our breath to be taken away, but in comparison to the salvation we have gained, these pains and losses are as nothing. Our hearts are laughing now and no longer sick, because they have found the "long" or everlasting peace of faith in a divine cause. Agony there is, but it is like Christ's agony, one that will end and, when ended, one that brings final peace and salvation. Hence Death is simultaneously an enemy and a friend, an enemy to the body but a friend to the soul; and therefore more friend than enemy.

Brooke's poem is built on a series of daring paradoxes and ironies, the greatest of which is that war is peace. War, by abrogating a world of uncertainty and individual happiness or unhappiness, brings moral renewal—"Honour has come back, as a king, to earth," as another one of the sonnets puts it. This statement makes use of another Christian allusion—war brings an inner sense of certainty and a willingness to sacrifice individual concerns for collective salvation that Brooke, relying on a Christian tradition that endorses similar values in a similar context, calls peace. The closing line of the sonnet, with its paradox of Death's being both friend and enemy, also echoes Christian doctrine, though it goes beyond Christianity to suggest that life is only worth living, is only healthy, when exposed to the risk of death. Readers of Hemingway will be familiar with this idea.

The closing line is also paradoxical in another, more immediately topical sense. The word *enemy* occurs only once in the sonnet (and only once in the whole series of sonnets, for that matter), and it is deliberately avoided until the last line. It is a word that by December 1914 could have evoked only one response: the Germans. But Brooke undercuts this expectation by defining the enemy (and friend) as simply Death. There is clearly a point to this. The omission confers upon the poem an intense, undiminished purity: the "shame" that we have known is our own, no one else's. The war in which by

God's grace we are allowed to participate is not *against* a particular nation but a war *for* our own salvation. Significantly, there is no mention of Germans, the Kaiser, the causes of the war, or any other recognizably topical reference in this or any of the other sonnets of the sequence. Those who have read through the long and often dreary list of poems produced in the early phases of the Great War will realize how unusual this is.

What is even more unusual, however, is that the significance of Brooke's sonnets seems not to have been understood at the time they were published. Or, if it was understood, then in a way that failed to reach expression. For if the sonnets had been fully understood, then the British would have had to come to grips with the problem that in idolizing Brooke and his war poetry, they were endorsing a position that, as far as almost all writers on the subject were concerned, was exclusively German: namely, the position that war, any war, war *per se*, was good. That the British failed at the time to see that Brooke was saying this very thing is perhaps understandable; it was a time when blind hatred and smoke and fire prevented all but the most clearheaded from seeing; and in Brooke's case, vision was additionally obscured by his early death and consequent symbolic apotheosis. Perhaps also the religious terminology and imagery in which Brooke cloaked his sonnets helped to disguise their deeper, underlying meaning.

As Albert Martin has shown in his study of the role of the Church of England in the Great War, numerous religious figures thought of Britain's entry into the war as a response "to a summons from the Beyond" and greeted the war as "splendid," "magnificent," and "divine." According to S. C. Carpenter, Britain was "divinely commissioned to end Prussian militarism," and the Reverend Basil Bourchier maintained that "we are fighting, not so much for the honour of our country, as for the honour of our God." Brooke's extraordinary vision in the fifth, last, and most famous of his war sonnets, "The Soldier," of an "eternal mind" that will preserve the Englishness of the dead soldier is easily matched by verses like the following:

> God of England! God Almighty!
>   God of England's children true;
> God of England's wondrous story;
>   England's God, we cry to Thee.

In such a context, it is hardly surprising that Brooke should have been misunderstood.[4]

Those who blamed Germany for glorifying war were not wrong. That there was a German tradition of this sort is undeniable. The notorious Treitschke is quite unambiguous on this point. "What," he asks rhetorically, "if war should really disappear and with it all movement and all growth? What if mankind should deliberately deprive itself of the one remedy for an ailing civilization?"[5] Treitschke made a whole philosophy out of applying some of Darwin's ideas on natural selection and evolution in a cultural context of the survival of the fittest through an eternal martial struggle to the death (that is, basically the social Darwinism of Herbert Spencer). But the philosophical glorification of war in Germany predates Darwin and Treitschke and goes back at least as far as Hegel, who, in the *Philosophy of Right and Law* (1821), concludes that waging war has a higher meaning in that through it "the ethical health of nations is maintained, since such health does not require the stabilizing of finite arrangements; just as the motion of the winds keeps the sea from the foulness which a constant calm would produce—so war prevents a corruption of nations which a perpetual, let alone an eternal peace would produce."[6]

What Hegel has in mind here is not total war but what he terms a "modern war," which is "conducted humanely and persons do not hate each other."[7] In fairness to Brooke, it should be admitted that this was also almost certainly the kind of war he was thinking of when he wrote the sonnets; and, indeed, the sestet of the fourth sonnet, "The Dead," contains an image that strikingly echoes Hegel's, though it is highly unlikely that Brooke had Hegel in mind.

But whether Brooke was influenced directly by Hegel or not, it is clear that his attitude toward war was not unique among British writers. The German tradition of glorifying war has a British equivalent, more muted certainly, but equally real. This is especially true of the nineteenth century. One recalls William Henley's "Song of the Sword" (dedicated to Kipling) in which there is an anguished cry for blood; or the conclusion of Tennyson's *Maud:*

> No longer shall commerce be all in all, and Peace
> Pipe on her pastoral hillock a languid note.

Carlyle—of whom more later—in *Chartism* (1839) and in *Past and Present* (1843) takes over Hegel's theory of the salutary function of war. In the latter work we are told that "man is created to fight; he is perhaps best of all definable as a born soldier; his life 'a battle and a march,' under the right General. It is forever indispensable for a man to fight: now with Necessity, with Barrenness, Scarcity, with Puddles, Bogs, tangled Forests, unkempt Cotton;—now also with the hallucinations of his poor fellow Man. . . . All fighting, as we noted long ago, is the dusty conflict of strengths, each thinking itself the strongest, or, in other words, the justest;—of rights which do in the long-run, and forever will in this just Universe in the long-run, mean Rights." Later on, in the same work, Carlyle goes on to praise the Army as "The One Institution" that can bring about the salvation of England.[8]

Carlyle's disciple John Ruskin is if anything more explicit in his praise of war. In the chapter "War" in *The Crown of Wild Olive* (1865), he sees, like Hegel, the origin of virtue in war. In words that strikingly anticipate Brooke's, Ruskin argues that "we talk of peace and learning, and of peace and plenty, and of peace and civilisation; but I found that these were not the words which the Muse of History [in the person of Hegel?] coupled together: that, on her lips, the words were—peace, and sensuality—peace, and selfishness—peace, and death. I found, in brief, that all great nations learned their truth of word, and strength of thought, in war; that they were nourished in war, and wasted by peace;—in a word, that they were born in war, and expired in peace."[9]

According to Edward Jenks's classic *A Short History of Politics* (1900), the ultimate and original foundation of all states, including England, is war; just as Walter Bagehot argued that the right of the Europeans in and to Australia consisted in their ability to kill the aborigines whenever they wished.[10] As late as 1915, W. L. George was able to maintain in the *English Review* that "the people do not want to abolish war; they talk of peace and that is lip service; they like blood as they like murders, boxing, the cinema." In illustration of this British attitude, George cites Nelson's celebrated command: "Boys! Love your enemies, but hate a Frenchman like poison!"[11]

D. H. Lawrence's story, "England, My England," first published by the *English Review* in 1915, confirms George's analysis. Lawrence's protagonist has no illusions about saving mankind when he sets out to fight the Germans in France: "He was out to kill and destroy; he did not even want to be an angel of salvation. As for the savior of mankind, well, a German was as much mankind as an Englishman. What are the odds? We're all out to kill, so don't let us call it anything else." To kill and to be killed, that is what matters; so, before dying himself, Lawrence's hero annihilates at least three Germans.[12]

Brooke's pro-war sonnets, then, are grounded in a genuine British tradition. Nevertheless it is not a poetry of hatred. It is rather a poetry of self-examination, of the "testing" of the self, of the self placed in a situation of risk. It is a kind of poetry that in this respect is very similar to the poetry of the thirties, though in all other respects utterly different.

Indeed, Brooke's letters dating from the last few months before his death, though as full as ever of high spirits and low humor, show an increasingly intense awareness of impending personal doom, of being literally half-in-love with easeful death. At the end of January 1915 he invites John Drinkwater to "come and die. It'll be great fun." Yet nowhere does he indulge in Hun-hating, and there are only very slight and occasional signs of adopting the official attitude of eminent friends like Eddie Marsh and Winston Churchill. After having himself witnessed the German investiture of Antwerp, he can still write that "the Germans have behaved fairly well in the big cities." He grieves for the "holocaust of the young poets, painters and scholars of

France and Belgium—and Germany." And he confesses that "it hurts me, this war. Because I was fond of Germany" (632).

The same kind of disinterestedness and purity of emotion infuses "An Unusual Young Man" (note the consciousness of being different in his response already signaled in the title), the brief, impressionistic, and memorable essay he wrote just after his twenty-seventh birthday, on the last day of peace. Representing the supposed thoughts of a twenty-four-year-old "friend" who is "active and given to music," these are quite obviously very much Brooke's own immediate reactions to the prospect of war. Almost at once his mind is flooded with epiphanic memories of Germany, of the "pompous middle-class vulgarity of the buildings of Berlin; the wide and restful beauty of Munich; the taste of beer; innumerable quiet, glittering cafés; the *Ring*; the swish of evening air on the face, as one *skis* down past the pines; a certain angle of the eyes in the face; long nights of drinking, and singing, and laughter; the admirable beauty of German wives and mothers; certain friends; some tunes; the quiet length of evening over the Starnberger-See."

Brooke's musician really can't imagine killing the friends he's made and got drunk with in Germany; and he is suddenly overwhelmed by a feeling of "ignorant helplessness," such as he had felt only twice before—when his mother had died and when he had broken with a lover. There is an immense feeling of loss, of emptiness, which is then equally suddenly filled with love for England. Images of remembered English landscape flash through his mind—like those of Germany a moment earlier—and "to his great disgust, the most commonplace sentiments found utterance in him. At the same time he was extraordinarily happy." So ends the essay: on a note of ironical patriotic joy, not hatred for an enemy.[13]

Brooke's general view of Germany, however, struck at least one other observer as less "unusual" and rather more conventional. When the English critic/philosopher T. E. Hulme met Brooke in Berlin in November 1912, they visited various theaters and exhibits together, and they also spent a good deal of time lounging at the *Café des Westens*. Hulme's biographer, Alun Jones, remarks of Brooke at this time that his attitude toward the Germans "was curiously insular for a poet." Why? Because Brooke "could not read German nor did he attempt to learn any, but delighted in reading *The Times* in German cafés in order to establish the superiority of his nationality and his visits to Germany merely confirmed his prejudices as to the German national character. He regarded the Germans as a nation of fat, uncouth, simple-minded peasants with a gift for military precision and punctuality who spoke in harsh, unbeautiful gutterals and displayed deplorable table-manners."[14] This attitude may very well have been insular for a poet but it was certainly not atypical for poets from the British isles. Even Hulme himself, who knew some German and had read a fair amount of modern

German aesthetics—which, translated into an English context in his essays, was to have a considerable impact on the development of poetry and criticism in Britain—even Hulme, as Jones readily admits, disliked the Germans not a whit less than Brooke.

Brooke had lived in Munich for three months during the winter of 1911 and for two months in Berlin in the spring of the following year. The letters he wrote home during both these periods show that most of the time he enjoyed himself and felt a kind of patronizing affection for the Germans he met. Drinking and singing with the German students and their professors in the beer halls was fun, but "extraordinarily different" from the King's College Discussion Society run by Goldie Dickinson back in Cambridge. And the German students were a simple lot, much given to beer and sentimental effusions. To E. J. Dent he wrote that he was full of "shallow generalizations about Munich and about Germany . . . mostly not very favourable to Germans as a race" (275).

Still, he clearly liked being in Germany well enough to go there again, staying with his friend Dudley Ward (who was engaged to marry a German girl) in Berlin. Brooke even took excursions into the immediate countryside, looking for a place where he and Ka Cox could stay when she came on her promised visit. The words he wrote to Frances Cornford probably capture Brooke's feelings toward Germany most succinctly: "I never talk or read a word of German. But I enjoy life hugely" (281).

Brooke's amiable contempt for Germans actually predates his first visit to Germany. In "Wagner" (1908), a short poem with a London setting, there appears a stereotypical German, "with a fat wide hairless face" and a "pendulous stomach," listening to the "love-music that is cheap" of his countryman: probably *Tristan and Isolde*. The music lover also fancies himself a woman lover, and the poem juxtaposes—*counterpoints* is perhaps a better word—the quasi-orgasmic shudderings of the female auditors with the "wheezy sighs" of the fat German's stomach; and the swelling of Wagner's music with the implied tumescence of other parts of the fat man's anatomy. Somewhere in the distant background, hidden behind the "noise," which the women are making, and the man's lips "bright with slime," there is a sense of Wagner's betrayal of the original lovers—Tristan and Isolde or Tannhäuser and Venus, it does not matter—in order to achieve his vulgar effects with a vulgar audience.

It is a remarkably successful poem. And it is clear that no less a poet than T. S. Eliot learned from it. The second stanza of "Wagner," especially, anticipates similar character studies in modern vulgarity by Eliot, "Sweeney Among the Nightingales" or "Whispers of Immortality":

> His heavy eyelids droop half-over,
>   Great pouches swing beneath his eyes

> He listens, thinks himself the lover,
>   Heaves from his stomach wheezy sighs;
> He likes to feel his heart's a-breaking.

Except for the last line, Eliot uses an identical stanza in "Sweeney"; he echoes directly the "heavy eyelids," as well as the general sleaziness of the fat German and his orgiastic women. Like Brooke, he also contrasts Sweeney's present vulgarity with a past in which love or death (or love-death) were noble and tragic themes. Brooke in this case handles the contrasts less obviously than Eliot, but he can be equally direct in other poems, as he is in "Menelaus and Helen," for example.[15]

Brooke's stay in Germany produced a couple of short poems with German settings, "Travel" and "In Freiburg Station," but neither poem uses Germany for anything beyond a vague, cosmopolitan background. This is not the case, however, with the one long poem that arose out of Brooke's visit, namely "The Old Vicarage, Grantchester," which Brooke had originally entitled "The Sentimental Exile." After the "1914" sonnets, "Grantchester" is Brooke's best-known poem, and one of the best-known poems in the English language. The poem is subtitled parenthetically, "Café des Westens, Berlin, May 1912," to allow the reader to fix this poetic monologue in a precise time and place. (Brooke really did start writing the poem in Berlin but in April rather than May.) It is a poem full of self-mocking nostalgia and homesickness, quite unlike in tone but still deeply evocative of Browning's "Home Thoughts from Abroad."

The poem opens with the speaker sitting in the Café des Westens, not reading an English newspaper for a change, but thinking out loud of home, of England and of Grantchester. His vision is one of Edenic rural beauty, of vernal splendor and youth—a vision abruptly shattered by an italicized German exclamation: *"Du lieber Gott!"* which brings the speaker, along with the reader, brusquely back to reality, an ugly, urban German reality:

> Here am I, sweating, sick, and hot,
> And there the shadowed waters fresh
> Lean up to embrace the naked flesh.
> *Temperamentvoll* German Jews
> Drink beer around;—and there the dews
> Are soft beneath a morn of gold.
> Here tulips bloom as they are told;
> Unkempt about those hedges blows
> An English unofficial rose;
> And there the unregulated sun
> Slopes down to rest when day is done,
> And wakes a vague unpunctual star,
> A slippered Hesper; and there are

> Meads towards Haslingford and Coton
> Where *das Betreten*'s not *verboten*. (67–68)

England, we learn here—the true England, anyway, the England of the Old Vicarage at Grantchester—does not possess an insalubriously hot and sweaty climate; has no *temperamentvoll* German Jews; is not given to swilling beer; does not attempt to tell the tulips how to grow; the sun when to rise and set; the stars to be on time; or people to keep off the grass. England, in other words, is rural, natural, quiet, free, refined, individualistic, and, most important, English. The grass is made for the Englishman, not the Englishman for the grass—though Brooke would be annoyed to see the "Keep Off the Grass" sign nowadays displayed at his old college, King's. Germany, on the other hand, is urban, unnatural, noisy, overregulated, vulgar, collective, and "cosmopolitan" (i.e., Jewish).

Of course, these clichés are treated to some extent ironically, but beneath the irony one senses a bedrock of solid *Lokalpatriotismus*—the poem is after all a celebration of Grantchester—which made it possible for Brooke a couple of years later to write the more grandly patriotic sonnets. This is a poem about belonging somewhere and having roots in a particular place, in a known and cherished tradition.

Beneath the surface of polish and charm, however, the same questions are being asked that Eliot was to ask a decade later in *The Waste Land:* where is my spiritual home? How do I get there?[16]

Significantly, Eliot asks these questions, or begins asking them at any rate, in a context very similar to and reminiscent of Brooke's. Like "Grantchester," *The Waste Land* opens in Germany; not in Berlin, to be sure, but still in Germany, in Munich and in the Alps. Eliot comments on no *temperamentvoll* German Jews drinking beer in the vicinity—though to judge from Bleistein or Silvero or Rachel née Rabinovich, Eliot had little love for German or other Jews—but he does comment on the rootless Marie who, during the war and immediately postwar period of starvation, fed her little life with dried tubers—potatoes, apparently, the archetypal German food. She too is *temperamentvoll,* skipping from one time and language to another, interlarding her conversation with German phrases, remembering, like Brooke's sentimental exile, a different, distant place where "you feel free."[17]

The poem, like Brooke's, begins in spring, but the memories drift to other seasons as well, to winter and summer, partly in accordance with Eliot's schemata of seasonal myth, but partly too with oblique historical reference. From the perspective of spring, Marie looks back through winter (war) to summer, the prewar summer of 1914:

> Summer surprised us, coming over the Starnbergersee
> With a shower of rain; we stopped in the colonnade,

> And went on in sunlight, into the Hofgarten,
> And drank coffee, and talked for an hour.
>
> (ll. 8–11)

The summer of 1914 was a surprising one—for all of "us." It was the last time it "rained" a life-giving rain, when the famous prewar sun shone and it was possible to drink coffee in the garden of the (royal) court—Marie, let us remember, is a cousin of the Austrian Archduke, who was assassinated in June 1914, the event that precipitated the war.[18]

But why the Starnbergersee? Just for the sake of local color, like Brooke's *Café des Westens?* Perhaps. But also, I think, because a famous King died there, mad Ludwig II of Bavaria who plunged—or was pushed—into its waters and drowned. Like Hieronymo at the close of Eliot's poem, he is "mad againe"; and like Eliot's drowned and yet not drowned Shakespearean Fisher King, "those are pearls that were his eyes" (1. 125).

Ludwig II was Wagner's most distinguished admirer and patron, which is one reason—not, of course, the only reason—why a few lines from *Tristan and Isolde* are included in the opening section of *The Waste Land.* The suggestion here, I think, is that sexual love is not enough to serve as a basis for individual and cultural renewal, just as Brooke had maintained in the opening sonnet of "1914." In Brooke's "Grantchester" the sense of place, the *genius loci magnacastrani,* is enough to ensure abundant fertility of the land and the happiness and faith of its inhabitants, just as the old Wych Elm, the hay, and the spirit of Mrs. Wilcox are enough in Forster's *Howards End.*

Brooke's Grantchester is not only a place, but, like *The Waste Land,* also a time. To be in Grantchester is to be young, to inhabit an eternity where the Church clock is forever stopped at ten to three, a time for perpetual afternoon tea rather than an omen of impending crucifixion. For here the Church, like Arnold's bible, fulfills a purely decorative function. At Grantchester the Church is fitted into a natural context, and it is nature that really tells the hours and not man or God. The river of life runs on joyously—and Brooke's repeated "under the mill, under the mill" catches that movement beautifully—runs on immortally in this natively English pleasure dome. Grantchester is of the imagination, a land of milk and honey, but like other such places—Yeats's Innisfree or Proust's Combray—it exists because a poet had been there.

In *The Waste Land,* however, the genius of the place is no longer a sufficient god. He too is moribund of thirst and inanition. Without real exaggeration, one may say that it was trench warfare and artillery bombardment that transformed the Old Vicarage into the Chapel Perilous; and say too that it was the war that transformed Brooke's sentimental exiles into the hardbitten refugees of Eliot's poem.

Brooke, and especially Brooke's "Grantchester," is, as Douglas Goldring puts it, "the swansong of the British middle class before the war"; to which it should be added that *The Waste Land* is its dirge.[19] But just as at the end of the *Twilight of the Gods*, the music rises and thereby suggests a new dawn that will follow upon the night, so too *The Waste Land* closes with an expression of hope. Here we find no offering of thanks for matching us with the hour of cultural and religious crisis, but the questing knight does hear the voice of God speaking through the thunder. It tells him to give, sympathize, and control. The giving is remarkably like Brooke's: the giving of the self, "the awful daring of a moment's surrender" (1. 404). The sympathy is the escape from the prison of the self, even if the escape is to death, as the case of the broken Coriolanus; the control is that of a well-captained ship, whose course is set toward the unknown future, leaping into cleanness, as it were. The command here, as in "Prufrock" or in "1914," is risk: to dare to transcend one's past self, to surrender that self to faith and to the possibility of death. Only through such risk can there ever come a real rebirth, and the waste land revert to Grantchester.

Unlike Brooke, Eliot seems anything but an insular poet. When the sometime resident of St. Louis; Cambridge, Mass.; London; and Oxford came to Germany, it was not to read *The Times* ostentatiously in cafés. Eliot had first visited Germany in the summer of 1911, chiefly Munich and the Alps; indeed, he finished "Prufrock" while in Munich. One critic, at least, sees his stay there as a time of extraordinary happiness.[20] Eliot came to Germany again in 1914 to study at Marburg, but soon after the outbreak of war returned to England. There is no sign that his experience of Germany left a significant trace, except perhaps in a musical sense, with Wagner especially leaving a profound impression on *The Waste Land*.

Eliot seems, like his sometime teacher George Santayana, a citizen of the world; seems, but is not always. In fact, he is occasionally just as insular as the insular poet who had traveled to islands as far away as Tahiti. In an infamous passage in *After Strange Gods* (1934), Eliot proposes a program more stringently insular than anything the Fabian socialist Brooke had probably ever dreamed of: a bourgeois, homogeneous population, sharing a common religious background, where "reasons of race and religion combine to make any large number of free-thinking Jews undesirable." If there is an influence of Germany to be discerned here, it is of that Germany which came officially to power a year before Eliot published these words. Much later Eliot came to regret what he had written, but even as late as his *Notes towards the Definition of Culture* (1948), he argued that "it is important that a man should feel himself to be, not merely a citizen of a particular nation, but a citizen of a particular part of his country, with local loyalties. . . ."[21] This is exactly what Brooke had believed. Brooke and Eliot are not so far apart after all.

This is true not only of their ideas but, as we have seen, of some of their poetic methods as well. Brooke felt that it was his debt to Browning and Donne that distinguished him from the other Georgians;[22] and these are influences not foreign to Eliot's poetry either. Anyone who has read through Brooke's *Poetical Works* will also not miss the note of Laforgue—and behind Laforgue, Heine—a note that sounds discordantly in much of the early poetry of Eliot as well. To contemporary students of poetry it may come as a surprise that Brooke was once thought of as the initiator of "ugly" and "shocking" poetry in England or that he should have had his poems rejected, as Siegfried Sassoon points out, because they were too "audaciously outspoken."[23] Though not exempting Brooke entirely from the charge of being "lucent-siropy," Eliot does recognize his "really amazing facility and command of language."[24] Small wonder then that Arthur Waugh, in his survey of modern literature, *Tradition and Change* (1919), should quote as a horrific example and without attribution, a line from "Prufrock" amid a discusion of Brooke's lapses in taste and supposed poetic "blots."[25]

George Bernard Shaw may seem an odd figure to link with Brooke and Eliot. He belongs to an earlier literary generation and he has rarely been included in the ranks of the poets at all; on the contrary, he is usually viewed, even in his dramas, as eminently prosaic. It is a view of Shaw that is, I think, radically mistaken, though that does not matter particularly in this context, since what connects Shaw with Brooke and Eliot is more an attitude toward life and English society than questions of aesthetics. This attitude I have defined as one of risk and, as we have seen, at the beginning of the Great War it came to be identified exclusively with Germany and especially with Treitschke and Hegel, a tradition entering the English intellectual mainstream primarily through Carlyle.

Shaw has very little to say about either Treitschke or Hegel, just as little, in fact, as Brooke and Eliot do. Shaw, however, acknowledges his debt to German culture more openly and readily. In the preface to the first German edition (1907) of *The Perfect Wagnerite* (1892), Shaw admits that he is unable to love the "typical modern German," whom he finds given to indulging excessively in duty, industry, education, loyalty, patriotism, and respectability. But for the great Germans of the past Shaw proclaims his absolute love: for the "great dynasty" of musicians beginning with Bach, without whom Shaw would "have perished of despair" in his youth. Shaw repudiates the English as his teachers in anything but words; his "masters" were, rather, "the masters of a universal language," of music. For the sake of these masters "Germany stands consecrated as the Holy Land of the capitalist age. . . ."[26] Of this great musical tradition, Shaw writes elsewhere, that he probably knows more about it than most Germans do themselves, though of the German literary tradition, except for Goethe, Schiller, Wagner, and the first volume of Marx's *Das Kapital*, he knows virtually nothing.[27] In *Sixteen Self Sketches* (1949), however, Shaw admits that he is able to read German, though only with some difficulty, but is hopeless at conversation. And, speaking in the third person about himself, he concludes that "Shaw was full not only of Ibsen, but of Wagner, of Beethoven, of Goethe, and, curiously, of John Bunyan."[28] With all this, it is remarkable that there are almost no German characters in Shaw's plays. There is the portrait of the Kaiser, drawn with mixed satire and sympathy, in the wartime one-acter, "The Inca of Perusalem"; the Austro-Germans in *Jitta's Atonement* (really more of an adaptation than Shaw's own creation); and the German Ernest Battler in the late play, *Geneva,* not a specially memorable or attractive figure either.

But the absence of German characters does not tell the whole story. *Man and Superman* is obviously indebted to Mozart's *Don Giovanni,* as well as— rather less obviously—to the opening section of Goethe's *Faust. Saint Joan* is deliberately anti-Schilleresque; and *Heartbreak House,* as recent critics have shown, is Wagnerian to the point of allegory.

Of Shaw's attitude toward Germany at the outbreak of the Great War, there are conflicting reports. Lytton Strachey has him filled with patriotic desire to smash the Germans. This, to put it mildly, seems unlikely, but it is true that Shaw was not neutral nor pretended to be. He was definitely not, in respect to the war at least, "one of our country's worst enemies," to quote from a letter that Shaw's sometime friend and colleague, Henry Arthur Jones, wrote to him in 1915.[29]

Shaw, in fact, was so little neutral or pro-German that in November 1914 he urged the Irish, in an appeal published in the *Freemen's Journal,* "to remember their debt to France, forget British tyranny, and help the French Republic to shatter the Prussian military machine." Shaw even agreed to assist the Irish Under-Secretary in a recruiting campaign.[30]

It is therefore ironic that during the course of hostilities Shaw should have been the best-known opponent of the war. As the periodical essays that he wrote at this time, later collected as *What I Really Wrote About the War* (1931), make clear, Shaw was an opponent of a very special type. He was not *really* against Britain's entry into the war, or, more precisely, once Britain had joined, he thought she might as well continue, since any likely outcome was certain to help the international socialist cause. In adopting this line, Shaw later concluded, he had been quite right, even more right than he had originally supposed. In the 1931 preface to the reprint of his *Fabian Essays,* he interprets the Great War as the bloodiest revolution the world has ever known, a revolution that has brought about more changes in four years "than Fabian constitutional action seem[s] likely to do in four hundred." One of the most important direct consequences of the war, the Soviet Revolution of 1917, established socialism by force, by the simple expedient of killing all those who opposed it. From the socialist point of view, the war had been an immensely profitable investment.[31]

Shaw, then, despite all rumors to the contrary, was not neutral or pro-

German. He might be given to quixotries like drafting, together with Count Harry Kessler, a manifesto affirming an *entente cordiale* between England and Germany to prove that England had not exhausted her cordiality with France, but Shaw was not in principle opposed to shedding blood.[32]

Nevertheless, for most Englishmen at the time Shaw was a manifest villain who was splitting moral hairs at a moment when England was being scalped, a vile cad for presuming to utter England's name in the same breath as Germany's (after Belgium)—suggesting, for example, that there might be English junkers as well as German ones—and mad in any event for believing he could change a right-thinking person's mind. "If the truth must be told," Winston Churchill was later to write, "our British island has not had much help from Mr. Bernard Shaw." But in the final analysis Shaw was considered to be relatively harmless: a frivolous Irishman who, as Churchill put it, had played the role of court jester for years past.[33]

It was because of this ambiguous attitude to the war that Shaw never became part of the celebrated pacifist movement that had its focal point in the Morrell country house at Garsington, a few miles outside Oxford. Bertrand Russell, one of the Garsington habitués, clearly saw in him a kindred spirit in the struggle against the "hypocritical high moral tone of the Government and its followers," but he recognized just as clearly that Shaw "did not write as a Pacifist."[34] On Shaw's part too there seems to have been a reserve toward the militant pacifists that prevented him from getting involved in the uncompromising anti-war effort characteristic of Russell and many of the other Garsington pacifists, despite his sharing their socialist views about the reformation of British society. Shaw never visited Garsington, though he was personally acquainted with its eccentric mistress, Lady Ottoline Morrell, and exchanged a number of letters with her.

Given this distance, both physical and spiritual, between Shaw and Garsington, it seems clear that Garsington cannot be identified with the English country house that is also the title for Shaw's play, Heartbreak House. Shaw after all began the play a year before the war started, though it is true he did not finish it until a year after it ended. And, although there is some justification for reading *Heartbreak House* as an anti-war play, the action paradoxically climaxes in a *Walpurgisnacht* of wartime destruction, with bombs dropping out of the sky and with Germans acting almost as the agents of God, wreaking vengeance upon Satanic capitalists in the Garden of England. Even more paradoxically, perhaps, Shaw's remarkable preface to the play acclaims, for reasons I shall examine shortly, the British Army as the one social institution worthy of admiration and able to serve as a model for regenerating a diseased society.

Garsington, then, cannot be Hearbreak House. Indeed, just how absurd such an identification is emerges clearly from a letter Aldous Huxley wrote in December 1921 to Lady Ottoline after publishing *Crome Yellow* (1921) and "discovering" he had hurt her with his satire upon what she took to be herself and Garsington. Protesting his innocence, Huxley claims that it would be as absurd to think of Crome and its eccentric menagerie as a portrait of the real Garsington as Heartbreak House. Since Crome is, however, quite "obviously" Garsington and informed readers like T. S. Eliot immediately recognized that fact, it would seem to follow logically that Garsington is also Heartbreak House.[35] While I do not think that such is the case, it does seem suggestive that a link between Garsington and Shaw's play should have crossed Huxley's mind at all, even if only to be dismissed (supposedly) at once. Garsington was probably not a model for the country house in Shaw's play, but in some sense and to some degree *Heartbreak House* did evoke Garsington in the minds of those who knew both. Shaw himself, though aware of Garsington only from a distance, wrote in May 1940 to one of the most prominent sometime visitors to that place, Virginia Woolf, amid the shadows of another German war, referring to a "play of mine called Heartbreak House which I always connect with you because I conceived it in that house somewhere in Sussex where I first met you and, of course, fell in love with you. I suppose every man did." Shaw seems here to be identifying Woolf with one of the central characters of the play, the oldest daughter of Shotover, Hesione, the embodiment of the irresistible woman.[36]

Despite the sometimes striking resemblances, one is still forced to agree with Huxley. In the final analysis Garsington is a very different sort of place. Garsington is as intellectual as Heartbreak House (more so, in fact); as preoccupied with the arts; as contemptuous of Horseback Hall; as concerned with the question of "whither England?" But at the same time Garsington, unlike Heartbreak House, is prepared to dirty its hands, as it were, in the manure of Horseback Hall: literally so, in the farm attached to Garsington and managed by Philip Morrell; figuratively so, in Philip Morrell's courageous attempt to avert England's entry into the war; in Bertrand Russell's even more courageous attempts to get England out of that war; and in Lady Ottoline's efforts to mitigate the "horsebackian" effects of the war, as in, say, the case of the suppression of *The Rainbow;* or in seeking to avert Sir Roger Casement's execution; or in providing alternative service for conscientious objectors. Garsington, in fact, gives the lie to *Heartbreak House* because it demonstrates, sometimes heroically, sometimes almost farcically, that its heart is not broken, that it is still capable of generous action that is creative rather than destructive.

But if Garsington denies Heartbreak House, Shaw could have countered that there was only one Garsington, and that the betrayal by all the other prewar would-be Garsingtons of the values for which they supposedly stood is more than sufficient reason for the charges he levels in his play against intellectual England. Garsington, after all, failed: it was the attack of a maddened nightingale against the mechanical juggernaut of modern bureaucracy and modern war. The fundamental thesis of Shaw's play remained unanswered: Britain was suffering from a severe, perhaps fatal illness; the connections between mind, heart, and hand were severed; there were neither whole and healthy human beings, nor a whole and healthy society. The fact that a limb could be made to move at Garsington may have been an encouraging sign to the utterly dispirited, but it was not enough to alter the diagnosis of imminent death.

The illness that Shaw describes in its last stages in *Heartbreak House* was first diagnosed by Thomas Carlyle in *Past and Present*. Carlyle's is the often unacknowledged voice that echoes through many of the Cassandran prophecies of doom during the first quarter of this century. Long years after his death in 1881, Carlyle's voice was still booming—though at times, as in the case of Lytton Strachey, ironically—through the minds of everyone who thought seriously in England. In every essential point, the attack against democracy by Shaw was anticipated by Carlyle.

Of all the modern spiritual heirs of Carlyle, Shaw must seem one of the least likely. After all, Shaw spent the greater part of a long lifetime working and writing and propagandizing for what, to Carlyle, would have been the damnable doctrine of socialism. Shaw himself, though sometimes confessing to unexpected spiritual ancestors like Bunyan or Dickens, usually preferred to be identified with a more respectable social and intellectual tradition: Nietzsche, perhaps, or Marx, or Tolstoy and Ibsen. This was no doubt understandable, for to be linked too closely with Carlyle was, by the beginning of this century, to be known as an old-fashioned biblical moralist.

Yet *Heartbreak House* is marked indelibly with Carlyle's thought, despite never once mentioning his name.[37] Characteristically, Shaw refers to Chekhov instead, in the subtitle of the play ("A Fantasia in the Russian Manner on English Themes") and more explicitly in the preface, as his primary influence. What Shaw is attempting in this play is to draw up the accounts of England's spiritual bankruptcy, much as Carlyle had done earlier in *Past and Present* or T. S. Eliot was to do in *The Waste Land* a couple of years later.

Heartbreak House is a profoundly symbolic play. Captain Shotover's country house stands for an entire culture that, ineffectual despite great incidental charm, has reached a dead end. Put on the simplest level, it poses the old problem of the division between action and contemplation, the heart and the hand, Heartbreak House and Horseback Hall. Power is vested among the ignorant barbarians, culture among the knowledgeable decadents. Nowhere, except in a qualified sense in Captain Shotover, do the two meet.

Even some of the very terms of Shaw's version of The Condition of England Question are identical with Carlyle's. So, for instance, much like the workhouse in Bury St. Edmund's at the beginning of *Past and Present*,

Heartbreak House is described as a "palace of evil enchantment," which has worshiped false gods. More important, England, according to Shaw, has failed to heed nature's immutable and implacable laws. To be sure, there is no one so graphic and tangible as Carlyle's Irish widow to infect those who would deny her human existence. But Shaw's nature does enter in the guise of an indifferent banker who extends long credits to a society, but in the end expects to be paid and will be paid. As Shaw points out in the preface to the play, generations of doctors may neglect sanitary conditions in hospitals with impunity until it seems as if cleanliness were nothing but a fad or a hoax for selling soap. "Then suddenly," Shaw warns, "Nature takes her revenge." She strikes a whole city down with pestilence, killing indiscriminately "until the innocent young have paid for the guilty old."[38] For Shaw the socialist, quite as much as for Carlyle the Calvinist, capitalist Nature's accounts always balance.

How then is England to be saved? Neither play nor preface tells us directly. But the latter does suggest a possibility that partially echoes Carlyle's solution. In a section called "The Dumb Capables and the Noisy Incapables," Shaw describes the articulate incompetence of every English institution but the army and large industry. "To pass from the newspaper offices," he writes in orthodox Carlylese, "and political platforms and club fenders and suburban drawing-rooms to the Army and the munition factories was to pass from Bedlam to the busiest and sanest of workaday worlds" (29). This "effective England" did its work in silence while the "ostensible England" was bawling like a baby in its crib. But unfortunately, in Shaw's view, the silent, effective men of action, occupied as they were with getting things done, allowed the idle professional rhetoricians to take over entirely the presentation of the war, to the point of themselves believing things belied by their own daily experience. Heart and hand were still disconnected.

Within the limits of Shaw's inveterate verbosity, *Heartbreak House* reveals the same distinction between active men of silence and passive men of words. The most obvious exemplar of the former type is the ancient Captain Shotover, whose very name is a reworking of Carlyle's would-be Captain of Industry, Plugson of Undershot. But Shotover's son-in-law, Hector Hushabye, is also in some way to be seen as a doer rather than a sayer. Though he is an inveterate liar and fabulist and deceiver of young innocents like Ellie, his boastful lies are nevertheless matched by unspoken acts of at least equal daring. His name too suggests that he prefers silence (though perhaps only the silence of sleep) to puffery. This is not true of most other characters in the play, especially not of the liberal Mazzini, the capitalist Mangan, or the representatives of Horseback Hall: Ariadne, Randall, and Hastings Utterword (whose surname is sufficiently revelatory by itself).[39]

Though Maurice Valency is quite right in arguing that there is nothing narrowly allegorical about *Heartbreak House*—and that this is the real strength of the play—still it is apparent that the play derives some of its significance through its implicit reference to Wagner's *Ring*. Shaw's debt to Wagner in this play has often been pointed out, though not always in the same ways. Margery Morgan maintains, for example, that we should read *Heartbreak House* in the context of *The Rhinegold*, thereby making Ellie into a kind of Freia, "bartered by the gods and offered up by the giants in return for Alberic's gold."[40] This is persuasive but only, I think, because the context is so narrow. In the larger context of the whole cycle, Ellie seems more like Brynhilde or even Krimhilde, drawn as she is to the obvious Siegfried figure, Hector. Hector, like Siegfried, is boastful, but he is also a true hero, and in the end he girds himself to kill Alberic in the shape of Mangan/Dunn. Ariadne, I think, is the real Freia, the daughter of Wotan/ Shotover, who has married into the stupid giants of Horseback Hall. That she has done so voluntarily is all the more devastating a comment on the degeneracy of Valhalla/Heartbreak House. One personification of Brynhilde, Hesione, the other daughter of Wotan/Shotover, has been unable to persuade Siegfried to undertake his true mission; and the other personification, Ellie, fails equally. The solution, it would seem, is for Wotan and Ellie/Brynhilde to join in producing another and more heroic Siegfried, though for this task Wotan's failing vitality seems to disqualify him.

The "god" Shotover and the "demi-god" Hector struggle together to overcome the giants. Contemplating what is to be done in order to save England, Shotover proposes a brutally simple solution: exterminate people like Mangan and Randall Utterwood, and exercise power in their stead. Hector agrees with the need to seize their power, but refuses to accept the preconditions of doing so. The rest of the play, and its violent conclusion, demonstrate to him (and to us) the profounder insight of Captain Shotover.

The progress of the play reveals too the illusions under which most of the inhabitants and guests of Heartbreak House have been laboring or, rather, idling. It is the process of stripping each person down to his essential nature that so disturbs Mangan and leads him to protest that everyone should undress physically to match his moral nakedness. For him, this is heartbreak—the shattering of every illusion about himself and others. Ellie, his youthful betrothed, undergoes exactly the same experience, with Hector, with Hesione, with Mangan, and with her own father. Even Ellie has been, as her name hints, living a lie. As Hector explains it: "In this house we know all the poses: our game is to find out the man under the pose" (133). The catch is that this search for the truth is merely a pose as well. Only at the very end do they discover that under the pose there is nothing at all. Only then do they start playing the game in earnest.

In *Past and Present* Carlyle had put forward the Captain of Industry, the arch-Millocrat, as his candidate for saving England. In *Heartbreak House* Shaw dismisses that possibility in the figure of Alfred Mangan. But this dismissal is only a seeming denial of Carlyle. For as we discover when the layers of sham are gradually stripped from Mangan, this Captain of Industry is in reality only a corporal of finance. Mangan turns out to be as much a victim of financial manipulators greater than himself as Mazzini is a victim of Mangan's monetary strategems. Mangan is only an unproductive, ineffectual braggart, a little boy playing at being a man. The real Captain of Industry is Shotover.

Shotover is the force that keeps Heartbreak House going. Even if his work is the work of death, devising infernal weapons for the War Office, it is still real work. There is nothing ordinary or petty about this man. Though it is helpful to know, as Shaw hints several times in the play, that he sold his soul to the Devil in the South Seas, even without that rumor it is amply apparent that we have to do here with a reincarnation of Faust. Like Faust, who would rather endure eternal damnation than accept a moment's static happiness, Shotover still prefers work to pleasure even at the brink of senility. Faust's contempt for mere happiness saved him from damnation; so too it saves Shotover. "I feel nothing," he complains to Ellie, "but the accursed happiness I have dreaded all my life long: the happiness that comes as life goes, the happiness of yielding and dreaming instead of resisting and doing, the sweetness of the fruit that is going rotten" (130). Like Faust, he recognizes in stasis the stigma of hell:

> Werd' ich zum Augenblicke sagen
> "Verweile doch, Du bist so schön,"
> Dann magst Du mich in Fesseln schlagen,
> Dann will ich gern' zugrunde geh'n.[41]

Shotover represents the old England. The Devil to whom he sold his soul is not only Goethe's Mephistopheles, he is also—and far more significantly—the devil of British imperial expansion. In Shaw's view, England sold its soul, in the South Seas and elsewhere, to gain an empire. Despite its evil past, however, or even possibly and unavowably because of it, the old England possessed a sense of mission in the world that the present England utterly lacks. Shotover was an effective captain of the ship of state. Drunk though he may have been with rum, he still knew how to steer a straight and steady course. Now Shotover's shot is over. "The last shot," he tells Ellie, "was fired years ago." As for the present captain, he is drunk on ditchwater while his crew is gambling away its fate in the forecastle. In a splendid biblical declamation worthy of Carlyle, Shotover foretells how Britain will "strike and sink and split," concluding with a rhetorical flourish by asking Hector if he thinks "the laws of God will be suspended in favor of England because you were born in it?" In reply, Hector poses a question of his own: what is to be done? "Navigation," comes the answer, almost as if from

Conrad's aged imperialist, Stein. "Learn it and live; or leave it and be damned" (156). But like Lord Jim, Hector has great difficulty in making reality and dream fit.

The real hope lies in Ellie. She is the embodiment of hope in the play, the principle of *das ewig Weibliche* that performs the work of the life force in drawing mankind farther up the ladder of evolution, farther along the Hegelian pilgrimage of progressive spiritualization and consciousness. She is both Margaret and Helen to Shotover's Faust, with the way to salvation leading, as in *Faust,* through death and destruction.[42] "The Life Force," Shaw observed in 1944, when he had reached a Shotoverian age himself, "however benevolent, proceeds by trial and error and creates the problem of evil by its unsuccessful experiments and its mistakes."[43] Ellie may be a mistake—a "lie"—but only by giving ourselves wholly up to that lie or that truth, only by the awful daring of a moment's surrender, will there ever be a hope of success.

Hence, when the Zeppelins come and the bombs begin dropping from the dark nocturnal sky, at the Passover of modern man, only the practical men— Mangan and the burglar, William Dunn—try to make their escape. The others exult in the coming destruction, in the end of the old disorder, turning on the lights so that Heartbreak House might become all the more visible a target.

"The judgment has come," Shotover announces prophetically. "Courage will not save you; but it will show that your souls are still alive" (159). The call is for all hands on deck. Tense with expectation, they await their doom, only to be disappointed when the Zeppelins turn away in another direction. Ironically, the only destruction that takes place is that of Mangan and Dunn, killed when a bomb explodes in Shotover's dynamite storage dump. The courageous are spared and Heartbreak House has been given a new lease on life. But for how long?

For as long, I think, as Heartbreak House remains ready to risk death. In Shaw's view, as in Brooke's, death is the only friend and enemy; death and war bring renewal, make mankind leap out of the ineffectual past of Randall's "dirty songs and dreary," or Hector's little games of love, into a future where life is more intensely lived because it is subject to death. The symbol of the zeppelin, with its phallic rigidity and elongation, its insemination of the earth with a death that brings new life, is peculiarly apt. It is a symbol that is at one and the same time both death-dealing and life-giving, just as the thunder at the close of the *The Waste Land* is.

For another believer in the life force and passionate adherent of *das ewig Weibliche,* for D. H. Lawrence, who chose the phoenix as his personal symbol of renewal through death, for Lawrence too the zeppelin had a powerful fascination. After watching a zeppelin raid in September 1915, Lawrence reacted almost ecstatically. "So it seems our cosmos has burst," he wrote to Lady Ottoline Morrell, "burst at last, the stars and moon blown away, the envelope of the sky burst out, and a new cosmos appeared; with a long-ovate, gleaming central luminary, with its lights bursting in flashes on the earth, to burst away the earth also. . . . But there must be a new heaven and a new earth, a clearer, eternal moon above, and a clean world below. So it will be."[44]

A clean world—it is almost as if the voice of Brooke were speaking through Lawrence; a clean world, cleansed by the iron broom of war and death. For Lawrence too was a believer in the life-giving power of death. In a remarkable essay written at about the same time as Lawrence watched the "long-ovate" zeppelin in the sky, ready to burst forth with new life and new death, in the strange and powerful essay entitled "The Crown" (October-November 1915), Lawrence argues that insofar as there is any passion in the war, "it is a passion to deal death and to take death. The enemy is the bride whose body we will reduce with rapture of agony and wounds." Here again death is but the worst friend and enemy, and again the passion and agony are like Christ's, bringing forth new life out of the embrace with death: "it is not really a question of victories or defeats. It is a question of fulfilment, and release from the old prison-house of a dead form. The war is one bout in the terrific, horrible labour, our civilisation labouring in child-birth, and unable to bring forth."[45]

Lawrence goes on to describe how, not long before, while stopping at the seaside, he had watched a maimed soldier surrounded by a group of excited women watching him and *wanting* him. "It was horrible, rather sinister, the women round the man . . ." (401). Horrible, but in some strange way invigorating, productive of new life. It is a vision of the war very different from that of a similar scene described only a short time later by Wilfred Owen in his poem "Disabled," in which the young maimed soldier in his wheelchair remembers how women looked at him before he was mutilated and how they look at him now:

> To-night he noticed how the women's eyes
> Passed from him to the strong men that were whole.[46]

For Owen the war brings suffering, physical and mental, to which at best we can react with pity; for Lawrence it brings, or at least can bring, a pitiless renewal of life.

As with Shaw, only those who courageously face destruction can be saved: "we may give ourselves utterly to destruction, then our conscious forms are destroyed along with us, and something new must arise" (404). Destruction is, for Lawrence, a divine spirit, when it breaks, like the zeppelins, the shell of the ego and opens the soul up to the wide heavens. For him it is divine for the same reasons it is divine for Shaw, because it does the work of the Life

Force. The evolution of consciousness—or, in Hegelian terms, the march of the Idea through history—demands the breakdown of the old forms of consciousness to permit the buildup of the new. Without a dialectic of continual opposition and recreation of consciousness, consciousness and history reach dead ends. Such dead ends possess an undeniable but horrible kind of perfection, a perfection of being finished, of a cessation of growth. Perfection, as Lawrence well knew, has as its root meaning in Latin a word defining a completely finished action. Such perfection is, according to Lawrence, the state arrived at by the baboon, who instead of becoming a man "arrested himself and became obscene, a grey, hoary rind closed upon an activity of strong corruption . . ." (405). The same is true of those other "perfectly-arrested egoists," the dog, the hyena, and the louse. These animals and insects are, of course, not just animals and insects; they are symbols—symbols of Germans, English, Tories, Liberals, bankers, moneygrubbers, all the sad perfection of the modern world.

It is the attempt to fix forever into finished form the ideals of democracy and aristocracy that Lawrence finds most horrifying in the war. Both Britain (democracy) and Germany (aristocracy) want to entomb their ideals, make whited sepulchers of them: sepulchers for the lion become a dog and the eagle turned into a vulture. Out of the perfect triumph of the dog or the vulture there can emerge no new consciousness, only the perpetuation of the old, "petrified, frozen falsely, timeless" (407). That, for Lawrence, is the final manifestation of evil, the betrayal of the dynamic life force, "not death, nor the blood-devouring Moloch, but this spirit of perpetuation and apparent timelessness, this obscenity which holds the great carrion birds, and the carrion dogs . . ." (407).

In the unfinished "Study of Thomas Hardy," also written during the war, Lawrence returns to the same subject and reaches similar conclusions. Almost as if rephrasing Brooke's "Peace," Lawrence here calls for an end of hating Germany and urges the British to be grateful to their enemy for still retaining the power to break out of the bonds of unproductive stasis. "Where do I meet a man or a woman," he asks, "who does not draw deep and thorough satisfaction from this war? Because of pure shame that we should have seemed such poltroons living safe and atrophied, not daring to take one step to life. And this is the only good that can result from the 'world disaster': that we realize once more that we can still squander life and property and inflict suffering wholesale."[47] Anything is better than the damnation of hollow men, forever pirouetting in perfect circles. Better the zeppelins, better the waste land, better the war.

For Lawrence, anticipating Eliot, nothing matters "so long as life shall sprout up again strong after this winter of cowardice and well-being, sprout into the unknown." For life has only one great aim and purpose, namely, the

Hegelian aim and purpose of bringing "all life into the human consciousness" (408). Unlike Shaw, Lawrence does not see this progressive consciousness as purely intellectual; his dream is not of a succession of sexless, solitary, and wholly spiritualized longlivers. For Lawrence such beings would be one with the dog, the vulture, and the hyena: perfect—and perfectly horrible. But although Lawrence's consciousness is much fuller—not just Hegel, but also Jung and Gross and Klages—it shares its dynamic aspect with Shaw's Life Force; and it is equally convinced that the only way to life is through death.

Like Shaw, Lawrence draws on Nietzsche and Carlyle, but also rejects them. He accepts Nietzsche's idea of an *ewige Wiederkehr* or eternal cyclical recurrence, but only after qualifying that acceptance by adding that "each cycle is different. There is no real recurrence" (461). Lawrence also admits the possibility, indeed the necessity, for a kind of superman, though one very different from Shaw's and much closer to Nietzsche's *Uebermensch* or Carlyle's hero, though here too there are important deviations. Lawrence admires power and the powerful man. He sees in power a mystic, semi-divine quality, an attribute of God in man, a kind of impersonal magnetism like Shotover's Seventh Degree of Concentration or Weber's charisma. But it is not a will-to-power but rather a gift of grace: "Power is beyond us. Either it is given us from the unknown, or we have not got it" (442). Power is what brings the new thing or the new man into the world. Or, as Lawrence puts it at the end of *Aaron's Rod* (1922): "The will-to-power—but not in Nietzsche's sense. Not intellectual power. Not mental power. Not conscious will-power. But dark, living, fructifying power."[48]

The Lawrentian hero appears in the "living periods" of mankind when mankind moves upward "through the zones of life-expression and passionate consciousness, upwards to the supreme utterer, or utterers" (609). Lawrence seems to consider himself one of these supreme utterers who bring a new idea into the world, but nowhere else does he see any sign of a new idea or feeling, or any trace of the new man.

More than any of the other writers considered here, Lawrence's life and intellectual development were connected with Germany. This is most obvious in Lawrence's marriage to a German, Frieda von Richthofen; but even before his marriage Lawrence had studied German and had written a novel, *The Trespasser* (1912)—originally entitled "The Saga of Siegmund"—that is steeped in Wagnerian symbolism and allusion.[49] One of Lawrence's aunts was married to a German, Fritz Krenkow, who was eventually to become a distinguished Arabicist. Lawrence knew him well and visited him at one time fairly frequently. Frieda no doubt taught Lawrence a great deal about Germany, by simply talking, by making trips to Germany with him and having him meet with her relatives—Lawrence was especially close to his mother-in-law, to whom he wrote letters in faulty but fluent German—but he was also prepared for a "German" experience in a way that few other writers of his generation were.[50]

Frieda's impact on Lawrence can hardly be overestimated. She was nearly as extraordinary a woman as he was a man; and Lawrence's life with her, intense, tumultuous, frustrating, and immensely exciting, provided abundant matter for Lawrence's own fiction, as well as for Frieda's memoir of their life together, *Not I But the Wind* . . . (1934), and innumerable biographies. More recently, Martin Green has shown in *The von Richthofen Sisters* (1974), that Frieda's family, especially her sisters, their husbands, lovers, and friends, also exercised an enormous influence on Lawrence's outlook on life and therefore on his creative work.

Green's work is fascinating and often persuasive, but he was not the first to observe that through Frieda, Lawrence had come into contact with an important body of German ideas. Robert Lucas's *Frieda Lawrence* (1973, English ed.) deals, as Green's study does, with Frieda's love affair with Otto Gross and with the circle of Bohemian artists she knew in Munich during the early years of this century. Émile Delavany's massive *D. H. Lawrence* (1969, French; 1972, English) is especially good at tracing some of Lawrence's ideas back to Schopenhauer, Otto Weininger, and the Anglo-German "renegade," Houston Stuart Chamberlain. So too Ernest Seillère, in his *David-Herbert Lawrence et les récentes idéologies allemandes* (1936), suggests Frieda's importance as a conveyor of German neo-Romantic ideas for Lawrence; and he makes specific connections with Bachofen, Klages, Steiner, and Frobenius.[51]

None of these writers, of course, "discovered" Lawrence's links with Germany; they have simply elaborated and clarified those links. Lawrence never hid his debt to German thought, nor did he in any sense take it over wholesale or accept it uncritically. Lawrence considered himself archetypically English. Amid the fury of the war, he learned to curse the Germans as thoroughly as any Tory hun-hater. "I hate Germans so much," he told Lady Ottoline Morrell in May 1915, "I could kill every one of them . . ."; and then, as if to make an exception of his wife, he lowered the numbers a little: "I would like to kill a million Germans—two million." He was deeply hurt by the continual attacks on him as a pro-German; by the experience of being turned out of Cornwall for being a German spy; and by being hounded by the British police throughout the war. The literary result of these traumatic experiences is the unforgettable "Nightmare" chapter in *Kangaroo* (1923).[52]

The immediate sources of Lawrence's thought are often English: Hardy, Carlyle, Ruskin, Arnold, Morris, though these are often admittedly writers who are themselves partly rooted in German thought—in Goethe, Hegel, Schopenhauer, and Marx. It is possible to exaggerate Lawrence's debt to Germany, to see him, as Martin Green does, imitating Gottfried Keller's *Der*

Grüne Heinrich in *Sons and Lovers,* or to read *Aaron's Rod* as a German novel in English guise, though I believe Green is right in arguing that Lawrence extended "the British tradition in fiction by introducing German elements."[53]

Green may be right too in seeing *The Rainbow* (1915) as a novel essentially inspired by the von Richthofen milieu, even if one has qualms at accepting all of his specific identifications, such as Will and Anna Brangwen as the Baron and Baroness von Richthofen. And, in a way, Green may even be understating his case here, since Lawrence may be indebted to Thomas Mann's *Buddenbrooks* (1902), which, like *The Rainbow,* tells the story of the development in pseudo-Darwinian terms of a single family. Mann, let us recall, was one of the German novelists whom Lawrence had actually reviewed.[54] But whatever the specific influences, certainly *The Rainbow* and its successor, *Women in Love* (1920), reflect many of the "German" ideas expressed in Lawrence's wartime nonfiction.

Overtly *The Rainbow* seems to have little to do with Germany and rather more with Poland, since two important characters in the novel either come directly from that country or have Polish ancestry: Lydia Lensky, Tom Brangwen's wife, and Skrebensky, Ursula's lover. Beneath the surface, however, a few German links appear. Lydia turns out to be half-German; and the self-assured foreigner who so fascinates the provincial Tom in an early scene in the novel is almost certainly based on a man Lawrence knew personally, Baron Rudolph von Hube.[55] In *The Rainbow,* this figure is associated with images of monkeys; and it seems clear that Lawrence intends us to see him as an embodiment of a "perfection" beyond the reach of the inchoate Tom Brangwen, but at the same time means us also to recognize Tom's potential for development and the "monkey man's" dead end.

The novel spans about seventy years, from around 1840—the dawning age of industrial and imperial expansion—to about 1910, the beginning of the end. It traces the gradual increase of consciousness and individuality in the three generations of the Brangwen family, starting with the mindless yet angelic marriage of Tom and Lydia; the partially conscious yet antagonistic connection between Will and Anna; and the fully conscious individualism of Ursula, which rejects the "mechanism" of Skrebensky and, at the close of the novel, is left waiting for an equally conscious individualistic male counterpart.

The Rainbow displays, in almost classic Hegelian terms, the development of consciousness in history. The increasingly larger element of "truth" or "consciousness" at each stage of progressive individualization does not deny, though it does negate, the preceding stage. The new consciousness is based on and yet supersedes the old. The movement is always unmistakably toward a greater comprehensiveness, a greater totality of consciousness. The novel moves inexorably toward the light—toward the great arc of the heavens, the span of the rainbow; but the rainbow keeps both of its feet on the ground, or as Hopkins puts it in a very different context, "man's spirit will be fleshbound when found at best, / But uncumbered: meadow ground is not distressed for a rainbow footing it." The confrontation of opposites, the chthonic horses, the past, the Marsh and the dark unconscious origins of the world on the one side, and the spiritualized, highly self-conscious rainbow, the future, on the other.

The same kind of dialectic informs the novel that continues the story of *The Rainbow. Women in Love* was originally conceived as an integral part of a larger novel that Lawrence planned to call *The Sisters,* a novel that would have told the story that Lawrence eventually concluded would have been too long to tell in a single book. As a title, *The Sisters* seems especially appropriate for the later novel, since *Women in Love* is largely built on a contrast between the loves and fates of the two Brangwen sisters, Ursula and Gudrun. But even Lawrence's final title emphasizes the importance of the female element in the novel at the expense of the novel's real hero, the semi-autobiographical Rupert Birkin. For Lawrence, as for Shaw, it was clearly the woman who was the principal bearer of the Life Force; for him too it was the *ewig Weibliche* that drew mankind forward into the light.

Ursula's "conjunction" with Birkin serves this larger evolutionary purpose, whereas Gudrun's with Gerald Crich does not. Significantly, however, the ultimately successful pairing of Ursula and Rupert does not issue in any tangible biological result, that is, there is no child—as there was in the successive generations of the Brangwens in *The Rainbow*—to represent a further stage in progressive consciousness. While the conclusion of the novel does not rule out the possibility of children, there is nothing in the novel itself that suggests that continued human development is contingent on biological descendants. On the contrary, in the fragmentary continuation of *Women in Love,* which Lawrence did not include in his final version of the novel, Gudrun bears a child—whether Gerald's or Loerke's is not clear—a fact that seems to indicate that children are to be understood as results of a failed "conjunction." The development of consciousness, Lawrence appears to be suggesting, will hereafter take on an inward dynamic form, through a stable alternation of attraction/repulsion between the male and the female—like two paired stars—rather than an outward pattern of a Hegelian dynamic.[56]

The births that do take place in *Women in Love* are therefore appropriately inner births and rebirths. Birkin undergoes three such rebirths: the first when he leaves Breadalby in haste after Hermione Roddice has attempted to kill him with a piece of lapis lazuli; the second, when Birkin and Gerald Crich wrestle each other; and the third when Ursula throws Birkin's rings back at him, symbolically repeating Hermione's earlier "murder." In each case, an act of destruction precedes an act of regeneration or rebirth; in each case, Birkin is either stripped naked physically or spiritually and reverts to an original state of primitive consciousness before rebounding toward a higher level of consciousness. It is only by exposing himself to the risk of personal annihilation that he is able to accomplish this forward movement. Only the death of the old self permits a leap into the new.

As in *The Rainbow*, the action of *Women in Love* develops by means of contrasted pairs, but now synchronically rather than diachronically. The two sisters are obviously one such pair, but so are Rupert Birkin and Gerald Crich. Though on the surface they are only friends, on a deeper level they are also brothers, that is, blood-brothers or at least would-be blood-brothers. In the chapter "Man to Man," Birkin proposes to Crich that they swear a "Blutbrüderschaft" in the way "the old German knights" used to do, swear that they will "be true to each other, of one blood all their lives." By this Birkin does not mean any "sloppy sentimentalism" but rather "an impersonal union that leaves one free."[57] This proposal is, *mutatis mutandis*, precisely the one he later makes to Ursula. Crich is interested but afraid, and in the end backs off from Birkin's offer; but, though never sworn, for Birkin at least the blood-brotherhood exists and is confirmed in the ritual samurai wrestling match he later has with Crich.

The pairing of Birkin and Crich is carefully delineated in other ways as well: just as Birkin passes through a love affair with Hermione (or willful intellectuality) before he finds Ursula, so too Crich has a futile love relationship with Minette (or mindless sensuality) before reaching out for Gudrun. The affair with Gudrun ends with Crich's death, partly because Crich, the man of the machine, refuses to acknowledge the animal vitality that lies deep within him; but also partly because Gudrun is incapable of an Ursula-like "conjunction." In the final section of the novel—set in the Austrian Tyrol but populated by refugees from a German urban Bohemia very much like Frieda's Munich—Gudrun rejects Crich in favor of the German sculptor Loerke, who is variously described as an insect, a mouse, a rat, and a snake. Snake calls to snake, as it were, and rat to rat. In yielding to Loerke, Gudrun brings the action of the novel full circle. Loerke is the twentieth-century embodiment of the strange little monkey-man whose perfect self-assurance had so fascinated Tom Brangwen generations earlier. In Gudrun, the rat lover, the Brangwen spirit has reached a similar stage of perfection and petrifaction, very much like the perfect little works of art she produces—perfect and utterly dead. Going off with Loerke, she chooses death in life, chooses the man who puts a sexless nymphet on a bronze horse rather than the man who places himself on a living horse, even if only to make that horse obey his fatal will and the collective will of a mechanized state.

Gerald himself also goes off with and to death, but real death, not death in life. He risks death on a journey upward along the mountain of truth rather than returning to the corrupt cities of the plain. His is a leap into cleanness, away from the dirty songs and dreary, the corrupt art and empty life that, in his limited consciousness, he sees as the only alternative. Such a death is final; but it is not a dead end.

8

No Salvation for the Hun

It is safe to say that there has been no crisis in which the public opinion of the English people has been so definitely opposed to war as it is at this moment. . . . This spirit is reflected in the House of Commons and it is everywhere recognized that a Minister who led this country into war would be responsible for a war as causeless and unpopular as any war in history, and that he would cease to lead the Liberal Party.
Lead editorial in The Nation, 1 August 1914

"That a rat has as great a moral right to exist as myself I am ready to concede. But if I can kill it I will kill it, and its death seems to me to end its right to existence."
Ford Madox Hueffer, When Blood
Is Their Argument (1915)

As the lights began to dim all over Europe, England along with the other belligerents plunged into a spiritual darkness from which it was not to recover for years. Even those who struggled fiercely to keep a little light burning were touched by it. Bertrand Russell, who was later jailed and nearly lynched for opposing conscription, remembers in his *Autobiography* how his friend and former colleague, Alfred North Whitehead, became "savagely warlike"; and even a longtime pacifist propagandist like J. L. Hammond was swept off his feet by the invasion of Belgium. Russell himself was tortured by intense patriotic feelings. "The successes of the Germans before the Battle of the Marne," he writes, "were horrible to me. I desired the defeat of Germany as ardently as any retired colonel. Love of England is very nearly the strongest emotion I possess."[1]

In an essay "Some Psychological Difficulties in Wartime," written for a pacifistic collection edited by Julian Bell, *We Did Not Fight* (1935), Russell goes into greater detail about the overwhelming pressure of mass suggestion to which everyone was subject during the first months and years of the war.

"As much effort," he recalls, "was required to avoid sharing this excitement as would have been needed to stand out against the extreme of hunger and sexual passion, and there was the same feeling of going against instinct." No one was exempt from being touched to a greater or lesser degree by this epidemic of hysteria, not even the pacifists themselves. Russell, for instance, cites the case of a woman getting up at one of the pacifist meetings to announce with great passion that, if her own son were wounded, she would not lift a finger to help him. And Cecil Gray recalls how, when he objected "mildly" to his father's prayer that "all German males should be castrated, all German women sterilized, and all German children exterminated," his father replied that "he hoped to see the day when I should be put up against a wall and shot."[2]

Of course, for most people and particularly for the young, there was no need for much investigation into, or consideration of, the whys and wherefores. Even Compton Mackenzie, no longer quite so young at thirty-one, was barely able to concentrate on finishing *Sinister Street* (1913–14), so much was he longing to be in the midst of the fray—not, however, really out of patriotic reasons or indignation at the fate of Belgium, but because he knew that this was "the greatest moment in the history of my time and that somehow I must be sharing in the excitement of it."[3] Similarly unvarnished motives inspired Siegfried Sassoon, R. H. Mottram, and Richard Aldington.

These were individual reactions. What did the psychological—and diplomatic—trick was the German invasion of Belgium. Seventy years after the event most historians are agreed that Britain would have entered the war on the French side in any case: that is, even if Germany had not violated the 1839 treaty guaranteeing Belgian neutrality. The story of apparent British hesitation, of the manner in which the Foreign Secretary misled the German ambassador about Britain's commitment to France, this story is most briefly, and perhaps most truthfully, told in John Viscount Morley's *Memorandum on Resignation* (1928).

Morley, who had served the Asquith government first as Secretary of State for India and then as Lord Privy Seal, was a distinguished man of letters and an influential Liberal statesman. He was present at *all* the crucial meetings of the Cabinet in the turbulent two weeks preceding Britain's declaration of war on Germany. According to Morley's account, a scant majority of the Cabinet initially followed his lead in urging that Britain remain neutral in a war between France and Germany unless directly attacked. Up until 3 August, at any rate, the question of Belgium was strictly "secondary to the pre-eminent controversy of the Anglo-French Entente." Well before that date, however—at least a week and possibly as much as ten days earlier—Grey had already threatened to resign if the Cabinet was determined to pursue a policy of neutrality. Together with the rest of the war party in the

Cabinet, including Churchill and Haldane but not at this point Asquith himself, Grey was for supporting France from the very outset, just as Britain was supposedly committed to do under the provisions of the Entente—this, despite the well-remembered fact that both Asquith and Grey had previously repeatedly assured both the House and the Cabinet that the Entente provided for no binding engagements. Yet suddenly such engagements were said by Grey to exist. Small wonder that Morley concluded that "an entente was evidently something even more dangerous for us than an alliance. An alliance has definite covenants. An entente is vague, rests on points of honour, to be construed by accident and convenience." Many members of the Cabinet, including Lloyd George, felt that they were "being rather artfully drawn step by step to war for the benefit of France and Russia."[4]

Morley was particularly outraged that Grey failed to respond to the German ambassador's query, on 1 August 1914, whether Britain would remain neutral if Germany promised to respect Belgian neutrality (as Gladstone had stipulated in 1870), or, failing that, if Grey would state clearly what conditions—even including an explicit guarantee of the integrity of France and her colonies—Britain would accept. To all of these questions Grey felt obliged, as he wrote to his ambassador in Berlin that very day, "to refuse definitely any promise to remain neutral on similar terms, and I could only say that we must keep our hands free."[5] Free for what? the German ambassador must have wondered.

The terrible irony, of course, as Morley saw at once, was that Grey's hands were anything but free. They were inexorably tied to France. Hence, when the expected German invasion of Belgium finally occurred, Morley concluded that "the precipitate and peremptory blaze" it produced "was due less to indignation at the violation of a treaty, than to natural perception of the plea that it would furnish for intervention on behalf of France, for expeditionary force, and all the rest of it. Belgium was to take the place, that had been taken before as pleas for war, by Morocco and Agadir" (14).

Morley's friend John Burns resigned from the Cabinet even before Belgium became the principal issue, in protest over Grey's blunt warning to the Germans that any attack on their part on the north coast of France would be construed as an act of war. Morley himself sent in his resignation on the morning of 3 August. Two other ministers, Simon and Beauchamp, also resigned but immediately afterward reconsidered. Lloyd George, along with the remains of the so-called Peace Party, went over completely to Grey's side after having, in Morley's words, "one of his customary morning talks with the splendid *condottiere* at the Admiralty" and "made up his mind to swing round, as he had done about the *Panther* in 1911, to the politics of adventure . . ." (24).

The German invasion of Belgium brought with it a massive propaganda war in the British press. It quickly overwhelmed public opinion of all political shades. William Watson voiced the general mood of righteous indignation in his poetical address "To the Troubler of the World":

> At last we know you, War-lord. You, that flung
> The gauntlet down, fling down the mask you wore,
> Publish your heart, and let its pent hate pour,
> You that had God forever on your tongue.
> We are old in war, and if in guile we are young,
> Young also is the spirit that evermore
> Burns in our bosom ev'n as heretofore. . . .
> We are not on such cosy terms with Heaven;
> But in Earth's hearing we can verily say,
> "Our hands are pure; for peace, for peace we have striven";
> And not by Earth shall he be soon forgiven
> Who lit the fire accurst that flames to-day.[6]

Germany and the Kaiser stood revealed in their true colors: a ruthless, unscrupulous, barbaric nation of Huns, ruled by the iron fist of the imperial devil incarnate. Now the Huns were preparing to crush civilization once again. With the French armies in full retreat, all that seemed to bar their way was Field-Marshall John French's British Expeditionary Force—or what the Kaiser had been pleased to call "the contemptible little army."[7]

With astonishing swiftness, British historians and eminent literary figures turned to reexamine the evidence of history in the light of their new experience. What they came up with confirmed only too copiously the malignity of Germany's traditions and people. It soon became obvious that the war was no mere accident, but a plot that had been decades in the hatching. In *Germany and the Next War* (1912), General Friedrich von Bernhardi had written large the Prussian masterplan for world domination, but the English had been too good-natured to take him seriously. Even to so apolitical figure as the seventy-one-year-old Henry James, it was obvious in 1915 that "the German powers had, up to a twelvemonth ago, been for years conspiring to let loose upon the world . . . such appalling engines and agencies as mankind had never before dreamed of." (Notice the distinction implied here between Germans and mankind.) Austin Harrison, in *The Kaiser's War* (1914), ventured to identify the precise date and place of Germany's implacable hatred of England: Versailles, 1871, the moment of German unification. His father, Frederic Harrison, for long an observer of Germany and a prophet of the wickedness of German intentions, confirmed his son's analysis in *The German Peril* (1915), where the war is seen as the result of "a perfectly regular and continuous chain of political design; and it is not the conspiracy of a Minister or a Sovereign, but essentially the national ideal of a people." Hilaire Belloc dug even deeper into the past in his *Elements of the Great War*

(1915) to find the root of the evil in the "Frederician tradition"—roughly equatable with the doctrine that the King of Prussia can do what he likes—which is "the principal cause of the war." Gilbert Murray, adopting a somewhat broader view in his study of Grey's diplomacy, concluded that the German peril that "Europe had to face in the preceding generation was similar to that of Napoleon or the invading Turks in the sixteenth century, though more scientifically prepared and more self-conscious."[8]

Just how self-conscious German aggression was emerged only after its philosophical underpinnings were laid bare. As Crane Brinton was to observe many years later, "In the first few months of the war, Nietzsche, Treitschke and von Bernhardi were linked together in British propaganda as mainly responsible for working the Germans, leaders and led alike, up to an immoral lust for conquest never yet seen on this earth." For many British commentators at the time, however, Treitschke and Bernhardi were merely symptoms; the underlying cause was Nietzsche. No one saw this more clearly than William Archer, the translator of Ibsen and friend of Shaw. In *Fighting a Philosophy* (1915), Archer asserts that "in a very real sense, it is the philosophy of Nietzsche that we are fighting." He concedes that while it is possible that Nietzsche's Prussian countrymen may have misread him, nevertheless "the trouble is that no human being can say how he is to be read aright." And besides, "wherever his ideas are clear, definite and easily translated into action, they are aggressively inhuman; wherever they stray in the direction of humanity . . . they are vague, visionary, and irreconcilable with the general trend of his doctrine."[9] As Archer was well aware, there were definite advantages in having for one's philosophical enemy a man who had been a certified madman.

A year later Archer returned to the same subject in an open letter to the famous German professor of Classics, Ulrich von Wilamovitz Möllendorf. "There can be no joining of hands with Germany," he writes in the published version of that letter, *The Villain of the World-Tragedy* (1916), "until she has washed her hands of the pernicious theories of statecraft and military policy which have made her conduct of this war one long succession of crimes. . . ." The man partly responsible for this "enormous excess of savagery" is again "your old schoolmate, Nietzsche."[10]

The aged Thomas Hardy—so often described as deeply indebted to German idealist philosophy, especially to Schopenhauer—also recognized in Nietzsche the chief culprit. "What a disastrous blight," he wrote, "upon the glory and nobility of that great nation has been wrought by the writings of Nietzsche, with his followers! I should think there is no instance since history began of a country being so demoralized by a single writer." Even Norman Angell, usually reluctant to join such campaigns, agreed that this war was "the result of a false national doctrine, which is in its turn the work of half a dozen professors and a few writers and theorists—Nietzsche,

Treitschke, and their school." But, according to Angell, the Germans were not entirely to blame. After all, Nietzsche and Treitschke were not really Germans. "Is there no meaning at all," he inquires in *Prussianism and Its Destruction* (1914), "in the fact that Nietzsche was not a German, but a Slav; that his great pupil in the philosophy of history, to whom more than to any other man we ascribe the fatal turn in our generation of German policy, Treitschke, was also a Slav?"[11]

Others sought to trace the origins of the evil even farther back into the German philosophical tradition. For some it was Hegel, with his naive idealization of the Prussian state, who was principally to blame; for others it was Fichte's rabid nationalism and exaltation of the German "virtues." Even Immanuel Kant did not escape censure. "I trace back to Kant," writes P. Chalmers Mitchell in *Evolution and the War* (1915), "the dreaming megalomania that destroyed the German sense of reality and that has made German 'Kultur' the enemy of the human race. . . . Nietzsche, of whom so much has been made, is a terminal flower in the tree of idealistic thought, beautiful, poisonous, sterile." How corrupted German culture was by this cloudy barbarism was apparent also in the music of Beethoven. Listening to his music after the war, the eminent aesthetician of Bloomsbury, Roger Fry, wrote home that "I also heard the *Pastoral Symphony*, which I hadn't since my youth. That shocked me profoundly and the essential barbarity and want of civilization of the German spirit and the worst of it is he is such a musician."[12]

The Germans were guilty, of that there could be no doubt. What still remained in dispute, however, was whether this guilt was wholly or partially to be imputed to the German government or to the German people, or to both; and whether this guilt could be atoned for or was ultimately unforgivable. At first, it looked as if there might still be hope for the Hun. "Germania" might be saved, so Eden Phillpotts maintained, by rapid and massive surgery:

> Surgeon her world! Let myriad scalpels bright
> Flash in her sores with all thy bitter might,
> So that their aching cease.
> Cut clean the cursed canker that doth foul
> Her spirit; and cleanse her sorry soul,
> And give her bosom peace.[13]

The same idea of saving the best that is in Germany by a beneficial excision of the worst underlies A. C. Bradley's essay "International Morality" (1915), where we are told that "any Englishman who reveres and loves that soul of her [Germany] which speaks in her music, philosophy, and poetry, must desire her total defeat for her own sake as well as for his country's and the world's."[14]

H. G. Wells, in a work whose title was to become one of the rallying cries of the conflict, *The War That Will End War* (1914), made a clear distinction that was frequently echoed by other writers of the time: "Be it remembered that Europe's quarrel is with the German State, not with the German people; with a system, and not with a race. The older tradition of Germany is a pacific and civilizing tradition. The temperament of the mass of the German people is kindly, sane and amiable."[15] This doctrine of the two Germanies was also available in the more popular version of the "good" German and the "bad" German (or Prussian), a distinction that was to do yeoman's service over a great period of time and that is not wholly dead today.[16] Arnold Bennett took up with gusto the subject of the Prussianization of Germany in *Liberty, A Statement of the British Case* (1914), where he showed how "the best qualities of the race were turned to evil, and its worst quality, a certain maladroit arrogance, was appealed to." As a consequence of years of such conditioning, "ladies have to take to the gutter in order to make room for the swagger of Prussian officers three abreast on the pavements of enlightened German cities." According to Robert Vansittart, who spent some time in Germany in the nineties, going about the German streets as a civilian meant taking one's life in one's hands, since the military "Code of Honour" required German Officers summarily to "cut down" anyone who offended them. The violation of Belgian neutrality, as the joint publication by members of the Oxford Faculty of Modern History, *Why We Are At War* (1914), urged us to remember "in justice to a great people," was the result not of "the doctrine of Germany, but rather the doctrine of Prussia. . . ."

In another donnish collection, *The War and Democracy* (1915), Alfred Zimmern lamented that "the German people, so kindly and, alas! so docile, is suffering, not for its sins, but for its deficiencies; not for its own characteristic acts or natural ambitions, but for what it has too tamely allowed others, Prussian statesmen and soldiers, with alien ideas and an alien temper, to foist upon it, until it has become an integral part of its natural life and consciousness." It is very likely this distinction (originating in the War of 1870) that led to the idea, "definitely suggested in various quarters" according to Norman Angell, of partitioning Germany after her defeat. But perhaps the case against Prussia and for Germany is stated most straightforwardly in a speech of Lord Rosebery's given on 22 September 1914: "What is it we are fighting against?" he asks his hearers. "It is not the German nation, though, of course, the German nation is fighting us. We have no particular quarrel with the German nation, which is a peaceful, quiet domestic race, liking their quiet beer saloons and their music; we are fighting against the military caste of Prussia. (Cheers.) I distinguish most broadly and strongly between Prussia and the rest of Germany." For the mass of the English reading public, however, these arguments were rather too sophisticated to be telling. In order to reach them, the journalist and financial swindler Horatio Bottomley put into effect the principle first enunciated by Leonard Hobhouse some years earlier: "Savage tribes advance upon the enemy with yells; we hurl defiance at them through a certain portion of the press."[17]

Indeed, Bottomley wished to do both. In his *John Bull*, besides openly advocating the extermination of the "Germhuns," he suggested that Zulus and Basutos be armed and allowed "to run amok in the enemy's ranks." Well before the time the Germans got around to using poison gas, he urged the army to employ this weapon. He even went as far as to pressure the army to adopt a policy of taking no prisoners. On the home front, all German civilians resident in Great Britain were to be imprisoned and their property confiscated. Those who had succeeded in being naturalized should be subjected to a curfew and forced to wear an identifying badge. Their children were to be forbidden to attend any school whatever. Nor was this all. If, after the war, any wretched Germhun were lucky enough to survive and find work in England again, and "if by chance you should discover one day in a restaurant that you are being served by a German waiter, you will throw the soup in his foul face; if you find yourself sitting at the side of a German clerk, you will spill the inkpot over his vile head."[18]

As the war wore on and the casualty lists mounted and nothing seemed to change for the better, saner heads than Bottomley's began to doubt the existence of the "good" German or the possible salvation of the Hun. Of course, a few farsighted thinkers and poets had been convinced from the very outset of the utterly irremediable nature of Germany's sin.[19] Among these was Arthur Conan Doyle, who told his readers in *The German War* (1914) that "it is not on the chiefs of the army that the whole guilt of this terrible crime must rest, but it is upon the whole German nation, which for generations to come must stand condemned before the civilised world for this reversion to those barbarous practices from which Christianity, civilisation and chivalry had gradually rescued the human race."[20] Others, however, only reached this position over a long period of time. For example, before the war the distinguished novelist Mrs. Humphry Ward had believed that "the hatred and envy of England, so apparent in German newspaper writing, was but the creed of a clique, and that the heart of the laborious and thrifty German people was still sound." With the outbreak of the war and the outrageous behavior of various German professors (some of whom she had in happier days entertained at her house in London), it became apparent that they were rotten to the core. In 1916, having gained special permission to visit the front for the purpose of composing a propaganda work specially suited to an American audience, she got her first glimpse through captured fieldglasses of the German trenches. "At last we are within actual sight of the *Great Aggression*," she noted in her diary, "the nation and the army which have defied the laws of God and man, and left their fresh and damning mark to all time on the history of Europe."[21]

Speculating on the same subject from the loftier perspective of Oxford, Sir Walter Raleigh, probably the most inspiring professor of English of the period, whose lectures and personality influenced minds as good and diverse as Lytton Strachey's and Aldous Huxley's, reached roughly similar conclusions. By the beginning of the war the Germans had grown to be indistinguishably Prussian, Raleigh argued, since the march of history in the last half of the nineteenth century had paid them to do so. They were a brave, faithful, and stupid people; and as such there was only one way to instruct them: namely "rough proofs." More specifically, Raleigh was reminded of the educational theory advanced by a "genial and humane Irish officer" of his acquaintance, who had been anxious to teach the leaders of the Zulu rebellion a lesson. " 'Kill them all,' he said, 'it's the only thing they understand.' " Raleigh goes on to explain that what this military man meant was that the Zulu chiefs would mistake moderation for fear, lacking the tuition of a little blood. Raleigh concludes that "this sentence has become almost true of the great German people," who must be given an advanced course in ethics, even though they are the authors of the "structure of modern metaphysics."[22]

Just where Raleigh's Irish officer had learned this particular theory of education we are not told. But it is possible that he may have run across it in Kipling's novel *Kim* (1906), where another British Colonial officer attributes a native rebellion to "not smashing them thoroughly the first time" and considers the action he proposes to take against them to be "punishment— not war." Less likely is the possibility that the Irish officer would have been reading Conrad, but if he had been, he would have found in "Heart of Darkness" the Imperialist Kurtz's succinct instructions for the education of primitive peoples: "Exterminate all the brutes!" Or he could have found it in the *Daily News*, where on 1 October 1914 he would have been informed by Arnold Bennett that "nothing will impress the Potsdam mentality so much as a public humiliation. . . . Many a savage brute has been permanently convinced of the advantages of civilization by the idiom of one knock down blow." The distances from Fleet Street to Oxonian ivory towers and Sussex country houses, it appears, was rapidly diminishing. Everyone was beginning to settle down comfortably into the mental slum.[23]

Though every day provided new and incontrovertible evidence of the stupidity and malignity of the Germans, it was nevertheless equally certain that these malicious fools had somehow managed to put one over on the British. While the government, in the person of the Lord Admiral Winston Churchill, assured the nation that its navy was in tip-top shape and possessed sufficient ammunition to last out the next five years, and while the same government had dispatched with admirable efficiency an Expeditionary Force of six crack divisions "ready down to the last gaiter button" to positions agreed upon with the French and the Belgians as long ago as 1906, the government nevertheless staunchly maintained that it had been caught unprepared by the declaration of war. When more than a year later Mrs. Humphry Ward paid a visit to the Foreign Secretary with a view toward gathering materials for a book on the theme of British unpreparedness, Sir Edward Grey was moved to discourse at length on that subject, touching on "the utter absence of any wish for war in this country, or thought of war. No one wished for it. I thought of his long, long struggle for peace. It was pathetic to hear him talking so simply—with such complete conviction."[24]

Was this actually the case? It is difficult to say. George Bernard Shaw remarked with consternation when faced with this dilemma that "it is hard to please a lion who, whilst delighting in being king of the beasts, terrible and mighty in battle, nevertheless insists on clothing itself in lamb's wool as the Prince of Peace all the time." No one, however, at this time seemed to remember Jeremy Bentham's observation in the *Essay on Universal and Perpetual Peace* (written 1789; published 1843) that one of the principal characteristics of British public life had always been a paranoic fear of being duped by foreigners who were at once more intelligent and less honest than themselves.[25]

What the violation of Belgian neutrality revealed from the outset and what was to be fully confirmed as the war progressed was that the Germans were not willing to fight fair. In short, as news of the shooting of civilians, the destruction of cathedrals, drunken looting and raping, dropping bombs on defenseless women and children, the maltreatment of prisoners, the use of poison gas, the sinking of unarmed vessels with mines and submarines—as reports of all these horrors came pouring in in ever vaster numbers, even those who might have remained skeptical at first were reluctantly convinced that the Germans were no gentlemen. A few literary figures had realized all along that this was precisely what was going to happen. H. G. Wells had foretold in his *The War in the Air* the horrors the Germans intended to visit upon the world, and nearly every one of the invasion stories had foreseen the Teutonic preference for efficiency over chivalry. Arthur Conan Doyle even went as far as to chide the English for their Romantic conceptions of war. In his short story "Danger" (1911), Captain John Sirius, standing on the conning tower of his submarine and sailing past the defeated and sullen men of the British navy, comes to realize that they are resentful because "they thought it cowardly to attack merchant ships and avoid the warships." This, observes Sirius, addressing himself directly to his audience, is like the Arabs who believe that any attack on the flank of an enemy force is mean and unmanly. No, Sirius concludes, "war is not a big game, my English friends.

It is a desperate business to gain the upper hand, and one must use one's brain in order to find the weak spot of one's enemy."[26]

Once the war actually broke out and Conan Doyle got down to the business of analyzing *The German War,* he used his brain to discover that matters were not so simple. After all, he pointed out that, although the French and English had been frequent enemies in the past, they had always fought decently against each other; even in the darkest days of Napoleon's ambition to dominate the world there had been no atrocities. But then Britain and France were Christian, chivalrous, and civilized nations. Germany, on the other hand, was something else—barbaric, ruthless, careless of chivalry, and motivated only by hate. The English, however, "have never been a nation who fought with hatred. It is our ideal to fight with a sporting spirit." A thorough examination of English history failed to reveal a single instance in which the English had ever behaved otherwise.[27]

Alfred Harmsworth, First Viscount Northcliffe, owner and publisher of *The Times* and the mass-circulation *Daily Mail,* toured the front in 1917 and arrived at similar conclusions. In *At the War* (1917), he describes a prison camp in France for members of the contemptible big army. " 'What a pity your Highlanders cannot meet these fellows in fair fight,' said a French officer, as we reviewed a gang of prisoners. 'The war would be over in a month.' " Drawing closer, Northcliffe inspected an ill-favored specimen hailing from Berlin who was barely above five feet tall, narrow-chested, and peak-faced, who "seemed far better fitted for his stool as railway clerk than for the life of the trenches or for the ordeal of attack." It was regrettable that gentlemen had to fight such an enemy; these were not only barbarians, but also lower-class barbarians.[28]

How striking an effect the war had on the British psyche can be seen from the hallucinations it evoked, particularly during the first few months after it began. To be sure, much of the overheated imagination is immediately attributable to industrious stoking by the press. But even so, there was a considerable remnant that had its direct origin in the people and that the press merely reported.

That the war on the home front should have begun with wild rumors of insidious German governesses secreting explosives all over England and of malignant German waiters poisoning innocent diners is only natural. After all, it was well known that foreigners were capable of doing almost anything. But the enormous dimensions as well as the ingenuity of German spying and fifth-column activity were surprising. Viscount Haldane was questioned in Parliament as to "whether he had any information that there were 66,000 trained German soldiers in England, or that there were in a cellar, within a quarter mile of Charing Cross, 50,000 stands of Mauser rifles and 7½ millions of Mauser cartridges, or 150 rounds per rifle."[29] Haldane himself, who had been educated in Germany and whose sympathies for German philosophy were well known, was eventually forced to resign from the Government, though it was chiefly due to him that the British Expeditionary Force (which he called a "Hegelian Army") was brought, in his words, "to such a degree of perfection as might make it in point of quality the finest Army for its size on the earth." Haldane, as he later recounted in his *Autobiography* (1929), was suspected of being a spy, and possibly even of being an illegitimate brother of the Kaiser.[30]

Probably the most industrious, as well as imaginative, spy-hunter was William Le Queux, already well known as the author of *The Invasion of England* (1905) and *Spies of the Kaiser* (1909). In the latter book he had drawn the public's attention to the Kaiser's five thousand spies working in Britain and had recounted how some of these spies had attempted to blow him and a friend up by means of explosives secreted in bonbons. In *Britain's Deadly Peril* (1915), he made the spectacular revelation that as long ago as 1908 he had provided the British Secret Service with a copy of a secret speech in which the Kaiser boasted of his "army of spies, scattered over Great Britain and France, as it is over North and South America." Le Queux also revealed that "in the obscure foreign restaurants in the neighborhood of Tottenham Court Road" men and women were meeting nightly and toasting "to the Day of Britain's destruction," and, moreover, were in possession of facts concerning the movement of German aircraft unknown to the British authorities.[31]

Sensational as this was, it still moved on a human level. Divine revelation only occurred with the first major engagement between British and German troops, at Mons in the closing days of August 1914. It was on this occasion that God, by making hosts of angels appear to the British Expeditionary Force, gave a sign in the heavens that He looked with favor on the Allied cause. On the ground, however, matters were progressing less satisfactorily and the British were eventually forced to yield their positions. For a few days the papers were full of these angels and their significance. And even after it was proved that they were merely part of a journalistic daydream of Arthur Machen's, people persisted in believing in them. Nor did the facts deter members of the British Expeditionary Force from being prepared to vouch for having seen these angels in action. As Richard Aldington, a veteran of nearly the whole war, was to observe some years later, "any real old sweat would swear to a wagonload of angels or cherubim or any other supernatural phenomenon for a couple of pints of beer. As for journalists, they don't even require beer—*c'est leur métier*."[32]

The most dramatic instance of mass hallucination at this early period of the war, however, was the famous passage of a whole Russian army corps through Great Britain. People from all over the country reported seeing them, calling out for vodka at Berwick-on-Tweed and Carlisle, scraping the snow off their boots on train platforms (in September!), even jamming a candy machine with a Russian coin in Durham. On 9 September the *Daily Mail* secured permission from the official Press Bureau—which, however, would neither confirm nor deny the report—to publish a telegram from Rome with "the official news of the concentration of two hundred and fifty thousand Russian troops in France."

Even so, the newspapers remained skeptical and hung fire. The report was published, but with reservations. However, the rumors were so persistent and their confirmation so widespread that, as the *Daily News* noted, it would have been almost more incredible if they were false than if they were true. The *Daily Mail*, though conceding that there might have been something in the story, refused to commit itself. On 14 September, however, the *Daily News* managed to secure some specific information. Its special correspondent, P. J. Philip, sent in a long dispatch confirming the Russian presence in Belgium and their cooperation with Belgian forces to cut off the German army. "For two days," he circumstantially informed his readers, "I have been on a long trek looking for the Russians, and now I have found them—where and how it would not be discreet to tell, but the published statement that they are here is sufficient, and of my own knowledge I can answer for their presence."[33]

On the same day, Aldous Huxley wrote to his father informing him that he had just received a letter from Captain Bertie Stobart, a family friend stationed in Belgium, bearing the news that the Russians had arrived at their base in that country, presumably Ostend. After checking with relations in the railways and in the Foreign Office, Huxley felt that he could not say for certain that Russian troops had actually passed through Britain. (After all, why should they?) But he did decide that it was very probable Russian reinforcements had arrived in Belgium via some sea-route.[34] Meanwhile, that evening Arnold Bennett noted in his diary that there was "no certainty yet as to the alleged Russian army in France." He was not altogether sure what to think but he knew that "military officers up to yesterday have always believed the tale, and indeed positively asserted it, here."[35]

What was the actual basis for this elaborate story? As far as is known, nothing at all. On 19 November 1914, in reply to a question from the floor, the Undersecretary of State for War replied in the House of Commons that no Russian troops had ever passed through Britain on their way to the Western Front. Certainly, postwar historians tell of no Russian armies fighting in Belgium or France. How, then, is one to account for this mysterious business? Clearly—since neither the British nor the German secret services were likely to have been imaginative or industrious enough to dream up so preposterous a story—what confronts us here is an authentic case of mass hallucination much like those provoked by the witch-hunts of earlier ages. Though, certainly, another explanation cited by Arthur Ponsonby is worth repeating. According to Ponsonby, a very excitable French officer whose English was less than perfect had been overheard rushing about near the front, shouting, "Where are de rations, where are de rations?" The Russians themselves, when they were approached by the British ambassador, Sir George Buchanan, with a proposal for transferring an army corps to aid the Allies, concluded that the poor man had gone mad.[36]

Naturally, in conditions so charged with the desire for good news about the Allies—or bad news about the enemy, which amounted to nearly the same thing—practically anything stood a chance of being taken seriously. Hence, when in August and September, amid a stream of German successes, the first reports of German atrocities began pouring in, it was natural that the initial reaction of horror and disbelief would soon change to an almost pornographic lust for more and gorier details. With the influx of great numbers of Belgian refugees (one of the by-products of war that Western Europe had almost forgotten); with the authenticated news of summary executions by the Germans of civilians suspected of being snipers or of aiding snipers; with the destruction of Louvain and its churches and precious collection of books; with the sinking of unarmed vessels, it gradually grew absolutely certain that the atrocities must be true. As in the case of the mysterious Russian army, it was hardly possible that so many, so various, and so well-confirmed reports could be mistaken.

Henry James, who had devoted nearly a lifetime to persuading his readers that the truth was invariably a relative quantity and that omniscient narration of any event could only be untrustworthy, felt no hesitation whatsoever about informing his readers that the Germans had a peculiar relish for destroying anything marked with a Red Cross. However, powerful as his indignation was, it was not enough to unhinge his prose style. Here is a part of his reaction to the onslaught of the Hun: "If it would have been hard really to give the measure of one's dismay at the awful proposition of a war squeezed together in the huge Prussian fist and with the variety and spontaneity of its parts oozing in a steady trickle, like the sacred blood of sacrifice between those hideous knuckly fingers, so, none the less, every reason with which our preference for a better condition and a nobler fate could possibly bristle kept battering at my heart, kept, in fact, pushing into it, after the fashion of a crowd of the alarmed faithful at the door of a church."[37] Naturally, with so many reports of the most outrageous German brutalities coming in from all sides, the British government—like the Belgian and French—felt it incumbent upon itself to examine and report upon this matter. To do so, it appointed a commission in September 1914 and selected as its chairman the seventy-six-year-old James Viscount Bryce, a man who had been partly educated in Germany and spoke the language well enough to be able to converse in it with Queen Victoria. After lengthy hearings and much sifting of evidence, this commission finally published the *Report of the Committee on Alleged German Atrocities* (1915) and *Evidence and Documents Laid before the Committee on Alleged German Outrages* (1916). The latter contains hundreds of cases of horrendous barbarities, of which the following are by no means atypical.

According to a Belgian soldier, who vouched for the truth of this account, on 7 August 1914, he saw a twelve-year-old boy with a bandage where his hand should have been. After inquiring about what had happened, he was told that the Germans had cut off his hand because he would not let go of his parents when these were being flung into the fire. The soldier, however, did not attempt to examine what was or was not underneath the bandage, and therefore testified that he was not wholly certain that the story was true. At the same time, however, he saw a little ten-year-old girl who, as her mother told him, had had her ear cut off by the Germans for listening to their orders. This was an act of extreme cruelty, since the girl was far too young to have been able to understand what they said. Again the soldier did not look under the bandage.[38]

Another report by a Belgian refugee related circumstantially how at seven o'clock of an evening at the beginning of October 1914 he had paused momentarily in his flight from the Germans in a farmhouse about ten minutes' walk from Louvenier, near Spa, in Belgium. He was in the kitchen with the farmer, his wife and baby, two other men, and a servant girl, when suddenly three Germans, an officer and two privates, came into the farmhouse. As soon as the occupants of the kitchen became aware of this, they all, except for the mother who was just nursing her child, fled post-haste into a butter-churning room adjoining the kitchen. From this room it was possible to watch the proceedings in the kitchen through a small window, approximately two-and-a-half feet square, but so high up that one had to stand on a bench to see from it. This the refugee and his companions at once set about to do. What they saw filled their hearts with terror and amazement. The Germans had seized the baby out of the arms of the farmer's wife, and while the two enlisted men held the baby, the officer drew his sword and decapitated it. The soldiers kicked the body of the child into a corner and then kicked the head, which was lying on the floor, after it. As soon as the farmer saw this happening, he attempted to shout and come to the aid of the victims, but the others prevented him by holding him back and stuffing a cloth into his mouth to stifle his outcries. After the farmer had been removed from the bench, the refugee continued his observations. He saw the two privates stripping the farmer's wife and, holding her steady by the arms and shoulders, allowed the officer to rape her. Then, in turn, the other two raped her. After they had finished, the officer once again drew his sword and cut off her breasts. Still not satisfied, he took out his revolver, pointed it at her bleeding body and—at that moment the farmer broke loose and everyone made wildly for the fields. From there the refugee could see how the farmhouse had been set afire and was being consumed by flames.[39]

Other stories were equally horrible. One dealt with the priest of Gelrode who, before he was shot, was made to stand on his toes with his hands above his head for two hours while the people imprisoned in his church were forced to urinate and defecate on him. Another had a woman being tossed into a cesspool after being raped by four or five soldiers. Others still recounted how scores of civilians had their hands cut off, or how babies were decapitated and their heads displayed prominently on bayonets. There was also a special class of atrocities, focusing on crucifixion, the most famous of these probably being that of the Canadian soldier, much in the press at approximately the same time the Bryce Report was published. *The Times* of 10 May 1915, carried an account of this, relating how a Canadian officer in Ypres had been found by his men pinned to a wall with bayonets thrust through his hands and feet, and with another bayonet stuck in his throat. In addition, his body had been riddled through with bullets. The Bryce Report also included testimony regarding the nailing by Germans of a child two or three years old to the door of a church.[40]

How much truth was there in all of these stories? No certain and precise answer can be given to this question, but what *is* certain is that almost everyone who dealt with the verification of atrocities in the less feverish times following the war concluded that there was practically no evidence supporting any of the alleged atrocities on either side. In any event, no case, on either side, involving crucifixion, cutting off of hands or breasts, or gouging out of eyes was ever confirmed by any postwar investigator. Time and again, as soon as the attempt was made to pin down an incident, it evaporated into thin air.[41]

How closely these stories were connected with hallucinations like the passage of the Russian army through England is suggested by the story of the mutilated nurse, which was widely circulated in mid-September 1914. This was an account of how Nurse Grace Hume of Dumfries, late of the Huddersfield Hospital, had been brutally tortured and murdered by German soldiers while serving at the camp hospital in Vilvorde, Belgium. The *Dumfries Standard* even carried a facsimile of the letter she had written to her sister, Kate Hume, on her deathbed. "Dear Kate," she wrote telegraphically, "this is to say good-bye. Have not long to live. Hospital has been set on fire. Germans cruel. A man here had his head cut off. My right breast has been taken away. Give my love to ————. Good-bye. GRACE." This letter had been personally delivered by a certain Nurse Mullard from Inverness together with a letter of her own, describing in greater detail the circumstances of Grace's death. This document recounted how the Germans had attacked and burned the hospital, killing all but 149 of 1,517 wounded men and nineteen of twenty-three nurses. Grace herself had been attacked while she was out in the fields looking for wounded soldiers. The two Germans were busy cutting off her second breast when an English soldier happened by and killed them. But it was too late to save Grace. She barely had time to scrawl her brief note before she died.

This story, sensational as it was, held up for all of a day. Grace Hume turned up safe and sound in Huddersfield, protesting that she had never been to Belgium, though she had volunteered to go there. When the *Yorkshire Post* checked back with Kate, she claimed that she had been wholly taken in by Nurse Mullard and the forged letter of her sister. *The Times* of 18 September 1914, commenting editorially on these latest developments, speculated that German agents might have had a hand in this affair, intending to discredit atrocity stories in general.

But the German agents did not hold up for very long either, as Nurse Mullard soon turned out to be a canard. On 30 September 1914 seventeen-year-old Kate Hume was charged before the Dumfries Sheriff with having committed a forgery. When she was finally tried and convicted in December, it was found that extenuating circumstances warranted a mild sentence. She had been much affected by the death of her brother, who had been the bandleader aboard the *Titanic,* and her doctor testified that, deranged by reading too much about German atrocities, she had actually persuaded herself that her sister had been killed. When the jduge released her on the grounds that she had already served three months in prison, his verdict was received with applause.[42]

The German newspapers, of course, gleefully picked up this story, while the English looked on with chagrin. Not long thereafter, however, the heroism of British womanhood was vindicated by a German atrocity of which there could be no doubt. The imagined mutilation of Nurse Hume was submerged entirely in the genuine martyrdom of Nurse Cavell. Her execution raised one of the greatest propaganda storms of the whole war and caused the Germans great harm in neutral countries, possibly even as much as the sinking of the *Lusitania.* Indeed, the Bishop of London, taking Miss Cavell's death as the subject for his Trafalgar Day sermon in the Church of St. Martin-in-the-Fields on 12 October 1915, proclaimed that "the cold blooded murder of Miss Cavell, a poor English girl, deliberately shot by Germans for housing refugees, will run the sinking of the *Lusitania* close in the civilized world as the greatest crime in history." Laurence Binyon was moved to compose a poem in fourteen uninspired stanzas depicting the various stages of German barbarity, with the following lines being fairly typical:

> And now that the deed was securely done, in the night
> When none had known her fate,
> They answered those that had striven for her, day by day:
> "It is over, you come too late."

In the lonely, dedicated, utterly proud and yet gentle figure of this woman the English at last found someone who could adequately symbolize for them their sense of outraged innocence, of a sweet virgin brutally and monstrously manhandled by the Prussian bully.[43]

The truth, perhaps unfortunately, is rarely as emotionally satisfying as fiction. Just as the *Lusitania* was later shown to be illegally transporting munitions along with its legitimate passengers, so too Nurse Cavell was not quite so innocent as she appeared to most English observers. As A. E. Clark-Kennedy was to conclude in his *Edith Cavell, Pioneer and Prophet* (1965), "in no sense was Miss Cavell a martyr, unless the meaning of that word is stretched to include every soldier who gives his life for his country in war-time." After all, as she herself admitted at her hearing, from the beginning of the war and in full knowledge of what the consequences might be, she had helped approximately two hundred French, British, and Belgian soldiers (the Bishop of London's "refugees") to escape to England and France via Holland. According to German martial law then in force in Belgium, this was unquestionably a capital offence.[44] Aware of this, she nevertheless continued, though repeatedly warned by her fellow nurses to refrain from doing so. When the German commandant of Brussels issued an order that all aliens (non-Belgians) were to carry on their persons an identity card, she failed to secure one. What is astonishing about this case is not that the Germans should have arrested Miss Cavell, but that they should have waited so long to do so. Nor was her execution quite so extraordinary an event as all the hue and cry suggested. After all, the French by this time had already shot three women and were later to shoot more, including the other famous female victim of the First World War, Mata Hari.

The British, however, whose law did not sanction the execution of women—and who were disposed to believe in German brutality in any case—were not impressed by such arguments. The soldiers at the front reacted rather differently. "I see from the papers," Frederick Keeling wrote on 11 November 1915, "that the silly sentimental agitation about Nurse Cavell still goes on at home. A good many soldiers out here don't think much of it. I have discussed it with many and found them all of my opinion—while admiring the woman immensely, I think the Germans were quite within their rights in shooting her. The agitation reveals the worst side of the English character." As the anonymous author of *War Is War* (1930), writes " . . . . we have not done booing the Germans for killing Nurse Cavell. Will nobody understand that if she did not knowingly and wilfully break the barbarous laws of war in the service of her country, well knowing the penalty, she would not have been the magnificent heroine that she undoubtedly was. If in in similar circumstances the French had shot a German nurse I think we should have managed to repress our indignation."[45]

After the war, Edith Cavell's body was exhumed and brought under Belgian army guard across Flanders to Ostend. There, draped in a Union Jack, she was placed aboard the destroyer *Rowena* and carried, under the constant watch of an officer and two men standing at attention with bayonets mounted and sword drawn, to Dover. In London she was placed atop a gun carriage drawn by six horses and accompanied by several details of cavalry and infantry. The streets to Westminster Abbey were lined ten to twenty deep with people come to pay their last respects. The ceremony in the Cathedral was headed by the Dean, and afterward her body was carried by noncommissioned officers of the Regular Army, including some she had helped to escape, to the Cathedral Close at Norwich, where she was buried, five miles from her childhood home in Swardeston.

The King of Belgium now awarded her posthumously the Cross of the Order of Leopold; the Belgian government gave her the *Croix Civique*. France made her a Chevalier of the Legion of Honor. Britain, however, could make no corresponding honorary gesture, since it possessed no decorations or honors with which to decorate deserving women—just as it had no laws to execute undeserving ones. Ironically, the martyr to Prussian militarism was given a burial with the highest military honors. And the nurse whose last and most famous words were, "patriotism is not enough," came to be one of the major focal points of British patriotism.

Not everyone succumbed to atrocity mongering. A few—a very few— insisted that the actual evidence was not conclusive and that the ultimate cause of the atrocities might lie in mass hysteria rather than in the Germans. "Personally, I would advocate much suspension of judgement," wrote Harold Picton in *Is It To Be Hate?* (1915), "as regards what went on in Belgium. Experience teaches us that at times like the present a very strange psychological atmosphere is created and the stories materialize somehow out of the air. Governesses with bombs appeared thus in the early weeks of the war. They appeared on every hand, but on official investigation they vanished away." George Bernard Shaw could not resist pointing out at least some of the irony of a situation in which the British were on the one hand protesting violently against the cruelty of the Hun while at the same time crushing the Irish Easter Rebellion with Hunnish efficiency. In the preface to "O'Flaherty, V. C., A Recruiting Pamphlet" (1916), Shaw provides some of the gruesome details of how the English used artillery in the center of Dublin and of how they executed the leading rebels, and then goes on to observe that "really it was only the usual childish petulance in which John Bull does things in a week that disgrace him for a century, though he soon recovers his good humor, and cannot understand why the survivors of his wrath do not feel as jolly with him as he does with them. On the smouldering ruins of Dublin the appeals to remember Louvain were presently supplemented by a fresh appeal. *Irishmen:* DO YOU WISH TO HAVE THE HORRORS OF WAR

BROUGHT TO YOUR OWN HEARTHS AND HOMES? Dublin laughed sourly."[46]

To some undefinable degree it is clear that the atrocity stories gained the great prominence and credence they did partly because the British public had been conditioned to expect atrocities for years beforehand—by the invasion stories and their horrific image of the cold-blooded Prussians. Some of the "favorite" varieties of atrocity had also been prefigured in other, earlier contexts, suggesting that they may have had a peculiarly horrifying attraction for the British imagination. So, for instance, there were the accounts of the crucifixion of British soldiers by the Burmese in the colonial wars of the 1880s. And at the turn of the century there was a great public outcry against the atrocities perpetrated—ironically—by the Belgians themselves in the Congo, where a considerable number of children had their hands cut off and were subjected to other kinds of torture.[47]

The most obvious connection, however, is with the Boer War. In comparison with the First World War, this conflict took place on an insignificant scale, but in terms of its psychological impact it was tremendous, anticipating in almost every respect the later reactions of the British public. In *The Pre-War Mind in Britain* (1928), C. E. Playne recalls vividly "making an appeal for a more reasonable conception of Boer women to the wife of a clergyman whom I had long known as a kindly and most hospitable person, and of the slow, deliberate answer I received: 'I hope these women will be killed, every one of them.'" And Norman Angell writes in *The Public Mind* (1927) that "in the Boer War we vilified the enemy much as later we did the Boche. Not only do we find the *Mail* telling us that the Boers are 'neither brave nor honorouble,' that they are 'cowardly and dastardly,' 'semi-savage' and 'inhuman,' 'filled with satanic premeditation,' but Mr. Swinburne gives us this picture:

> Vile foes like wolves set free,
> Whose war is waged where none may fight or flee,
> With women and with weaklings. Speech and song
> Lack utterance now for lo[a]thing. Scarce we hear
> Foul tongues that blacken God's honored name
> With prayers turned curses. . . .
> To scourge these dogs agape with jaws aflame."

This kind of "poetry" bears unmistakable promise of future effusions of the Muse of the Great War, just as Playne's kindly clergyman's wife or Swinburne's "whelps and dams of murderous foes" anticipate stories like Kipling's "Mary Postgate" and "Swept and Garnished."[48]

Perhaps we should not be unduly surprised by this sort of psychological phenomenon. The modern practice of "total war" requires atrocities, whether real or imagined, to work the population up to the fever pitch necessary to sustain the will of the government, especially in a long and arduous conflict. No doubt in the course of the war many genuine atrocities were committed, although almost certainly fewer than the Bryce Report indicated. Guilt for these atrocities, however, was shared by both sides; indeed, one American historian, H. E. Barnes, was later to maintain in *The Genesis of the World War* (1926) that ". . . the one true and perfectly authenticated 'atrocity' in the World War, and the situation which produced by far the greatest suffering and death among the civilian population was the illegal blockading of Germany, continued for months after the Armistice."[49]

Where the guilt lay and just how it should be apportioned are not questions that need concern us here. What does concern us is that these atrocity stories about the Germans were believed by virtually the whole of the British population during the war and, despite evidence suggesting they were untrue, after the war. Hence Stephen McKenna could assert unabashedly in 1921: "It is not surprising that among those who remember, the name of a German stinks and the presence of a German is an outrage." It sometimes seems almost as if the Germans behaved with the real brutality they did in the Second World War because no one would have believed they could have behaved otherwise. In this way the horrors of the imagination can help provoke the horrors of reality.[50]

The stench of the Hun was vile and it infected the atmosphere for many years after the war. But to a lesser and more tolerable degree other foreigners stank too. Morally, no inhabitant of another nation could match an English gentleman, who had achieved, as H. Rider Haggard once put it, "the highest rank to which we can attain." The consciousness of their innate moral superiority was the cause in the British public mind of the very natural conviction that any foreigner who opposed himself to the British will was *ipso facto* opposing the virtues of gentleness, chivalry, honor, sportsmanship, democracy and, in a word, civilization. Hence, by a simple but extremely persuasive logical step, an enemy could not help but be barbaric and brutal. How very powerful this feeling was can best be judged by Bertrand Russell's relieved remark in the Preface to *Justice in War Time* (1917) that the actual Bryce Report had turned out to be milder than what the great mass of people actually thought had taken place. Undoubtedly all the nations of Europe at this time shared the conviction of inevitable superiority about themselves, particularly the Germans. But even they did not have the complete assurance that centuries of peace at home and a nearly unbroken record of military success abroad can confer. With the citizen of another country it was, my country right or wrong; with the typical Englishman at the beginning of the Great War, it was inconceivable that his country might be wrong.

Conclusion

You will always be fools and we shall never be gentlemen.
Captured German officer to his British interrogator

If only God had forgotten to create male Germans and
female Germans I should have no complaint to make.
Virginia Woolf to Angus Davidson, 4 April 1927

The shift in the British conception of Germany, which had begun in the last years of the nineteenth century, inevitably gained tremendous force and momentum during the war. By 1915, as we have seen, the German cousin was dead, never again to be resurrected except by cranks and Nazi-sympathizers at the fringes of British political life.[1] "It was in 1915," D. H. Lawrence was to recall in his novel *Kangaroo* (1923), "the old world ended."[2] From then onward, the German national character was to remain indelibly fixed in the British psyche. It was, in its main outlines and extreme form, efficient, disciplined, humorless; cold yet paradoxically sentimental; dull, vulgar, and barbaric, yet inordinately proud of its "Kultur"; viciously cruel on "principle"; unbearably arrogant when victorious, abjectly cringing in defeat. In short, it was the "hun." By 1970, it had become obvious, as one critic put it, that in contrast to the nineteenth century, "today a serious interest in German life and thought is the exception among English novelists. Almost invariably Germans and their way of life are only portrayed from a negative point of view."[3]

During the interwar years and once more after the Second World War— that is, at times when the hun seemed more ridiculous than dangerous—the British press became the site of a sport known as hun-baiting. There, in articles, reviews, and letters-to-the-editor, the antics of the hun, especially of the Herr Professor variety, would be detailed and subtly mocked. A. E. Housman was particularly adept at the game; he kept in readiness a notebook filled with ironic barbs, with blank spaces where the name of some unfortunate Herr Professor could be inserted.[4]

After the Great War even those who felt some sympathy with Germany's claims that she was not the only guilty party or that the Versailles Treaty was a vindictive attempt to humiliate her, could not summon up equal sympathy for the individual Germans whom they actually met (or, if they did, then only by a supreme effort). John Maynard Keynes—who better than any other Englishman of the time recognized the potential for disaster built into the treaty's reparations clauses and who did his utmost to try to get food to Germany during the blockade—even Keynes could not free himself from stereotypical responses. Going to meet a German delegation from the new revolutionary socialist government shortly after the Armistice, he found that they "satisfied wonderfully, as a group, the popular conception of Huns. The personal appearance of that race is extraordinarily against them. Who knows but that it was the real cause of the war!"[5] This remark, though meant to be humorous, serves more to mask Keynes's prejudice than to disclaim it.

During the late 1920s and early 1930s, there was a brief resurgence of interest in Germany and things German among British intellectuals. The interest was chiefly artistic, sexual, and political, and showed itself most powerfully in the poetry and fiction of the so-called Auden group. Auden himself was the first of this group of young men to go to Berlin in 1928, and it was the glowing reports he sent back to his friends of the excitements of sexual freedom and political conflict there that led them to follow. The result was, aside from Auden's own remarkable *Poems* (1930), Christopher Isherwood's wonderfully evocative Berlin novels—later to reach a mass public in two film versions, *I Am a Camera* and *Cabaret*—as well as Stephen Spender's poems and translations of Rilke. For a very short time, until the Nazis came to power, Germany came once again to seem to a few but quite influential English writers a model that Britain might well emulate.[6]

Of the members of the Auden group, however, only Auden himself was to preserve more than a passing sympathy for Germany. For the rest—for Isherwood, Spender, and Edward Upward—the interest had never really gone beyond politics and sex to culture.[7] With Auden it did. He continued to steep himself in German existential philosophy and theology, to translate German literature (Goethe and Brecht), and in 1956 even to purchase a small farmhouse in the provincial Austrian village of Kirchstetten. It would not be too much to say that it was due to Auden, more than to any other single Englishman, that the flow of German art and thought into the English-speaking world was reestablished after the traumas of two world wars.

But Auden was—and remains—very much an exception. Much more typical is a response like George Orwell's. In his well-known essay on Kipling (1942), Orwell tries to exonerate Kipling from some of the charges of "fascism" and racism that are often leveled against him. Taking the line "Lesser breeds without the Law," from "Recessional" (1897), Orwell observes that it does not refer, as is so often taken for granted in "pansy-left circles," to the Indians or the Chinese, but "almost certainly to the Germans." Somehow, though Orwell does not explain how, that makes everything all right. Thinking in terms of "lesser breeds" and "higher breeds" is apparently not reprehensible as long as it is confined to Germans.[8]

It would appear that, as D. C. Watt remarks in his *Britain Looks to Germany* (1965), that the British view of Germany resembles the mentality of the Bourbons on their restoration to the French throne in 1815: they had learned nothing and had forgotten nothing. So it is, writes Watt, with Britain twenty years after the conclusion of the Second World War; but so, he adds, it was also with Britain and France: "After the twenty years war with France in its revolutionary and Napoleonic phases it took British opinion nearly half a century to recover its sense of balance."[9] Fifty years, then, is the period necessary for a sane reassessment of national character after a great war. In the year 2,000 the British view of Germany will once again be more or less what it was in 1865, fifty years before the outbreak of the First World War. Perhaps Watt is right. But one may be permitted to have one's doubts. The hun, I suspect, is too deeply rooted in the British psyche to wither away even after half a century. Like his infamous predecessor and namesake, it is more likely that he will be haunting the memory—and the imagination—of Englishmen for centuries to come.

Appendix: The Nature and Uses of Imagology

Imagology can be broadly defined as the study of national/ethnic/racial/cultural images or stereotypes as they appear in literary contexts. Imagology explicitly includes the study of literary images of other groups (hetero-images) as well as images of one's own group (auto-images). Indeed, as I shall argue later, the one is not possible without the other.

Under other names, imagology has had a fairly long if not overly respectable history, one that has been surveyed most sympathetically and thoroughly by the Belgian comparatist Hugo Dyserinck in his 1966 *Arcadia* essay, "Zum Problem der 'images' und 'mirages' und ihrer Untersuchung im Rahmen der Vergleichenden Literaturwissenschaft," and, with somewhat different emphases, in two sections of his book, *Komparatistik: Eine Einführung* (1977; 1981), entitled "Franzoesische und amerikanische Komparatistenschule" and "Komparatistische Imagologie." Indeed, Dyserinck may be credited with adopting and adapting this word for use in literary study—and for having done more than anyone else to make it theoretically and academically respectable.

That different national, ethnic, regional, racial, and cultural groups have had quite specific and often (supposedly humorous) derogatory "images" of other corresponding groups is a fact which is so obvious that it requires no further discussion. That such images or stereotypes frequently appear in significant literary contexts should be equally obvious, since literature always reflects, directly and/or indirectly, the culture out of which it springs. More problematic is providing a convincing rationale for the study of such images.

A common—and by no means irrelevant or unimportant—justification is that they should be investigated because, like Mount Everest, they are there. This seems to be the reasoning behind a work like Salvador de Madariaga's *Portrait of Europe* (1952), which seeks to categorize the major European population/language groups according to their supposed group characteristics, partly on the basis of linguistic and literary data. The same is true of a now largely discredited but formerly highly influential kind of imagological study based on the assumed climatic differences between northern and southern Europe. Of these, Madame de Staël's *De l'Allemagne* is perhaps the best-known example.

Here, however, one already recognizes another, not always openly acknowledged rationale for the presentation and study of group images: a rationale one might broadly call political—which, if "political" is indeed broadly enough defined, forms the real basis for the study of such images and stereotypes. For the "polis" ultimately includes all of the important social aspects of humanity, including the literary aspects.

Madame de Staël's book (like Tacitus's *Germania* before it) may be understood more accurately as an attempt to change/correct the auto-image of her primary audience—France at the close of Napoleon's reign—than really to portray the Germans in an objective fashion. The same is true, it must be admitted, of even some of the most distinguished modern practitioners of comparative literature: even of, say Ernst Robert Curtius's *Die franzoesische Kultur* (1920) or of Jean-Marie Carré's *Les Ecrivains français et le mirage allemand, 1800–1940* (1947). As late as 1978 the latter book was praised by another distinguished French comparatist, Marius-François Guyard, in a reprint of *La Littérature comparée* (1951), as "un livre precieux" and presented as a model of imagological study, despite the fact that it fails utterly to live up to its stated standard of objectivity and is in reality a topical book meant to arouse the French of the immediate postwar period to the danger of succumbing once again to a "mirage" of Germany. Carré's book is, in fact, the mirror image of Madame de Staël's, presenting as it does a Germany populated not with "Dichter und Denker" but "Richter und Henker."

It should not be surprising, therefore, that in the 1950s the great American comparatist, René Wellek, denounced all such work—that is, imagology both root and branch—as the mere products of their authors' national/cultural/ethnic prejudice, and as being wholly irrelevant to the study of literature. As even Hugo Dyserinck has admitted, it would be unwise to simply disregard Wellek's objections and proceed with business as usual. There can be no question but that Wellek is right in perceiving much if not most imagological work as partly or primarily motivated by political considerations which, in extreme cases, may render such work worthless as literary criticism, though it may provide valuable evidence for an imagological study of the persistence of group stereotypes among imagologists and comparatists themselves. Wellek is wrong, however, in suggesting that literary study can be conducted in an apolitical vacuum, for it should be obvious that insisting on being apolitical is itself a very political attitude. This must not be taken to mean, however, that it is legitimate to give rein to one's political views under the guise of literary criticism; it means simply that one must always be aware of the political context of one's work and not pretend to a non-existent objectivity. The objectivity lies *not* in the absence of politics; but in the consciousness of its presence. This applies as much to Carré's chauvinist politics as it does to the often pious expressions of hope at the close of discussions justifying the existence and practice of imagology—or of comparative literature, for that matter—that such study will serve to promote amity and better understanding among nations. I myself, I might add, share that view; but I also know that it is a political view.

That imagological study is not literary study is, in the mid 1980s, a charge that seems less forceful or threatening than it apparently did in the fifties. Wellek and Warren's famous theoretical fulminations against the introduction of so-called extrinsic methodologies (impurities) into the sacred realm of the intrinsic study of literature have largely gone up in smoke. The quest for pure "literariness" has passed the way of the quest for other absolutes; and methodology (whether structuralist, psychoanalytic, imagological or other) is no longer thought of as inexorably tied to a single discipline, like the study of literature. Literary study is today largely defined by its subject matter, not by its approach.

Nor, for that matter, are methodologies pure or absolute either. Inevitably, imagology shares certain methodological concerns with other more familiar critical procedures. Like Marxist and other socially oriented types of criticism, it focuses on the ways in which culturally, racially, or ethnically identifiable groups (e.g., blacks or Protestants or Italians) are presented in the literary productions of a definable historical period, and what assumptions underlie that presentation; though unlike such criticism—and including feminist criticism, for that matter—it does not necessarily center on oppressed or underprivileged groups, though it may do so. Imagology shares with *Geistesgeschichte* and especially with literary thematics a conviction that ideas, including preconceived ideas, exercise a determinable influence on group behavior and not merely social and economic power centers. In other words, imagology depends on the assumption that literature profoundly influences how we think and what we are.

Imagology deals with the literary "projections" of the group imagination; the relation between imagology and the imagination is not merely nominal. In this respect, imagology has affinities with some of the major concerns of psychoanalytic criticism, especially those with a Jungian orientation, since imagological projections are closely related to the conception of archetypes, being like them chiefly unconscious and nonrational. It is not surprising, therefore, that discussions of imagological theory and/or practice should find a welcome reception in the pages of *Ethnopsychologie, Revue de Psychologie des Peuples,* published by the University of Le Havre.

Though, as we have seen, imagology has a fairly long history, it should not be considered simply a continuation or modernized version of the so-called "Bild" or "image" studies of the past. While such studies were and often are useful for imagological work, they were too often content to be mere inventories of, say, Germans in English literature or blacks in American literature. Imagology, properly conceived, goes beyond such mere cate-gorizing and cataloguing, not only by problematizing its subject but by focusing on the ways in which the images of others help to define the group/national identity/solidarity of the author and his primary audience. In the present study, for example, Germans tend to function as the defective mirror image of the English. They represent a—or even *the*—difference by means of which English national self-awareness is maintained and reinforced. A study like this one, therefore, of English literary representation of Germans during the decades immediately preceding and following the turn of the century is *and must be* at least equally a study of English self-representation.

Imagology is potentially a valid methodological approach for the whole existing range of literary production, though there are good reasons for limiting imagological analysis to specific, easily definable areas, since the conclusions based on such analysis will obviously vary, depending on the audience(s) for whom a given literary work or category of works was originally designed. So it is clear that an imagological study of children's books, of horror comics, of supermarket romances, or of American intellec-tual quarterlies will be valid only for each category rather than for the target culture as a whole.

Imagological analysis of canonical texts, however, is especially valuable, since these latter may be said to incorporate the officially accepted values of a culture. They therefore function as exemplars of the most privileged literary experience available to the educated class of a given society and are usually mediated through elite institutions like universities. These institutions in turn influence the outlook of the mass media in a way quite disproportionate to their numbers.

Though in practical terms the canon is composed by definition of texts that are continuously and minutely picked over, these texts are nevertheless rarely examined from the point of view of how they represent ethnic or national groupings, and how such representation influences readers' percep-tions of those groups. Conrad's "Heart of Darkness," for example, is one of the classic testing grounds for innovative critical methodology. It is certainly among the four or five short novels that are most frequently taught in introductory literature courses all over the English-speaking world. It is the subject of at least a dozen critical essays every year. Yet how many teachers of—or students in—those courses, or how many of the authors of those essays, think it important, or perhaps even know, what the ethnic origins of the mysterious figure at the center of the story, Kurtz, are? Or what overtones of ethnic/cultural superiority the name of Conrad's narrator and alter-ego, Marlow, has? Or what the implied contrast between British and Belgian imperialism signifies? Or what the connection is between the Belgian conquerors (not colonists) in the Congo and the Roman conquerors (again not colonists) in Britain? Yet in the answers to these questions lie important clues to our response to this story and at least part of our final acceptance of Kurtz and Marlow as "superior" people—superior *English* people.

What the imagological critic hopes to demonstrate by answering questions such as these is that even the most serious kinds of literature function to reinforce stereotypes of our own group identity, usually by contrast with other group identities. Thus, in "Heart of Darkness" an initial contrast between Romans and Britons (and Rome and London) as imperial bearers of light into darkness, is followed by later (related) oppositions/contrasts between the Belgians (and by implication other imperialist nations like the Germans and French), between the Europeans as a whole and the Africans, between a Kurtz who has been partly educated in England and is partly of English descent and his nameless Russian admirer, and finally between Kurtz (a name with obvious German overtones) and super-English Marlow. All of these contrasts serve to isolate those characteristics that are supposedly peculiarly, as Conrad was fond of putting it, "ours."

The establishment of group identity by means of differentiation from other group identities is by no means an innovation of Conrad's fiction. It has always been one of the principal functions of literature from the very beginning of human literacy. The grandest of the ancient literary forms, the epic, is also the most immediately concerned with defining, by means of exemplary heroes engaged in exemplary actions, the nature of national/ cultural identity. Hellenic, as contrasted with Trojan, identity is an important aspect of the *Iliad,* just as Odysseus's identity as Greek and Ithacan is crucial to an understanding of *The Odyssey*—a point that James Joyce was well aware of when seeking to define Irish national identity some three thousand years later. So too with the *Aeneid,* where a new Roman identity is carefully established by contrasting it with Trojan, Greek, Carthaginian, and Latin models.

The imagological critic, however, is not confined to asking the same questions of a variety of discrete canonical texts. Such questions are only the first steps to another, broader inquiry relating to the ways in which literature both reflects and changes the consciousness of group identity. So, for example, the imagological critic might trace the development of English or German or French stereotypes of literary identity from the Renaissance to the nineteenth century, seeking to show how those stereotypes underwent significant change. Such self-definition must of necessity involve some degree of redefinition of other important rival groups. So the investigation of single-group stereotypes always involves investigation of the wider social/ cultural context of definition.

Imagology fully accepts the consequences of assuming that literature reflects, though by no means in a naive or uncomplicated fashion, the active forces in the society that produces it. To return to my earlier example, a proper imagological understanding of what Conrad is doing in "Heart of Darkness" needs to be based on a historical awareness of what was happening in King Leopold's Congo in the closing decade of the last century, how the British public reacted to reports of Belgian atrocities there, how—on a more general level—the British believed in their identity as not only a conquering but also as a colonizing people, how all this activity was clothed in an ethic of supposed national/racial duty to bring the benefits of civilization to what Kipling notoriously referred to as "lesser breeds without the Law." Finally, there is also a personal, autobiographical context that must be considered in Conrad's case—the special need of the outsider to urge his oneness with his newly chosen people. It is only when "Heart of Darkness"—and by extension, of course, any other literary work—is placed in these social, historical and biographical contexts that the imagological analysis becomes convincing.

There is a further step, however. For literature is not merely reflective; it is also active. The social and political context is a necessary precondition for a story like "Heart of Darkness," but the story, once it has come into existence, also serves to reinforce aspects of that context. The contemporaneous British reader—as some of the reviews of Conrad's work at this time testify—would have identified with Marlow and his group of similarly minded listeners aboard the *Nellie,* the self-conscious heirs of the great tradition of Elizabethan literature and world conquest, of explorers and pirates from Drake to Franklin—and would have understood Kurtz's famous "horror" as induced chiefly by an inefficient and un-English colonial master rather than due to any fundamental aspects of the human condition. In this way, Conrad's story served to reinforce existing group stereotypes rather than merely reflect them.

Imagology, then, is not simply a new critical game, designed to provide players at universities around the world with enjoyment and employment. It is that, undeniably, like all academic work, regardless of the discipline. But it is also more: it is a means of self-discovery, a way of looking at others which is also a way of looking at ourselves. It is also the discovery that only by looking at the other can we really see ourselves. Or that by changing the way we look at others, we can also change ourselves.

Notes

Introduction. National Character and "Race"

1. Ramsay Muir, *Nationalism and Internationalism* (London: Constable, 1917), p. 38. The best general overview of nationalism is Hans Kohn's *The Idea of Nationalism* (New York: Macmillan, 1948). But see also John Oakesmith, *Race and Nationality* (London: Heinemann, 1919); and Bernard Joseph, *Nationality: Its Nature and Its Problems* (London: Allen & Unwin, 1929).

2. Salvador de Madariaga, *Portrait of Europe* (London: Hollis & Carter, 1952), pp. 92–94.

3. Willa Muir, "Translating from German," in *On Translation*, ed. Reuben Brower (New York: Oxford, 1966), pp. 95–96. Muir may have borrowed this idea from Ezra Pound who in a 1917 review of Joyce's *Ulysses* blamed the "hell of contemporary Europe" on the lack of democratic institutions in Germany and on "the non-existence of decent prose in the German language. . . . The mush of the German sentence, the straddling of the verb out to the end, are just as much a part of the befoozlement of Kultur and the consequent hell, as was the rhetoric of the later Roman Empire's decadence and extinction." Pound goes on to single out Heine and Frederick the Great as the only "decent" prose writers in Germany, without appearing to be aware that the latter wrote only in French. See "At Last the Novel Appears," in James Joyce, *A Portrait of the Artist as a Young Man*, ed. Chester Anderson (New York: Viking, 1968), pp. 323–24.

4. E. H. Dance, *History the Betrayer, A Study in Bias* (London: Hutchinson, 1960), p. 9.

5. Max Müller, *Biographies of Words and the Home of the Aryas* (London: Longman's, 1888), p. 245. Quoted in the *Encyclopedia Britannica* (Eleventh ed.), under "Aryan."

6. Hilaire Belloc, *Cautionary Tales* (London: Duckworth, 1939), p. 127. That Belloc's well-known anti-imperialism did not preclude him from being a racist as well is evident from *The Modern Traveller* (1898), where one of the supposedly humorous sketches depicts an American black, with the following couplet attached: "Observe the face of William Jackson,/How typical an Anglo-Saxon!"

7. Isaac Taylor, *The Origin of the Aryans*. 4th ed. (London: Scott, 1914), pp. 73 and 244–46. As late as the twenties of this century, Taylor's views on the relation of "race" and character are repeated—even amplified—in supposedly serious works of history and cultural anthropology. Harold Peake, for example, asserts categorically that the Nordic Race shows "at all times . . . a marked degree of courage . . . both physical and moral," whereas the Alpines "are not as a rule a warlike people, or one possessed of courage in a high degree. . . ." *The English Village: The Origin and Decay of Its Community* (London: Benn Brothers, 1922), pp. 51–52. See also Dean William Ralph Inge's "The White Man and His Rivals," in *Outspoken Essays* (London: Longmans, 1923), pp. 209–11.

8. Arabella B. Buckley, *History of England for Beginners* (London: Macmillan, 1887), pp. 5–6. Attempts to discover remnants of the non-Germanic inhabitants of ancient Britain in the present population became increasingly frequent in the immediate postwar period. Hence, in

his chapter on "Race and Language" in *The Changing Face of England* (London: Nisbet, 1927), pp. 243–44, Anthony Collett informs us of the African and Asian origins of the Cornish in the following terms: "Watching the Cornish faces, all the old racial legends seem true. See that tall, lean, loose-limbed figure pitching swedes in a cow-barton. . . . That dark face and mop of frizzled hair make him almost more like a Somali than an Englishman—a Somali tempered by Western rain and school boards, and with fried locusts changed for pastries and cream. . . . Lift your elbows from the barton wall, or step from the little shop, and the next face you see may be straight from Mongolia. It is flat and round, and with the eyes as tilted as a Chinaman's. . . . Some ancestor whose face that lad's mirrors may have led a horde of the sons of Turan over the flats of the Dogger Bank on foot into England, crossing the great estuary of the joint Thames and Rhine. Africa and Asia confront each other in a Cornish street. . . ." D. H. Lawrence also writes occasionally of the Cornish in a similar vein. More "scientifically," the distinguished Cambridge anthropologist A. C. Haddon finds traces of prehistoric racial residue in his *Races of Man and Their Distribution* (New York: Macmillan, 1925), p. 86, where the "Beaker-folk"— characterized by a broad head and "flattened occiput" with a "fine but often receding forehead, long face, rugged features, prominent brow ridges, strong nose of moderate width"—are seen as belonging to a physical type "well known in the north and east of Ireland; a survival of the type appears to persist in some intellectual British families."

In much the same way, F. G. Crookshank notes that "any ordinary observer . . . may easily observe within the compass of a day's ramble in London a range of Mongolian or semi-Mongolian types amongst our native Cockneys." Also there are natively British "mongoloids of the higher grade" who "sometimes achieve marked success on the stage, in the professions, and even in Parliament." See *The Mongol in Our Midst: A Study of Man and His Three Faces* (London: Kegan Paul, 1924), pp. 15 and 18–19.

According to R. N. Bradley the aboriginal population of ancient Britain was Arabic-speaking and of African descent. The word *lad,* for example, is derived from the Arabic *walad,* meaning "boy"; *soot* comes from the Arabic word for "black"; many old river names, like Thames and Swale, are of Arabic origin; and Salisbury Plain especially is "full of Arabic place-names. . . ." The subsequent Celtic invaders, few in number, were "at an early date, swallowed up in the population," of which the "short dark Silures of South Wales" are a surviving representative sample. The dark Hamites, however, inexplicably turn out, later in Bradley's study, to be "always characterized by a tendency to blondness," though this still does not give them an edge over the third stratum of the population, the Nordics, who being "tall, blue-eyed, fair-haired, courageous, chivalrous," enjoy superior "sexual selection" and are "the backbone of our character and institutions. . . ." See R. N. Bradley, *Racial Origins of the English Character* (London: Allen & Unwin, 1926), pp. 6, 10, 26, 28, 182.

9. Thomas Nicholas, *Pedigree of the English People* (London: Longman's, 1868), p. 20.

10. A. H. Keane, *Ethnology* (Cambridge: University Press, 1909), p. 410. Keane probably picked this idea up from C. W. Dilke's *Greater Britain* (1868), where the phenomenon is attributed to "racial pride."

11. Ernest Baker, *National Character and the Factors in Its Formation* (London: Methuen, 1927), pp. 23, 26, 30, and 39.

12. William McDougall, *Is America Safe for Democracy?* (New York: Scribner's, 1921), pp. 79 and 182. The distinguished Liberal politician and social critic C. F. G. Masterman is similarly worried in *England After War* (New York: Harcourt, Brace & Co., 1923), p. 246, that the declining birthrate in Britain will mean the end of white supremacy. "If this process continues," he predicts, "we can see a world in which the dominant white races, dwindling in number, or outswarmed by others, will occupy but a tiny fragment of territory crowded with Jews and Chinamen and Indians, and the various races at present deemed 'uncivilised.' "

13. Havelock Ellis, *The New Spirit* (New York: Boni & Liveright, n.d.), pp. 20–21.

14. C. H. Pearson, *National Life and Character: A Forecast* (London: Macmillan, 1894), pp. 14 and 90.

15. Francis Galton, *Hereditary Genius* (London: Macmillan, 1914), p. x, 327 and 330.

16. Havelock Ellis, *A Study of British Genius* (London: Constable, 1914), p. 9.

17. Karl Pearson, *National Life from the Standpoint of Science* (Cambridge: University Press, [1905]), pp. 21–23, and 46. How widely these assumptions about Africans were shared is especially clear from the way in which others disagreed with Pearson. The distinguished anthropologist H. J. Fleure, for instance, writes in *The Races of Mankind* (London: Benn, 1927), p. 35, that "it is felt by many that the best Bantu stocks have large possibilities of development under the best European guidance, whatever may be the ultimate fate of the lowlier peoples, for the mere hunters can hardly survive the multiplication of European contacts. The need of stable and healthy African societies is a very great one, as the future of the world's civilisation is intimately bound up with the assurance of supplies from the intertropical lands, supplies that only native peoples can produce in such climates."

Chapter 1. The Death of the German Cousin

1. George Steiner, *In Bluebeard's Castle* (New Haven: Yale University Press, 1973), esp. pp. 47–48.

2. John Mander, "Must We Love the Germans?" *Encounter* 33 (December 1969): 36.

3. Fighting under Wellington's command at Waterloo was also "The King's German Legion," established in 1803 and composed chiefly of Hanoverians. They fought well enough to be considered by Wellington "worthy of being Britons." One of the Legion's officers was Count Friedrich Wilhelm von Bismarck, who was forced to depart hurriedly from England because of a duel.

4. Quoted in Sir Joshua Fitch, *Thomas and Matthew Arnold* (New York: Scribners, 1898), p. 115.

5. Charles Kingsley, *The Roman and the Teuton* (London: Macmillan, 1875), pp. 226, 95, and 305; Edward Freeman, *The Chief Periods of European History* (London: Macmillan, 1886), p. 64.

6. Quoted in Richard Faber, *The Vision and the Need, Late Victorian Imperialist Aims* (London: Faber & Faber, 1966), p. 76; and Cecil Chesterton, *The Prussian Hath Said in His Heart* (London: Chapman & Hall, 1914), p. 82.

7. Even as late as 1913, J. A. Cramb maintained in the series of lectures subsequently published as *Germany and England* (London: John Murray, 1914), p. 11, that "the war of 1870 with France was a war of great revenge, of *just* revenge, and for one of the greatest causes. No war in history, perhaps, was ever more just than the war which Bismarck and Moltke waged against France." Carlyle is, of course, always mentioned as the principal British champion of the German cause in 1870, and rightly so. Tennyson, however, also railed against the "red fool fury on their Seine" at the time of the Paris Commune; Charles Kingsley maintained that, had he been German, he would have sent his last son, his last shilling and even himself "to get that done which must be done so that it will never need doing again." His brother, Henry Kingsley, published a novel, *Valentin* (1872), on the whole sympathetic to the Germans; and Coventry Patmore and Alfred Austin published poems supporting Prussia. Others, pro-French or neutral at first, gradually drifted toward supporting Germany. "This war," Meredith wrote his son in October 1870, "is chargeable upon France, and the Emperor [Napoleon III] is the Knave of the pack." As for the German annexation of Alsace-Lorraine, it should be remembered that at the Congress of Vienna in 1815, the British mission had been instructed to cede to Germany not only Alsace-Lorraine but also Belgium and Burgundy. Even as late as 1915, W. L. George could

write openly of the "filching of Strasbourg" by the French. For the above citations, see Albert Martin, *The Last Crusade* (Durham, N.C.: Duke University Press, 1974), p. 85; Friedrich Brie, *Imperialistische Strömungen in der englischen Literatur* (Halle: Niemeyer, 1928), pp. 193–95; George Meredith, *The Letters*, vol. 1, ed. L. L. Cline (Oxford: Clarendon Press, 1970), pp. 424–41; Heinrich Fränkel, *Deutschland im Urteil des Auslandes Früher und—Jetzt* (Munich: Georg Müller, 1916), p. 21; and W. L. George, "The Price of Nationality," *English Review* 20 (1915): 195. According to Paul M. Kennedy's *The Rise of the Anglo-German Antagonism, 1860–1914* (London: Allen & Unwin, 1980), p. 92, British press opinion was largely on the German side in 1870.

8. George Bernard Shaw, *What I Really Wrote About the War* (New York: Brentano, 1931), p. 23; and Disraeli quoted in Kurt Meine, *England und Deutschland in der Zeit des Ueberganges vom Manchestertum zum Imperialismus, 1871 bis 1876* (Berlin: Ebering, 1937), p. 38.

9. This attribution is odd in view of Disraeli's strong public denunciation of *The Battle of Dorking*. By 1875 Disraeli believed that "Britain and Germany should always go hand in hand because they shared common interests and views, race and religion." See Kennedy, *Rise*, pp. 27 and 29.

10. Quoted in Michael Holroyd, *Lytton Strachey, A Critical Biography* (New York: Holt, Rinehart, & Winston, 1968), 2:59.

11. H. G. Wells, *The War in the Air* (London: G. Bell & Sons, 1908), pp. 242–43.

12. Charles Doughty's play *The Cliffs* (1909) also sees the submarine as a critical factor in a German invasion.

13. E. S. Turner, *Boys Will Be Boys* (London: Michael Joseph, 1948), p. 176.

14. "A World at Stake!" *The Magnet* 9 (31 October 1914): 1; Arnold Bennett, *Journals, 1911–1921*, ed. Newman Flower (London: Cassell, 1932), p. 122.

15. I. E. Clarke, *Voices Prophesying War, 1763–1914* (London: Oxford, 1966), pp. 144–45. For further discussion of invasion stories, see Samuel Hynes, *The Edwardian Turn of Mind* (Princeton: Princeton University Press, 1968), pp. 34–53.

16. Orton James Hale, *Publicity and Diplomacy, With Special Reference to England and Germany, 1890–1914* (New York: Appleton-Century, 1940), p. 374; and Laurence Thompson, *Robert Blatchford, Portrait of an Englishman* (London: Gollancz, 1951), p. 223; and Turner, *Boys*, p. 173.

17. H. H. Munro, *When William Came, A Story of London under the Hohenzollerns* (New York: Viking Press, 1929), p. 83. Saki's novel pretty clearly owes a debt to A. J. Dawson's invasion fantasy, *The Message* (1907), in which the Germans also initially overrun London but are eventually defeated, with the Kaiser having to abdicate (and Napoleon III thereby revenged) and a German republic proclaimed.

18. Lord Archibald Rosebery, *War: A Fight to the Finish* (Stirling: Eneas Mackay, [1914]), pp. 10–11. In *The War of Ideas* (London: Oxford University Press, 1917), p. 7, Sir Walter Raleigh claims that "if we were not sure of the ultimate issue of this great struggle, we should have no sufficient motive for continuing to breathe." How widespread this British Masada complex was may be judged from John Buchan's "The German Mind," *Land and Water* 5 (6 November 1915): 19, where we are told that "if Germany's claims were admitted few honest men would desire to continue their life on this planet."

19. Clarke, *Voices*, pp. 152–53; and G. H. Perris, *Our Foreign Policy and Sir Edward Grey's Failure* (London: Andrew Melrose, 1912), pp. 152–53.

20. Hale, *Publicity*, p. 338; Churchill quoted in F. W. Hirst, *The Six Panics and Other Essays* (London: Methuen, 1913), p. 91; and Kennedy, *Rise*, p. 253.

21. L. S. Amery, *My Political Life* (London: Hutchinson, 1953), 1:214, Hale *Publicity*, pp. 340 and 336.

22. The Earl Percy, "Military Policy and the War," *National Review* 57 (August 1911): 957

and 968. As early as 1904, Major-General Sir James M. Grierson, Director of Military Operations, conducted a "war game" with Germany as the enemy invading France through Belgium
and encountering "united Anglo-French opposition." In March 1905 Grierson assured the
French government of British support in the event of war. In January 1906 the new Liberal
Foreign Secretary, Sir Edward Grey, approved of continued military conversations with the
French. See J. McDermott, "The Revolution in British Military Thinking from the Boer Crisis
to the Moroccan Crisis," in P. M. Kennedy, ed., *The War Plans of the Great Powers, 1880–1914*
(London: Allen & Unwin, 1978), pp. 104–111. On 23 August 1911 the Committee on Imperial
Defence met with a select group of ministers to discuss strategy. General Sir Henry Wilson
outlined his plans for committing six or seven divisions of the British Expeditionary Force to the
Northwest European theater. Thereafter there was no doubt on the part of the French about
British intentions to intervene in their behalf. Kennedy, *Rise,* p. 449.

23. Bertrand Russell, *Portraits from Memory* (London: Allen & Unwin, 1956), p. 30; and
Perris, *Our,* p. 45. The anti-German attitude of the Foreign Office predates the Liberal Govern-
ment by several years, reaching back at least as far as the last year of the Boer War. See Chandran
Jeshuran, "Lord Lansdowne and the 'Anti-German Clique' at the Foreign Office." *Journal of
Southeast Asian Studies* 3 (September 1972): 229.

That anti-German feeling was by no means confined to the Foreign Office, which rather
reflected widespread public opinion, is suggested by I. A. R. Wylie in *The Germans* (Indianapolis: Bobbs-Merrill, 1911), p. 3. where the British are said to "go on, hating, despising,
tolerating, or ignoring the race to which we are so closely connected, not according to our
knowledge, which is often *nil,* but according to our characters and our inherited prejudices." So
too Lady Phillips, in *A Friendly Germany: Why Not?* (London: Constable, 1913), p. 2, assumes
at the outset of her argument that "a very great number of British citizens to-day, if not an actual
majority" are fundamentally hostile to Germany.

24. Zara S. Steiner, *The Foreign Office and Foreign Policy, 1898–1914* (Cambridge: Cambridge University Press, 1969), pp. 112–13; and Amery, *Life,* p. 227. See also Hale, *Publicity,*
p. 370, for the Foreign Office memorandum of April 1909, written by Charles Hardinge, in
which any agreement with Germany is described as a "trap," a view that "became a fixed dogma
in the influential circles that controlled British policy." Grey's Germanophobia was so extreme
that in 1907 he threatened to resign "if the band of the Coldstream Guards visited Germany";
and by May of the same year, even Edward VII was perturbed and thought that "Grey was too
anti-German for his tastes." Kennedy, *Rise,* pp. 283 and 403. See also Ronald W. Clark, *The Life
of Bertrand Russell* (New York: Knopf, 1976), p. 244, where Charles Sanger is quoted as writing
to Russell in August 1914 that "I have always regarded Grey as one of the most wicked and
dangerous criminals that has [*sic.*] ever degraded civilisation. . . ."

25. Robert Graves, *Good-bye to All That* (Garden City, N.Y.: Doubleday, 1957), pp. 58 and
39. Graves's friend and biographer, Martin Seymour-Smith, writes of his subject's early German
home environment as including Christmas celebrations "in the German tradition, which means
heavily, overjovially, and overactively." But Graves's honor is saved, since "he has only ever read
in the language with the greatest reluctance—and has never read a whole book in it." See *Robert
Graves, His Life and Work* (New York: Holt, Rinehart & Winston, 1982), p. 29.

As in Graves's case, a similar connection between Germanophobia and anti-Semitism is made
in Saki's *When William Came.* That it was not an uncommon connection is evident from works
like the anonymous *England Under the Heel of the Jew* (1918), which uncovers an "Ashkenazi-
German alliance" to conquer England. According to Norman Cohn's *Warrant for Genocide*
(New York: Harper & Row, 1967), pp. 150–51, leading members of the British establishment
endorsed the view that the Bolshevik Revolution in Russia was really a German-Jewish plot.
Even some intellectuals were taken in by this kind of mania, long after the war had passed. In
1924 Edmund Gosse could in good conscience refer to Leonard Woolf as "that half-educated
German," and Hilaire Belloc in 1932 went as far as to define the Nazis as a movement in which

"the wretched Hitler is a figure head and the clever Yid Rosenberg the manager." *Letters*, ed. Robert Speaight (London: Hollis & Carter, 1958), p. 227. In *Emmanuel Burden, Merchant* (London: Methuen, 1927), p. 198 (originally published in 1904), Belloc recounts how an honest British businessman is undone by two Jews, one of them a "greasy German Jew"; and in popular fiction generally, as in Buchan's *Greenmantle* or Sapper's novels, it is often German Jews who are the villains.

In 1915 *The English Review* calculated that "seventy-five per cent. of the foreign element in the City was born German and Jew;" and at the outbreak of the war, Leo Maxse's *National Review* conducted a vigorous anti-Semitic campaign, with remarks like: "Some of us are of the opinion that it would be scarcely worth while to knock out the modern Attila and his Huns—to reduce the German Empire to more reasonable proportions—if we are to leave the British Empire at the mercy of the German Jew"; or, further, "never again can we allow ourselves to be hocussed and bossed by German Jews or crypto Jews." It was this kind of thing that eventually drove Sir Edgar Speyer out of his adopted country. See Raymond Radclyffe, "The Germans in the City," *English Review* 21 (August-December 1915): 521; and [Leo Maxse], "The German Jew and the German Empire," *National Review* 64 (October 1914): 5–11.

26. Graham Greene, *The Old School* (London: Jonathan Cape, 1934), p. 187; and Julian Symons, *Horatio Bottomley* (London: Cresset Press, 1955), pp. 165–166.

27. Charles Hamilton Sorley, *Letters* (Cambridge: Cambridge University Press, 1919), p. 97.

28. Frederick Hillersden Keeling, *Letters and Recollections*, ed. E. T. (New York: Macmillan, n.d.), pp. 177–82.

29. The quotations from the *Guardian* are taken from Irene Cooper Willis, *England's Holy War, A Study of English Liberal Idealism During the Great War* (New York: Knopf, 1928), pp. 61–62, 78.

30. Charles Hamilton Sorley, *Marlborough and Other Poems* (Cambridge: The University Press, 1919), p. 73. In his *Anthology of War Poetry, 1914–1918* (London: Nicholson & Watson, 1943), p. 36, the poet Robert Nichols confesses that his repeated readings of Sorley's letters "have brought me to understand why the Poet Laureate [John Masefield] once said to me that Sorley was potentially the greatest poet lost to us in that war, and that, had Sorley lived, he might have become our greatest dramatist since Shakespeare." And in "Sorley's Weather" Robert Graves momentarily prefers Sorley to Shelley. *Fairies and Fuseliers* (New York: Knopf, 1919), p. 35.

31. Thomas Hardy, *Satires of Circumstance*, vol. 21 of *The Writings of Thomas Hardy in Prose and Verse*, Anniversary Edition (New York: Harper, n.d.), p. 230.

32. This action took effect on 13 May 1915 and included other members of the Hohenzollern family. The Japanese Emperor Hirohito was meted out the same punishment at the outbreak of World War II, but was readmitted into the Order in 1971. Eventually this mania for "expunging" came to include British citizens who were thought to be, or to have been, unduly sympathetic to Germany. George Bernard Shaw was asked to resign from the Dramatists' Club, Bertrand Russell was struck from the list of Fellows of Trinity College, and, in November 1916, it was proposed to raze Carlyle's statue on the Embankment in Chelsea. Paul Fussell, *The Great War and Modern Memory* (New York: Oxford, 1977), p. 176, quotes Graham Greene witnessing a dachshund being stoned by an angry mob in Birkhamstead.

33. J. M. Robertson, *The Germans* (London: Williams & Norgate, 1916), preface.

34. G. K. Chesterton, *The Crimes of England* (New York: John Lane & Co., 1916), p. 106. So too J. Ellis Barker, in *Modern Germany*, 5th ed. (London: Smith, Elder & Co., 1915), p. 119, contends that Bismarck's "appearance and his personality suggest that he had a considerable amount of Slav blood in him; at all events, Slavs and Slav methods were most sympathetic to him. . . . " Chesterton was later to mock the spy mania of the early stages of the war in "A Tall Story," in *The Paradoxes of Mr. Pond* (1936).

35. C. Chesterton, *Prussian*, p. 82. This would also appear to be the verdict nowadays, even

of British observers who are relatively sympathetic to Germany. John Mander, for instance, writes in *Our German Cousins* (London: John Murray, 1974), p. 174: "Today, we are not likely to be persuaded that it was the possession of Teutonic blood that conferred on us an unquenchable thirst for freedom. Nor does the Germanic basis of our language mean that our literature or our style of thinking, bear much relation to those of the Germans. There are parallels, of course; but no more than those with the cultures of France and Italy—to which we owe far more than we owe to Germany." After the war it was discovered that the Germans were not really Nordic after all. As a consequence, H. J. Fleure, Professor of Geography and Anthropology at the University College of Wales, was able to maintain in his *The Peoples of Europe* (London: Oxford, 1925), p. 43, that "the sharp criticism and startling clarity of French thought, growing where all the racial stocks of Europe jostle one another . . . stands in increasing contrast to the more laborious stodginess of the more or less Alpinized German with his heavier menu in both food and drink. The quick enterprising element is present here and there; but it is the Alpine patience and appetite for detail that has increasingly dominated the psychology of the German people, working out into a powerful combination that has had remarkable results in the industrial period."

36. Maurice Hewlett, *Letters*, ed. Laurence Binyon (London: Methuen & Co., 1926), p. 145; and Sir Walter Raleigh, *Might Is Right* (Oxford: Clarendon Press, 1917), p. 8. In his poetical contribution to *King Albert's Book* (New York: Hearst International, [1915]), p. 55, Hewlett also sees the Belgian resistance to the Germans as a racial phenomenon, though, oddly enough, in this instance the Iberians share the opprobrium with the Teutons:

> O MEN of mickle heart and little speech,
> Slow, stubborn countrymen of heath and plain,
> Now have ye shown these insolent again
> That which to Caesar's legions ye could teach,
> That slow-provok'd is long-provok'd. May each
> Crass Caesar learn this of the Keltic grain,
> Until at last they reckon it in vain
> To browbeat us who hold the Western reach.

It would also appear that Raleigh's ideas regarding the non-Germanic ancestry of the English are based on the theories of Pan-Celticists like Luke Owen Pike. In *The English and Their Origin* (London: Longmans, 1866), p. 177, Pike invites anyone to "go to the British Museum, and if I may use the expression, de-idealise the ideal Greek heads of the sculptures . . . and then let him ask himself in what European city he thinks he might with most success look for models for these works of art or for the originals of these portraits." In Berlin? Emphatically not. In Paris? No again, but not so emphatically. "In London? Yes, even in the lowest haunts of the lowest neighbourhoods."

37. Nottidge Charles MacNamara, *Origin and Character of the British People* (London: Smith, Elder & Co., 1900), pp. 222, 226; and Homer Lea, *The Day of the Saxon* (New York: Harper & Bros., 1912), p. 128.

38. J. A. Cramb, *Germany and England* (London: John Murray, 1914), pp. 136–137.

39. [P. C. Mitchell], "A Biological View of Our Foreign Policy," *Saturday Review,* 82 (February 1896), 118–120.

40. [Frank Harris], "England and Germany," *Saturday Review* 84 (11 September 1897): 278–79. For Harris's extreme Germanophobia in the late nineties, see Hugh Kingsmill, *Frank Harris* (London: Cape, 1932), pp. 109–10 and 209. An anonymous essay, "The German Peril," *Blackwoods'* (January 1898), p. 107, contends that Germany "or more properly Germans—since this is less a national than an individual question—are simply eating into us in the vital parts, intercepting off for their own use the stream of our national life, which is trade and manufac-

ture." William Archer was later to refer to Harris's article as "mad and wicked" in *The Villain of the World Tragedy* (London: Fisher Unwin, [1916]), p. 27. It was, according to Archer, an utterly isolated instance, "a freak of irresponsible and unprincipled journalism." However, Norman Angell relates in *After All* (New York: Farrar, Straus & Young, [1951]), p. 139, how at a dinner party before the war Leo Maxse (then editor of the *National Review*) told him that "Germany will fight because she must expand," and that the British empire had resources that Germany needed. Another guest then quoted Admiral Lord Fisher to the effect that "we have eventually to fight Germany . . . because she cannot expand commercially without it." According to Caroline E. Playne's *The Pre-War Mind in Britain* (London: George Allen & Unwin, 1928), p. 137, "the brutality of Lord Fisher's language did much to arouse alarm concerning British imperialist assumptions. Then he was known to be a personal friend of King Edward's, and, for this reason, sayings like the following, 'I hope to remain in office long enough to see the German Fleet at the bottom of the sea,' excited all the more angry attention in Germany." There was also a sociological version of this kind of Darwinian argument. This school of thought, heavily indebted to the French sociologist Gustave LeBon, traced the origin of national conflict to the behavior of rival crowds or herds. See W. B. Trotter's *Instincts of the Herd in Peace and War* (1916) and Sir Martin Conway's *The Crowd in Peace and War* (1915). In the latter work, for example, we are told that "the ideals that are tried in the furnace of war are not the cause of it, though they may contribute to the victory of one crowd and the overthrow of the other. Thus, at the present time, in spite of all we read and hear, we are not fighting Germany for righteousness' sake, but because Germany has been a strongly growing crowd which upset the equilibrium of Europe and aimed at the hegemony of the world" (London: Longmans, 1915), p. 288. Conway also goes on to single out P. C. Mitchell's "admirable essay" for praise (p. 316).

Chapter 2. Joseph Conrad's Diabolic and Angelic Germans

1. Joseph Conrad, *A Personal Record* (New York: Doubleday, 1925), pp. 37, 19.

2. Joseph Conrad, *Notes on Life and Letters* (New York: Doubleday, 1925), p. 95.

3. Ibid., p. 146.

4. Ibid., p. 164.

5. Jessie Conrad, *Joseph Conrad As I Knew Him* (London: Heinemann, 1926), p. 90. Just how well Jessie Conrad might have been able to judge her husband's fluency in German is open to question. According to the Conrad's close friend J. H. Retinger, Jessie's German vocabulary was limited to one word, *Donnerwetter!* See his *Conrad and His Contemporaries* (New York: Roy Publishers, 1943).

6. Conrad, *Personal,* p. 121.

7. Norman Sherry, *Conrad's Western World* (Cambridge: Cambridge University Press, 1971), pp. 325ff.

8. Jocelyn Baines, *Joseph Conrad, A Critical Biography* (New York: McGraw-Hill, 1967), pp. 221–22. Frederick Karl also notes (but makes nothing of) the curious fact that both Conrad and Ford changed their names to disguise their national origins. See *Joseph Conrad: The Three Lives* (New York: Farrar, Straus & Giroux, 1979), p. 432n.

9. Leo Gurko, in his *Joseph Conrad, Giant in Exile* (New York: Macmillan, 1962), p. 178, counts only three Germans, omitting Stein from consideration for unstated reasons.

10. Joseph Conrad, *Victory, An Island Tale* (New York: Doubleday, 1927), p. viii.

11. Conrad, *Notes,* pp. 105–6.

12. Ibid., pp. 147, 157.

13. Joseph Conrad, *Falk* (New York: Doubleday, 1914), p. 93. G. Jean Aubry's discussion of the story in *Joseph Conrad: Life and Letters,* vol. I (New York: Doubleday, 1927), 1:107–8, suggests that it is based on an actual encounter with a German Captain Hermann.

14. Joseph Conrad, *Lord Jim*, ed. R. B. Heilman (New York: Holt, Rinehart, and Winston, 1967), p. 35.

15. Walter Kayser, *Das Groteske: Seine Gestaltung in Malerei und Dichtung* (Oldenburg: Gerhard Stalling Verlag, 1957), p. 202. In English the German passage reads: "the attempt to interdict and exorcise the demonic on this earth" (my translation).

16. Frederick Karl, *Joseph Conrad, A Reader's Guide*, rev. ed. (New York: Farrar, Straus and Giroux, 1969), p. 127.

17. See George Bernard Shaw, *What I Really Wrote About the War* (New York: Brentano's, 1931), p. 23.

18. He is, however, a student of the grotesque and the sublime. "His collection of *Buprestidae* and *Longicorns*—beetles all," Marlow observes, "horrible miniature monsters, looking malevolent in death and immobility, and his cabinet of butterflies, beautiful and hovering under the glass of cases on lifeless wings, had spread his fame far over the earth" (pp. 174–75).

19. In *Victory*, as Alice Raphael has shown in *Goethe the Challenger* (New York: Cape, 1932), Conrad portrays a more credible Gretchen in Lena, and Faust in Heyst.

20. Frederick Karl was, I believe, the first to point out the close connection between Stein and Goethe. See his informative discussion in *Guide*, pp. 125–26.

21. Johann Wolfgang von Goethe, *Werke*, ed. Josef Kunz (Hamburg: Christian Wegner Verlag, 1960), 3: 84. The English sense, in my translation, of these lines is:

> So finally I've got it in my hands
> And call it in some sense my own.

22. It is only fair, however, to cite Norman Sherry's argument that Stein is based, in part, on a Dr. Bernstein, a German naturalist collecting specimens in Malaysia for the Leyden Museum. See his *Conrad's Eastern World* (Cambridge: Cambridge University Press, 1966), p. 143.

23. Goethe, *Werke*, p. 100. The two German phrases mean, respectively, "Permitted is what pleases" and "Permitted is what is fitting."

24. Goethe, *Werke*, p. 167. The sense of these lines, again in my translation, is as follows:

> The rudder's smashed and the ship
> Is splitting on all sides. The deck
> Bursts open underneath my feet!
> I seize you in both my arms!
> Just as the sailor at the very last
> Holds fast to the rock where he was doomed to wreck.

Chapter 3. E. M. Forster's Rainbow Bridge

1. E. M. Forster, "Recollections of Nassenheide," *The Listener* (1 January 1959), p. 12.

2. Elizabeth Beauchamp, Countess von Arnim, was actually Australian by birth, though English in loyalty and feeling.

3. Leslie de Charms, *Elizabeth of the German Garden* (London: Heinemann, 1958), p. 104. See also P. N. Furbank, *E. M. Forster: A Life* (London: Secker & Warburg, 1977), 1:127.

4. E. M. Forster, *Howards End* (New York: Vintage, n.d.), p. 30. This is a reprint of the 1921 Borzoi edition; all further references to it will appear in the text, by page number enclosed in parentheses and preceded by an "H."

5. E. M. Forster, *The Manuscripts of "Howards End,"* ed. Oliver Stallybrass (London: Edward Arnold, 1973), p. 70. I have omitted a number of editorial symbols in my citation.

6. In *E. M. Forster: The Critical Heritage*, ed. Philip Gardner (London: Routledge & Kegan Paul, 1973), pp. 150 and 153.

7. *Nordic Twilight* (London: Macmillan, 1940), p. 10, and *Two Cheers for Democracy* (London: Edward Arnold, 1972), p. 34.

8. In *Goldsworthy Lowes Dickinson* (London: Edward Arnold, 1962), p. 209, Forster quotes a letter to Bernard Berenson in which Dickinson praises Goethe as follows: "For years I have felt Goethe to be more important than any other man and now I see more clearly why."

9. Forster, "Recollections," p. 14.

10. *The Listener* (November 4, 1954), p. 756. Other members of the aging Bloomsbury circle were not quite so sure about Wagner's cultural value. According to John Maynard Keynes, *Two Memoirs* (London: Rupert Hart-Davis, 1949), p. 45, "one can believe sometimes that no greater responsibility for the war [World War I] lies on any one man than on Wagner."

11. In the manuscript Forster had included Goethe with Hegel and Kant but later decided to omit him, perhaps because Goethe does not fit so easily into the "idealist" framework. If so, that omission suggests that Forster was fairly well acquainted with the German idealist tradition. *Manuscripts*, p. 27.

12. It is also just possible that Forster may have picked up this quotation from Joseph Conrad's *Lord Jim* (1900), where it is used as the epigraph.

13. *Manuscripts*, p. 26.

14. Forster may have picked up the idea for Father Schlegel's decision to leave Germany from Hilaire Belloc's novel *Emmanuel Burden, Merchant* (1904), where the father of one of the principal characters is a German, "a patriot and idealist of the highest type" who "saw in the occupation of Frankfort in 1866, the advent at once of militarism and of foreign rule. He determined to abandon a town still dear to him, but intolerable since it supported an oppressor." Hilaire Belloc, *Emmanuel Burden, Merchant* (London: Methuen, 1927), p. 57. Ford Madox Ford's father, Franz Hüffer, actually did leave Westphalia after the Prussian takeover, something that Forster may very well have known. Hüffer, however, supported Prussia in the war against France.

15. See E. M. Forster's introduction to *The Longest Journey* (London: Oxford, 1960), p. xii. Forster had also considered Harold as another possible name for Stephen, again a German name.

16. *Aspects of the Novel* (New York: Harcourt, Brace & World, 1966), pp. 109–10.

17. See the relevant entries in the *Oxford Dictionary of English Etymology*. The fictional town of Hilton seems to be a fusion of Hitchin and Stevenage in Hertfordshire. Forster's boyhood home, "Rooks Nest," was located near the latter, and in *Marianne Thornton* (New York: Harcourt, Brace & Co., 1956), p. 301, Forster admitted that Howards End was modeled on this home. The name itself is probably derived from the "manor or tenement of Bromesend," also in Stevenage. See *A History of Hertfordshire*, in *The Victoria History of the Counties of England*, ed. William Page (London: Constable, 1912), 3:143. In the same volume (pp. 151–55) there are plans and pictures of "Rooks Nest," as well as a brief description of the house. That Stevenage, like Hilton, was linked with the Germanic past in the minds of others besides Forster is made clear by the assertion that "about three quarters of a mile south of Stevenage, lying beside the road, are six tumuli, known as the Six Hills, which point to the antiquity of this road" (p. 139), as well as by the description of Stevenage as "a good example of the development of the Teutonic type of settlement which is so frequently met with in Hertfordshire" (p. 140). Forster may also have been aware that "Libury," in neighboring Little Munden, was sold in 1899 to several Germans and converted "into a German Industrial and Farm Colony to provide work and shelter for German-speaking unemployed and destitute" (p. 132), so that his idea of implanting half-Germans in Hertfordshire may not have been entirely farfetched.

It should also be noted that, according to Furbank, *Forster*, p. 16n, "Rooks Nest" had once actually belonged to a family named Howard.

18. For a useful discussion in English of Heimdall's function, see E. O. G. Turville-Petre, *Myth and Religion of the North* (London: Weidenfeld & Nicolson, 1964), pp. 150ff. The

rainbow bridge, like Asgard, is linked to the World Tree. Heimdall is sometimes called the "Goldentoothed," which provides a roundabout and probably purely coincidental connection with Forster's wych-elm and its pigs' teeth.

I would also like to observe here that, while I have no convincing proof of sources, the last two sentences of the "rainbow bridge" passage are evocative of the form and tone of Anglo-Saxon and Old Norse poetry. Compare, for instance, those two sentences with the concluding lines of "The Seafarer," as translated by Burton Raffel in *Poems from the Old English* (Lincoln: University of Nebraska Press, 1964), p. 34:

> He who lives humbly has angels from heaven
> To carry him courage and strength and belief.
> A man must conquer pride, not kill it,
> Be firm with his fellows, chaste for himself,
> Treat all the world as the world deserves,
> With love or with hate but never with harm,
> Though an enemy seek to search him in hell,
> Or set the flames of a funeral pyre
> Under his Lord.

Or this passage from "The Words of the High One" (Hávamál), in *The Elder Edda: A Selection,* trans. P. B. Taylor and W. H. Auden (London: Faber & Faber, 1969), p. 43.

> A man should be loyal through life to friends.
> And return gift for gift,
> Laugh when they laugh, but with lies repay
> A false foe who lies.

19. Forster, "Recollections," p. 14.

20. For a brief account of Old Norse studies in England, see the introductory section of E. V. Gordon, *An Introduction to Old Norse* (London: Oxford University Press, [1927]).

21. *The Rhine Gold* (Mainz: Schott's Söhne, [1897]). From Forster's discussion of the libretto and Wolfgang and Wieland Wagner's deviations from Wagner's original stage directions it would appear that Forster was using the German text. In that text the bridge is even more prominent. Jameson, for instance, omits the following directions for Froh: "der der Brücke mit der ausgestreckten Hand den Weg über das Tal angewiesen, zu den Göttern." It is also possible that Forster may have consulted Jessie L. Weston's *The Legends of the Wagner Drama: Studies in Mythology and Romance* (London: David Nutt, 1896), which deals with and summarizes the main sources for Wagner's *Ring* (and his other operas).

22. Lionel Trilling, in *E. M. Forster* (Norfolk, Conn.: New Directions, 1943), p. 133n, associates Father Schlegel's sword with "Schiller's sword which Thackeray bought in Weimar and which he hung in his study over his books," but he does not explain why he thinks Forster might have known this.

Miss Avery's function in the novel is important but obscure. Her name seems to refer to *avera* (from the Danish *hoveri*), from the Domesday Book, and meaning "one day's work which the King's tenants give to the Sheriff," alluding perhaps to Miss Avery's feudal services to the Howard family. There is a mention of the performance of avera at Broadwater (near Stevenage) in *A History of Hertfordshire* (3:131). A more remote possibility is that Forster is thinking here of Andvari, the name for Alberich in the Old Norse *Volsunga Saga.* Though unlikely, this association might help account for Miss Avery's dramatic gesture of throwing the gold pendant she had bought for Evie's wedding—and which Evie had refused—into the duckpond. If so, this would be a symbolic reversal of Alberich/Andvari's theft of the Rhine gold.

Chapter 4. The Loves of English Women and German Men

1. P. N. Furbank, "John Bull in the German Garden," *Encounter* 22 (April 1964): 86. This self-centered quality of *Elizabeth and Her German Garden* was singled out in some of the otherwise favorable reviews of the book. So Arthur Quiller Couch's review termed Elizabeth "not only selfish, but quite inhumanly so and her mind . . . of that order which finds a smart self-satisfaction in proclaiming how thoroughly it is dominated by self. A husband is a nuisance, children are amusing toys—now and then. . . ." Quoted in Leslie de Charms, *Elizabeth of the German Garden* (London: Heinemann, 1959), pp. 78–79.

2. Bertrand Russell, *The Autobiography of Bertrand Russell, 1914–1944* (Boston: Little, Brown & Co., 1968) p. 57. Elizabeth's first husband, Henning von Arnim, was a grandson of Prince Augustus of Prussia, nephew of Frederick the Great. Her second marriage in 1916 to John Francis Stanley Russell ended in separation shortly after the war. In a postwar novel, *Vera* (1921), she writes that "perhaps husbands have never altogether agreed with me. It did in fact need the Great war, and a second husband, to make me really grow up." See Stanley Kunitz, ed., *Twentieth Century Authors* (New York: H. W. Wilson, 1942), p. 1217.

3. For biographical information about Katherine Mansfield, see Anthony Alpers's two studies of her work: *Katherine Mansfield* (New York: Knopf, 1954), and *The Life of Katherine Mansfield* (New York: Viking, 1980), as well as Sylvia Berkman, *Katherine Mansfield* (New Haven: Yale University Press, 1951). For Dorothy Richardson, see Gloria G. Fromm, *Dorothy Richardson* (Urbana: University of Illinois Press, 1977), and John Rosenberg, *Dorothy Richardson: The Forgotten Genius* (London: Duckworth, 1973). Information about Wylie and Spottiswoode is harder to come by, except for brief entries in biographical dictionaries; but for the former see *My Life with George* (New York: Random House, 1940). Critical or biographical discussion of Spottiswoode is virtually nonexistent.

Two other novels on Anglo-German themes by Spottiswoode, *Marcia in Germany* (1908) and *Hedwig in England* (1909), have nothing of the intensity of *Her Husband's Country*. But a postwar novel, *The Wheel in Turning* (1933) is quite remarkable for its dark, almost surreal quality. Its set of refugees from a happier world includes an impoverished Prussian general who wears his uniform only at home, having been forbidden to do so in public; a son who joins the Nazis and another who joins the Communists; a daughter who prostitutes herself for money and good times, and another who kills herself because she's unable to deal with the new world. Spottiswoode's starving and desperately disillusioned Germany—where once-brilliant officers eke out livings as attendants in public lavatories—is an utterly different place from that described by E. M. Butler in her autobiography, *Paper Boats* (London: Collins, 1959), p. 83. Here, at the height of the supposedly devastating inflation of 1923, we are told of a Germany where the tables are groaning "under heavy loads of food" and high-powered cars purr through streets lined with fashionable restaurants filled to overflowing by gluttonous ex-Huns. Butler, who had attended school in Germany before the war, eventually attained distinction as a professor of German at Cambridge. Her memories of her German schooldays are that she, together with the other English pupils, were contemptuous of "how sloppy and sentimental Germans were," and that, when she finally left Hanover, it was with the impression that "there was something inherently ridiculous about the Germans. I never quite lost it . . ." (pp. 16 and 20).

4. Sybil Spottiswoode, *Her Husband's Country* (New York: Duffield & Co., 1911), p. 59. All further references to this work will appear in the text, by page number enclosed in parentheses.

5. I. A. R. Wylie, *Dividing Waters* (Indianapolis: Bobbs-Merrill, 1911). All references to this work will be included in the text, by page number enclosed in parentheses. Elsewhere, however, Wylie does concede that German women are lamentably lacking in elegance, a fault that, in her view, is "entirely" their own fault. Still, the fact of German bad taste does not

altogether excuse the British from assuming naively that their local code of manners must constitute a Universal Code received from on high. See *The Germans* (Indianapolis: Bobbs-Merrill, 1911), pp. 151 and 179. Spottiswoode and, to a lesser extent, Wylie see German vulgarity as primarily a function of German poverty, but others—E. Phillips Oppenheim among them—attribute it to ill-gained and ill-spent wealth. "Wherever they have been, for the last few years," so Oppenheim's elegant protagonist, Norgate, observes in *The Double Traitor* (New York: A. L. Burt Co., [1915]), p. 2, "they seem to have left the trail of the *nouveaux riches*. It is not only their clothes but their manners and bearing which affront."

6. Wylie, *My Life*, pp. 127, 152, and 144.

7. Wylie, *Germans*, p. 40.

8. Wylie, *Life*, p. 143.

9. Wylie, *Germans*, p. 44.

10. Wylie, *Life*, p. 145. As late as 1919, Wylie depicts a British soldier murdering in cold blood a German prison guard whom he had befriended, and then pretending shamelessly to the German's mother that he had been his friend. See "John Prettyman's Fourth Dimension," in *All Sorts* (London: Mills & Boon, 1919).

11. Berkman, *Mansfield*, p. 35.

12. Alpers, *Mansfield*, p. 63.

13. John Carswell, *Lives and Letters* (New York: New Directions, 1978), p. 64. Carswell's view also does not seem to be shared by the later Mansfield, who came to think the book " 'a lie,' 'positively juvenile,' and 'not what I mean.' " Quoted in Alpers, *Life*, p. 129.

14. All quotations are from Katherine Mansfield, *In a German Pension* (New York: Knopf, 1926), pp. 15–69.

15. J. M. Murry, Introduction to Katherine Mansfield, *The Short Stories* (New York: Knopf, 1954), p. vi.

16. Dorothy Richardson, *Pointed Roofs* (New York: Knopf, 1919), p. 28. All further references to this work will be included in the text, by page number enclosed in parentheses.

17. Fromm, *Richardson*, pp. 77 and 81.

18. Violet Hunt, *Those Flurried Years* (London: Hurse & Blackett, [1926]); Douglas Goldring, *South Lodge, Reminiscences of Violet Hunt, Ford Madox Ford and the English Review Circle* (London: Constable, 1943); Arthur Mizener, *The Saddest Story* (New York: World, 1971).

19. Goldring, *South Lodge*, p. 98. All further references, unless indicated otherwise, will be included in the text, by page number enclosed in parentheses.

20. Ford Madox Ford, *Parade's End*, pt. 1, *Some Do Not . . .* (London: Bodley Head, 1963), p. 196. Further references to *Some Do Not . . .* will be included in the text, by page number enclosed in parentheses.

21. Ford Madox Hueffer, "High Germany—I: How It Feels to Be Members of Subject Races," *The Saturday Review* 112 (30 September 1911): 422.

22. Ibid.

23. Ford Madox Hueffer, "High Germany—II: Utopia," *The Saturday Review* 112 (7 October, 1911): 456.

24. Goldring, *South*, p. 38.

25. Violet Hunt, *The Desirable Alien: At Home in Germany*, with preface and two additional chapters by Ford Madox Hueffer (London: Chatto & Windus, 1913), pp. x–xi. All further references to this work will be included in the text, by page number enclosed in parentheses.

26. Violet Hunt, *I Have This to Say: The Story of My Flurried Years* (New York: Boni & Liveright, [1926]), pp. 244–48. Further references to this work will be included in the text, by page number enclosed in parentheses.

27. See Thomas Moser, *The Life in the Fiction of Ford Madox Ford* (Princeton: Princeton University Press, 1980), p. 196.

28. Mizener, *Saddest*, p. 282; David Garnett, *Great Friends* (London: Macmillan, 1979), p. 55. Significantly, as a Ruthenian, Ford would have been able to claim his sometime collaborator, Joseph Conrad, as a countryman. More ominous than Ford's change of name is the suspicion, voiced by Paul Delany in *D. H. Lawrence's Nightmare* (New York: Basic Books, 1978), pp. 101–3, that Ford may have engaged in spying on Lawrence at Masterman's instigation.

29. According to the entry on Ford in the *Dictionary of National Biography*, Ford was "registered at birth as Ford Hermann Hueffer, but adopted the additional Christian names of Joseph Leopold Madox." Hence it was only necessary to rid himself of the "Hermann" officially, since the "Joseph Leopold" could be dropped without bureaucratic sanction. As to the change of surname from Hueffer to Ford after the war, Stanley Kunitz's *Twentieth Century Authors* (New York: H. M. Wilson, 1942), p. 474, maintains that this was done "for reasons probably connected with his complicated marital affairs."

30. Ford Madox Hueffer, *When Blood Is Their Argument: An Analysis of Prussian Culture* (New York: Hodder & Stoughton, 1915), p. 302; Hunt, *I Have*, p. 247.

31. Ford, *When*, p. 302.

32. Robert Green's *Ford Madox Ford: Prose and Politics* (Cambridge: Cambridge University Press, 1981), p. 74, sees Ford's two propaganda books as only ostensibly concerned with Germany. Their actual subject is "British political institutions in peacetime. At the heart of these books lies his belief that Britain has become too much like Germany, too 'socialist,' too 'materialist.' "

33. Peter Buitenhuis, "Writers at War: Propaganda and Fiction in the Great War," *University of Texas Quarterly* 45 (September 1976): 283.

34. Ibid. Ford also translated Pierre Loti's *The Trail of the Barbarians* (1917), which in its dedication calls upon the youth of France to keep their hatred of the Germans alive after the war, as well as to "keep them out, as you would keep out wolves and vampires." Ford's brief "Translator's Note" describes Loti as a "great stylist."

35. Ford Madox Ford, *Return to Yesterday* (New York: Liveright, 1932), p. 350. In the preface (dated 3 February 1915) to *When Blood Is Their Argument*, p. vii, Ford claims that he "imbibed in my very earliest years a deep hatred of Prussianism" together with a "deep love and veneration" for France. Of the "protracted period" that he spent in Germany he now recollects that his admiration for "many institutions" there was purely "platonic" and merely "intellectual," while disliking "the idea of spending a moment longer than was absolutely necessary in that country." With respect to his "High Germany" hymns of praise, he is now struck to "find myself expressing in these articles the same feeling of unrest and anxiety to get away" (pp. 170–71).

36. Ford Madox Ford, *The Good Soldier* (London: The Bodley Head, 1962), p. 43.

37. Ford Madox Ford, *Parade's End: No More Parades* (New York: Vintage, 1979), p. 307.

38. Ibid., pp. 628–29.

39. Ibid., p. 629.

40. The entry on Ford in Kunitz, *Twentieth*—an account that bears all the traces of having been inspired by Ford himself—observes that "German poetry, particularly Heine, appealed to him, but he thought out his novels in French before writing them in English. . . ."

41. In the opening pages of *The Desirable Alien*, Hunt gives a somewhat different account of her early "German" upbringing. Her French governess turns out to have been a German spy in disguise, who was expelled from Paris shortly before the Commune took over. This story—with the appropriate moral plusses changed to minuses—may be the source of the German spy Franz Bamberger, who masquerades as a French Butler, Anatole, in Violet Hunt's novel, *The Last Ditch* (London: Stanley Paul & Co., 1926), pp. 108–9.

42. There is some mention of Bad Nauheim in *The Last Ditch*, Hunt's ambitious but flawed novelistic reply to Ford's *Good Soldier* and *Parade's End*. Even at this late date (1926) we still find Hunt, in the guise of her persona, *the* Lady Venice, fantasizing about marrying Ford. Here

her heroine finally manages to bag the portly and omniscient quasi-Ford, Audely. Now the world is saved, for "so long as Our Order breeds men like Audely and women like Venice . . . we shall get along all right" (p. 169).

43. Violet Hunt and Ford Madox Hueffer, *Zeppelin Nights* (London: John Lane, 1916), p. 2.

44. Hunt, *I Have*, p. 258. In *The Last Ditch*, p. 102, one of the principal characters recalls that the Germans "always hated and suspected us. . . . Oh yes, they hated us. No one ever smiled at us. Indeed, I never did see any one smile at all in Germany. They are a sour, dour, glum, sulky nation."

45. J. K. Prothero [Ada Elizabeth Jones], "Mr. Hueffer and His Cellar *Garnie*," *New Witness* 7 (6 January 1916): 293. Reprinted in Frank MacShane, ed., *Ford Madox Ford: The Critical Heritage* (London: Routledge & Kegan Paul, 1972), pp. 122–24. In Hunt's *The Last Ditch*, pp. 198–211, the sometime night hag is transformed, in the Lady Venice's eyes, into "a great pink pearl, so beautiful and eternal and serene . . . ," and another character remarks on the courageous and cheerful way his "barber in Bridgewood" greets the zeppelin threat. Hunt and Ford's wartime hysteria is transferred into the mouth of an absurd Mrs. Leahy who "began, now, to explain the Zeppelin agony in her own painfully, popular novelettish way," as follows: " 'It is the crystallized malevolence of the world, the father and mother of a Zeppelin are unspoken curses.' "

46. MacShane, *Ford*, p. 125.

Chapter 5. The Mental Slum: H. G. Wells and Rudyard Kipling

1. Wells's attitude was rather more complex than Kipling's. Before the war he had been a vociferous and uncompromising opponent of British military involvement on the continent. But faced with the actual event, his opposition crumbled. As a consequence, after the war Wells was sometimes viewed as a "Lost Leader." For instance, Douglas Goldring says of him in *Reputations* (New York: Thomas Seltzer, 1920), pp. 90–91:

> When the war broke out, while many of Mr. Wells' disciples were keeping alight the flame of those principles which by his eloquence he had instilled into their minds, Mr. Wells himself, like the majority of us, completely lost his head. At one moment he was urging all the middle-aged gentlemen living in the country to clean their rook-rifles so that, when the Hun invaded, they might lurk behind hedges and bag at least a victim apiece before their women were raped—regardless of the fact that, according to those laws of warfare which we observed so faithfully in South Africa, such a proceeding would have justified the Germans in burning every village they entered. This emotional episode . . . shows us how completely, as an intellectual leader, he is untrustworthy.

2. H. G. Wells, *The Outline of History* (New York: Macmillan, 1920), p. 572. Later still Wells was to recall that "in those days one relied very much on the common sense of mankind. I will confess I was taken by surprise by the Great War. Yet I saw long ahead how it would happen and wove fantastic stories about it. I let my imagination play about it, but at the bottom of my heart I did not feel and believe it would really happen. I did not suspect that Lord Grey, the German Emperor and the rest of them were incompetent to that pitch." See H. G. Wells, Foreword to J. M. Kenworthy's *Peace or War?* (New York: Boni & Liveright, 1927), p. viii.

3. H. G. Wells, *Mr. Britling Sees It Through* (Chicago: Donolme & Co., 1917), p. 67. All further references to this novel will be included in the text, by page number enclosed in parentheses and preceded by a "W."

This contrast between German rigidity and Allied spontaneity was one of the leading propagandistic themes of the war. That Wells thought of it in explicitly racial terms is confirmed by his contention, in *What Is Coming? A European Forecast* (New York: Macmillan, 1916),

p. 37, that "the Germans are racially inferior to both the French and English in the air." According to John Cowper Powys, *The Menace of German Culture* (London: W. Ridder, 1915), p. 126, Germany represents the state machine whereas the Allies stand for "the freedom and liberty of the human soul." However, the principal exponent of this view was undoubtedly the French philosopher Henri Bergson. In *The Meaning of the War: Life and Matter in Conflict* (New York: Macmillan, 1915), pp. 37–38, we are told that when the war broke out, "on the one side there was force spread out on the surface; on the other, there was force in the depths. On one side, mechanism, the manufactured article which cannot repair its own injuries; on the other, life, the power of creation which makes and remakes itself at every instant." With the aid of this philosophy, it was possible to have "Gott mit uns" even when one was an atheist. How deeply this notion of German "racial" rigidity and stupidity is still rooted in our consciousness can be gauged from Barbara Tuchman's *The Guns of August* (New York: Macmillan 1962), p. 228, which endorses this view and conceives of German arrogance as "that natural quality in Germans whose expression so often fails to endear them to others." Nature, we are made to realize, has created the Germans different from us.

4. Wells had earlier written a piece for the *Nation* (August 22, 1914) entitled "The Liberal Fear of Russia" in which he argued that Russia was too barbarous, too disunited, too thickly populated with Jews to be any danger for at least the next two centuries. Wells apparently did not notice the contradiction between this view and the one expressed earlier in *An Englishman Looks at the World* (London: Cassell, 1914), p. 144, that Britain's real enemy was Russia, not Germany. It is also worth noting that Britling's ideas bear a remarkable resemblance to those expressed by Jane Harrison in *Alpha and Omega* (London: Sidgwick & Jackson, 1915) on the same subjects. Like Britling, Harrison sees Germany as collectivistic and atavistic, a nation given over to abstractions, "drunk, not with beer, but with theories" (248).

5. Rudyard Kipling, *A Diversity of Creatures*, vol. 26 of *The Writings in Prose and Verse* (New York: Scribners, 1917), pp. 512–13. All further references to this volume will be included in the text, by page number enclosed in parentheses.

6. Bonamy Dobrée, *The Lamp and the Lute* (New York: Barnes & Noble, 1964 [1929]), as reprinted in *Kipling and the Critics* (New York: New York University Press, 1965), p. 53. An earlier version of the same essay appeared originally as "Rudyard Kipling," in *The Monthly Criterion* 6 (December 1927): 499–515, and has been reprinted in *Kipling: The Critical Heritage*, ed. R. L. Green (London: Routledge & Kegan Paul, 1971). The strongest case yet put forward for "Mary Postgate" as a philanthropic document is Nevill Coghill's 1965 essay in the *Kipling Journal* 32 (December 1965): 69: "To me 'Mary Postgate' is a masterpiece of utter beauty and sympathy," Coghill proclaims, adding a few sentences later that "it is the case of one step further than 'Father, forgive them; they know not what they do.' It is the step that we ought to imagine the dying German might have taken, had he known as much about Mary Postgate as we do."

7. Bonamy Dobrée, *Rudyard Kipling, Realist and Fabulist* (London: Oxford University Press, 1967), pp. 131–33.

8. C. E. Carrington, *The Life of Rudyard Kipling* (Garden City, N.Y.: Doubleday, 1955), p. 334.

9. An allusion to the death of Kipling's son at the front in late September or early October 1915, which, since the story dates from March of that year, can hardly be accurate.

10. W. W. Robson, "Kipling's Later Stories," in *Kipling's Mind and Art*, ed. Andrew Rutherford (Stanford: Stanford University Press, 1964), pp. 273–74.

11. J. I. M. Stewart, *Eight Modern Writers* (Oxford: Oxford University Press, 1963), p. 277. His later *Rudyard Kipling* (London: Gollancz, 1966) adds nothing to this interpretation. Probably Stewart also means to hint at what he takes to be the ultimate source of Kipling's misogyny: latent homosexuality.

12. J. M. S. Tompkins, *The Art of Rudyard Kipling* (London: Methuen, 1959), pp. 135–37.

13. C. A. Bodelsen, *Aspects of Kipling's Art* (Manchester: University Press, 1964), p. 102n.

14. Dobrée, *Kipling*, p. 131.

15. In Max Beerbohm's famous parody, "P.C., X, 36," Santa Claus is arrested for, among other reasons, being a German. The only essay wholly devoted to the subject of Kipling's attitude toward Germany is Basil M. Bazley's "Kipling's Opinion of the Germans," *The Kipling Journal* (July 1945), pp. 3–5. Bazley begins by asserting that Kipling's opinion was thoroughly consistent: a "dislike—hatred is perhaps not too strong a word—of everything German" which was "of no recent growth." Kipling is usually credited with first using the word *Hun* in its present sense, though Kaiser Wilhelm—a fervent admirer of Kipling—urged his troops during the Boxer Rebellion to "fight like Huns." (Undoubtedly, the word is first used—apparently favorably—in English poetry in Thomas Campbell's "Hohenlinden," "When furious Frank and fiery Hun [Austrian],/Shout in their sulphurous canopy!") By the time the war broke out, the word was in general use, by high, middle, and low brow alike. Writing to John Squire on September 25, 1914, Arnold Bennett has this to say about it: "Yes, my dear Squire, I deeply agree with your objection to that infernal word 'Hun,' but I think our objection is literary. The word is a most damnable cliché. . . . But I think it is a fairly descriptive word." Arnold Bennett, *Letters*, ed. James Hepburn (London: Oxford, 1968), p. 356. After the war, some intellectuals regretted their earlier hun-baiting. Siegfried Sassoon describes finding a book in Robert Bridges's library in which the word *Hun* had been carefully obliterated and *German* written in its place. *Siegfried's Journey* (London: Faber, 1945), p. 96. A fair sample of Bridges's wartime poetical efforts is the concluding stanza of "August 1914," taken from R. M. Leonard's *Patriotic Poems* (London: Oxford, 1914), p. 8:

> "Up, careless, awake!
> Ye peacemakers, fight!
> ENGLAND STANDS FOR HONOUR
> GOD DEFEND THE RIGHT!"

16. Rudyard Kipling, *The Eyes of Asia* (Garden City, N.Y.: Doubleday, 1918), pp. 7–8.

17. This was even too anti-German for the British Foreign Minister who was to reverse a century-old tradition in foreign policy by entering into an "entente" with France directed against Germany. On 2 January 1903 Lord Lansdowne wrote a letter in which he registered his astonishment at the violence of anti-German feeling in England during the Venezuela crisis, and observed that in particular "Kipling's poem was an outrage." Quoted in Thomas Wodehouse, Lord Newton, *Lord Lansdowne, A Biography* (London: Macmillan, 1929), p. 258.

18. That during his lifetime Kipling was generally thought of—and *not* for that reason necessarily thought ill of—as a racist is apparent from Dean Inge's reference to Kipling in his overtly racist "The White Man and His Rivals." There Inge's dread of the "yellow peril" is confirmed by the "horror which overpowered [Kipling] at the deadly efficiency of the Chinese. 'Soon there will be no more white men, but only yellow men with black hearts'. . . ." See William Ralph Inge, *Outspoken Essays* (London: Longmans, Green & Co., 1923), pp. 219–20.

19. The German airman, it might be recalled, attracts Mary's attention by his animalistic grunts. This swinish aspect of the Germans may be further suggested here by the name "Ebermann." ("Eber" is the German word for boar.) No doubt we are also intended to pick up an allusion to Matthew 12:34, "O generation of vipers, how can ye, being evil, speak good things?", since the title of the story, after all, is taken from Matthew 12:44, "Then he [the unclean spirit who is cast out] saith, I will return into my house from whence I came out; and when he is come, he findeth *it* empty, swept and garnished." The real point of this, as far as the story is concerned, emerges only in the following verse: "Then goeth he, and taketh with himself seven other spirits more wicked than himself, and they enter in and dwell there: and the last *state* of that man is worse than the first. Even so shall it be also unto this wicked generation." For the five good Belgian spirits, it seems, there are seven evil ones dwelling in Frau Ebermann.

20. Stewart, *Eight*, p. 277.

21. This is a story that should be read in the context of the German air invasion scare of 1913, when the *Daily Mail* (25 February 1913) published a lead article entitled "Unwelcome Visitors," concluding that "whether or not we accept the circumstantial reports that a strange airship was seen hovering over British territory on Friday and Saturday, it must be taken as certain that this country has recently been visited by foreign aircraft."

22. As a critical curiosity, one might mention here Malcolm Page's argument that the airman may not be a German at all. Noting that, aside from a few words of broken English, the airman speaks nothing but French, Page concludes that he may very well *be* French. "Otherwise," Page argues, "we must construct tortuous explanations: that a German speaks two languages, and does not know whether he has crashed in England or France." Kipling's point in all this, according to Page, is to "underline his picture of the consequences of war." ("The Nationality of the Airman in 'Mary Postgate,' " *The Kipling Journal* (June 1970), p. 15.) An article still remains to be written that would maintain, on the basis of Mary's demonstrated, though faulty, knowledge of German, that she is a spy.

23. A term Churchill is credited with inventing after the German bombardment of Scarborough. According to James Morgan Read's *Atrocity Propaganda, 1914–1919* (New Haven: Yale University Press, 1941), p. 53, Churchill was reminded on this occasion by the Manchester *Guardian* "that babies could be killed by hunger as well as by shells." For Murray's early views on the war, see Gilbert Murray, *Thoughts on the War* (Oxford: Clarendon Press, 1914), p. 9.

24. Siegfried Sassoon, *Memoirs of an Infantry Officer* (New York: Collier, 1969), p. 103. In *The Last Ditch* (London: Stanley Paul & Co., 1926), pp. 211–12, Violet Hunt has one of her principal female characters, Ida, declare that she would instantly kill any German airman if he happened to fall out of a zeppelin even if his back were broken and he begged for water. Like Mary Postgate—to whom Hunt is evidently referring—Ida sadistically relishes letting "him die as parched as a bone, thinking of the good beer of the Fatherland." In reply to Ida's conclusion that the victims of air warfare are innocent civilians, the Lady Venice (Hunt's alter ego) replies that "we made altogether too much of the innocent civilian business. There are, as a matter of fact, no innocent civilians left in England, except perhaps me and Mother, more shame for us! Even Ida, doing war work, isn't a civilian."

25. C. E. Montague, *Disenchantment* (New York: Brentano's, 1922), p. 279.

Chapter 6. Wellington House and the Strange Death of a Liberal Professor

1. Quoted in David Newsome, *On the Edge of Paradise: A. C. Benson, The Diarist* (London: John Murray, 1980), p. 312.

2. Peter Buitenhuis, "Writers at War: Propaganda and Fiction in the Great War," *University of Texas Quarterly* 45 (Summer 1976): 278. See also Ivor Nicholson, "An Aspect of British Official Wartime Propaganda," *Cornhill Magazine* 70 (June 1931): 593–606. Nicholson regrets that none of the chief creators and executors of British cultural warfare—Masterman, of course, but also G. H. Mair and Sir James Headlam-Morley—bothered to write a "full and authoritative history." For Bennett's role as a literary propagandist, see especially Kinley E. Roby's *A Writer at War: Arnold Bennett, 1914–1918* (Baton Rouge: Louisiana State University Press, 1972).

3. Quoted in Roger Lancelyn Green, *A. E. W. Mason* (London: Max Parrish, 1952), p. 134.

4. John Buchan, *The Clearing House*, Preface by Gilbert Murray (London: Hodder & Stoughton, 1946), p. viii.

5. John Buchan, *The Thirty-Nine Steps*, in *Adventures of Richard Hannay* (Cambridge, Mass.: Riverside Press, n.d.), p. 230; and Sir Arthur Conan Doyle, "His Last Bow," in *The Annotated Sherlock Holmes*, ed. W. S. Baring-Gould (New York: Clarkson Potter, 1967), 2: 793

and 802. As a young man Doyle had attended a Jesuit college in Feldkirch, Austria, for a year and learned some German. His attitude toward Germany ranges from patronizing amusement—as with the German von Baumser in *The Firm of Girdlestone*, who makes remarks like "Dot vos a mistake"—to admiring suspicion in *The Exploits of Brigadier Gerard* (New York: Appleton, 1896), p. 237, where the Germans, who "had always seemed to me to be a kindly, gentle people, whose hands closed more readily round a pipe-stem than a sword-hilt" hide beneath "that homely surface . . . a devilry as fierce, and far more persistent than that of the Castilian or the Italian." According to Jerome K. Jerome, *My Life and Times* (London: Hodder & Stoughton, [1926]), p. 263, Doyle once sent him an invitation—round about 1900— to join an organization called "Friends of Germany."

6. John Buchan, *Greenmantle* (London: Nelson, n.d.), pp. 68 and 90.

7. Ibid., p. 103.

8. Ibid., p. 135.

9. John Buchan, "The German Mind," *Land and Water* (6 November 1915), 17–18, and idem, *Clearing*, p. 79. Buchan's portrait of the Kaiser in *Greenmantle* is, however, not unique. In "The Price of Nationality," *English Review* 20 (1915): 186–87, W. L. George depicts the Kaiser as having "strong, if peculiar moral views . . . a clear idea of right and wrong; he is, in other words, a Truly Good Man. . . . Nothing is so dangerous. A Fouché, a Talleyrand will give way because they do not care; a Truly Good Man will drench the world in blood because he must do his duty." The most extraordinary picture of the Kaiser in prewar English literature is undoubtedly that of Baron Corvo's in *Hadrian the Seventh* (1904), with its vision of William II as the new ruler of a Northern European Roman Empire, stretching from Holland to the Urals and blessed by an English Pope. Corvo's Kaiser as the Savior of Christendom is admittedly extreme, but in a more sober and serious vein a similar argument is put forward in W. T. Stead's "The Lord Chief Justice of Europe," *The Contemporary Review* 71 (April 1897): 596.

10. Thomas Hardy, *Verse*, in *The Writings*, Anniversary Edition (New York: Harper & Brothers, n.d.), 21: 227. Another eminent writer of Hardy's generation who also wrote for Wellington House was Henry James. See J. D. Squires, *British Propaganda at Home and in the United States from 1914 to 1917* (Cambridge: Harvard University Press, 1935), p. 54.

11. Hardy, *Verse*, p. 228.

12. See Squires, *British*, p. 29.

13. Quoted in Buitenhuis, "Writers," p. 289. Masterman put Sir Gilbert Parker in charge of the American end of Wellington House propaganda, assisted by a distinguished team of British academics, including A. J. Toynbee. There were also subsections for French, Scandinavian (headed by William Archer), and Arabic propaganda, as well as the occasional employment of sympathetic writers of other nationalities (e.g., Salvador Madariaga). There was even a graphic arts section, which included painters of the caliber of C. R. W. Nevinson.

14. Buitenhuis, "Writers," p. 286.

15. *Gilbert Murray: An Unfinished Autobiography*, ed. Jean Smith and Arnold Toynbee (London: Allen & Unwin, 1960), p. 110. Murray himself remarks in *The Foreign Policy of Sir Edward Grey, 1906–1915* (Oxford: Clarendon Press, 1915), p. 122, that Grey's speeches are "almost dull." The Cabinet initially opposed Grey's efforts to intervene in the war on France's behalf. According to Winston Churchill, a three-quarters majority of the Cabinet was at first willing to support John Morley's proposal to remain neutral unless Britain were attacked directly. But, as Morley later put it, the question of Belgium soon became for waverers what in earlier times Morocco and Agadir had been "as pleas for war." Morley was convinced that Grey should have openly stated—and if necessary negotiated—the specific conditions under which Britain would remain neutral in a German war with France, when the German Ambassador Lichnowsky asked him to do so on 1 August 1914. Three days later, after Britain had declared war, Morley and John Burns resigned, the only Cabinet members to do so. In this way the victory went to the Liberal Imperialists, the bellicose and self-righteous wing of the party that

Murray had opposed before the war. Of this powerful group, R. J. Sontag writes in *Germany and England: Background of Conflict, 1848–1894* (New York: Russell & Russell, 1964), p. 308: "To the Liberal Imperialists, opponents of the chosen British race, opponents real or supposed, domestic or foreign, were enemies of God, morality, and progress." See also the entry for John Morley in the *Dictionary of National Biography*, as well as Morley's *Memorandum on Resignation* (New York: Macmillan, 1928).

16. Gilbert Murray, *Thoughts on the War* (Oxford: Clarendon Press, 1914), p. 4. A year later, Murray was still convinced that this breakdown of the traditional class divisions in Britain was one of the benefits of the war. See Gilbert Murray, *Ethical Problems of the War* (London: Thomas Nelson, 1915), p. 19. Murray's Oxford colleague, Professor Walter Raleigh, shares this view in *Some Gains of the War* ([New York]: Doran, 1918), p. 10. That both Murray and Raleigh's war hysteria reached a pitch that made it seem ridiculous even to interested observers is clear from Rupert Brooke's description of their rising, in December 1914, "at six every day to line hedgerows in the dark and 'advance in rushes' across the Oxford meadows." Rupert Brooke, *The Letters*, ed. Geoffrey Keynes (London: Faber, 1968), p. 644.

17. Gilbert Murray, "Oxford and the War," in *Faith, War, and Policy: Addresses and Essays on the European War* (Boston: Riverside, 1917), p. 224.

18. Murray, *Ethical*, p. 10.

19. Murray, *Autobiography*, p. 111.

20. Preface to Murray, *Faith*, p. ix.

21. Murray, *Ethical*, p. 9.

22. Ibid., p. 17.

23. Murray, *Faith*, p. 133.

24. Ibid., pp. 246–47.

25. Ibid., p. 254.

26. Gilbert Murray, *The Problem of Foreign Policy* (London: Allen & Unwin, 1921), p. 11.

27. Ibid., pp. 12, 27, and 21. In *War and the Liberal Conscience* (New Brunswick, N.J.: Rutgers, 1978), p. 83, Michael Howard remarks that "the Versailles settlement . . . lay on the liberal conscience like a burden of original sin. 'It was exactly as we had prophesied,' wrote Charles Trevelyan, 'the Imperialist War had ended in the Imperialist Peace.' Behind a façade of high-flown liberal sentiments about democracy and national self-determination, the British government and its allies had conducted the war as they had conducted all previous wars—for the national self-aggrandisement of their states, making secret agreements to distribute enemy possessions among themselves taking no account of the wishes of the peoples concerned." When the war broke out in August 1914, Trevelyan resigned his government position and, together with Ramsay MacDonald, E. D. Morel, Arthur Ponsonby, and a few others, founded the Union for Democratic Control, which sought to bring about a negotiated peace and an end to secret treaties. At the close of the war, he, along with others in the UDC, joined the Labour Party.

28. Charles F. G. Masterman, *England After War* (New York: Harcourt, Brace & Co., 1923), p. 15.

29. Murray, *Problem*, p. 31.

30. Ibid., pp. 9–10. Murray reverts to this issue in *Then and Now* (Oxford: Clarendon Press, 1935), p. 32, but with a less-understanding tone: "No doubt the War Office, by War Office standards, was right. War is Hell, and that is the sort of thing you do when you live under the laws of Hell."

31. Murray, *Problem*, p. 34. The classic statement of this position, as well as an almost clairvoyant prediction of its disastrous results, is J. M. Keynes's *The Economic Consequences of the Peace* (1919).

32. Gilbert Murray, *The Ordeal of This Generation* (New York: Harper & Brothers, 1929), p. 67.

33. Murray, *Then*, pp. 32–33.

34. Murray, *Thoughts*, p. 9. Murray's son-in-law, Arnold Toynbee, managed to keep his head better, despite being also involved in Wellington House work. Toynbee's major contribution to the propaganda effort, *Nationality and War*, bears many of the earmarks of the species, but even so contains patches of wonderful decency and generosity, as in the following instance: "In the moments when one realises the full horror of what is happening, the worst thought is the aimless hurling to destruction of the world's only true wealth, the skill and nobility and genius of human beings, and it is probably in the German casualties that the world is suffering its most irreparable human losses." *Nationality and War* (London: J. M. Dent, 1915), p. 7.

35. Douglas Goldring, *Reputations* (New York: Thomas Seltzer, 1920), p. 85.

36. Quoted in Newsome, *Benson*, p. 319.

37. Jerome, *Life*, p. 269.

38. For Bennett on Zangwill, see Arnold Bennett, *Journals, 1911-1921*, ed. Newman Flower (London: Cassell, 1932), p. 103; for the destruction of Bell's pamphlet, see David Gadd, *The Loving Friends, A Portrait of Bloomsbury* (New York: Harcourt, Brace, Jovanovich, 1974), p. 113.

Chapter 7. Into Cleanness Leaping: Brooke, Eliot, Shaw, and Lawrence

1. Quoted in Christopher Hassall, *Rupert Brooke: A Biography* (London: Faber & Faber, 1964), p. 210. In this connection, it is perhaps worth mentioning Philip Larkin's speculation that even fifty years after Brooke's death his *Collected Poems* "far outsell those of Eliot and Auden." See "The Apollo Bit," in *Required Writing* (New York: Farrar, Straus & Giroux, 1984), p. 177.

2. Rupert Brooke, *The Letters*, ed. Geoffrey Keynes (London: Faber, 1968), p. 662, and Rupert Brooke, *The Poetical Works*, ed. Geoffrey Keynes (London: Faber, 1974), p. 19. All further references to Brooke's poetry will be to this edition.

3. These ideas are not new for Brooke. In a 1913 poem "Love," Brooke uses a number of the same expressions relating to love as he does in "Peace." "They have known shame," reads part of one line, "who love unloved." Love can temporarily make the lovers forget their "agony," but it leaves them "lying" (with the pun intended here) with "their own poor dreams within their arms," each alone with a ghost in "his lonely night." Love is, in fact, "sweet lies at most." Brooke, *Works*, p. 55.

4. All quotations are taken from Albert Martin, *The Last Crusade: The Church of England in the First World War* (Durham, N.C.: Duke University Press, 1974), pp. 78, 80, 134, 140, 133. On 19 January 1915—three months before he died—Brooke wrote that he wished he were able to enter the Hereafter with his friend Dudley Ward: "He would be sensible about God: if we met him. He's English." Brooke, *Letters*, p. 656. All further references to this work will be contained in the text, by page number enclosed in parentheses. It is perhaps also appropriate to cite Jerome K. Jerome's dictum that "I have noticed that trouble invariably follows when God appears to be interesting himself in foreign affairs." See *My Life and Times* (London: Hodder & Stoughton, n.d.), p. 264.

5. Quoted in the introduction by the Rt. Hon. Arthur James Balfour to Heinrich von Treitschke, *Politics*, trans. Blanche Dugdale and Torben de Bille (New York: Macmillan, 1916), p. xxviii. R. J. Sontag's *Germany and England: Background of Conflict, 1848–1894* (New York: Russell & Russell, 1964), pp. 323–330, contains a good discussion of Treitschke's ideas and career. Broadly stated, Treitschke started off as a Liberal who admired Britain and disliked Bismarck, but after 1866 turned into something like a Prussian Liberal Imperialist. Henceforth his view was that Britain (as a nation of shopkeepers) had abandoned honor for the sake of trade; and that "this gospel of the service of Mammon threatened to mutilate mankind, to lop off from emotional life all heroic elements, everything that was sublime and beautiful, every-

thing that was ideal." Put succinctly, Treitschke's philosophy may be described as Hegel grafted on Darwin.

6. Georg Wilhelm Friedrich Hegel, *The Philosophy*, ed. C. J. Friedrich (New York: Modern Library, 1954), p. 324.

7. Hegel, *Philosophy*, p. 328. Hegel's theory of war, though in its original form discredited today, survives and even flourishes in the justification of revolutionary violence. According to Kennedy, *Rise*, p. 389, during the late nineteenth century Hegelianism in Britain "gradually became an accepted part of the philosophy curriculum and, under Bosanquet, Bradley and their colleagues, received further modification into English forms of thought." Bertrand Russell puts this more strongly in his *History of Western Philosophy* (London: Allen & Unwin, 1945), p. 701, by asserting that "at the end of the nineteenth century, the leading academic philosophers, both in America and in Great Britain, were largely Hegelians."

8. See William Henley, *The Song of the Sword and Other Verses* (London: David Nutt, 1892), p. 7; Alfred Lord Tennyson, *Complete Poetical Works* (Boston: Riverside, 1898), p. 217; Thomas Carlyle, *Past and Present* (London: Chapman & Hall, 1897), p. 190.

9. John Ruskin, *The Works*, Library Edition, ed. E. T. Cook and A. Wedderburn (London: George Allen, 1905), 18:464.

10. See Robert Nisbet, *The Social Philosophers* (Frogmore: Paladin, 1976), p. 102; and Walter Bagehot, *Physics and Politics* (New York: Knopf, 1948), p. 214. Ruskin was also an ardent imperialist who urged the British to expand their colonies: "This is what she must do or perish: she must found colonies as fast and as far as she is able . . . seizing every piece of fruitful waste [*sic*] ground she can set her foot on, and there teaching these her colonists that their first aim is to be to advance the power of England by land and sea. . . ." Quoted in George Haines, *Essays on German Influence upon English Education and Science, 1850–1919* (Hamden: Archon Books, 1969), p. 116.

11. W. L. George, "The Price of Nationality," *English Review* 20 (1915): 188, 190. Jerome K. Jerome (*My Life*, pp. 265 and 267) was later to recall that when war broke out the British were relieved and joyful. As far as he himself was concerned, "the animal in me rejoiced. It was going to be the biggest war in history. I thanked whatever gods there be that they had given it in my time." In October 1915 George Bernard Shaw observed in a lecture on "Some Illusions of the War," that war, "though both a sport and a romance, is something more than either because, although it has lost its subtlety and conflicts violently with morality and religion, it has not lost its necessity." See Allen Chappelow, *Shaw—"The Chucker-Out"* (London: Allen & Unwin, 1969), p. 362. One of the most extreme statements of the pro-war point of view occurs in Sir Walter Raleigh's *Some Gains of the War* ([New York]: Doran, 1918), p. 27, where we are told that "there is something absurd in the pacifist of British descent. He has fighting in his blood, and when his creed, or his nervous sensibility to physical horrors, denies him the use of fighting, his blood turns sour." And further: "No one can do anything to prevent war who does not recognize its splendour, for it is by its splendour that it keeps its hold on humanity, and persists."

12. D. H. Lawrence, "England, My England," *The English Review* 21 (August–December 1915): 245.

13. Rupert Brooke, *The Prose*, ed. Christopher Hassall (London: Sidgwick & Jackson, 1956), pp. 196–200.

14. Alun R. Jones, *The Life and Opinions of T. E. Hulme* (London: Gollancz, 1960), p. 100.

15. The fat man's "great pouches" swinging under his eyes—separated undoubtedly by a big nose—carry obvious sexual overtones. Less obviously, these pouches would have suggested to contemporaneous readers that the fat man was given to masturbation. George Orwell, for example, recalls in "Such, Such Were the Joys," that in his school he first learned the true significance of rings around the eyes.

That Brooke's poetry, especially "Wagner," influenced Eliot has been noted before. Timothy

Rogers maintains in his *Rupert Brooke: A Reappraisal* (London: Routledge & Kegan Paul, 1971), p. 15, that "in Eliot's own early writings there are some suggestions, if only slight, of . . . kinship" between Brooke and Eliot. And according to Robert Brainerd Pearsall's *Rupert Brooke: The Man and the Poet* (Amsterdam: Rodopi, 1974), p. 63, Eliot liked "Wagner" and imitated it.

16. It should not really come as a surprise to link Brooke with Eliot in this way. Brooke's credentials as an intellectual are impeccable, something that was recognized early in his election as an Apostle at Cambridge. While it is true that his fellowship thesis on Webster was turned down, it is also true that the same thing happened to as respectable an intellectual as Lytton Strachey. Virginia Woolf is surely right in seeing in Brooke a wide-ranging sensitivity and intelligence, one that, had he lived, "would in the end have framed a speech that came very close to the modern point of view." See Woolf's "Review of the *Collected Poems of Rupert Brooke*," *TLS* (8 August 1918), p. 371. B. C. Southam, in *A Student's Guide to the Selected Poems of T. S. Eliot* (London: Faber & Faber, 1968), pp. 72–73, was the first to point out the connection between "Grantchester" and the opening section of *The Waste Land*, though Grover Smith hints at it in *T. S. Eliot's Poetry and Plays, A Study in Sources and Meaning* (Chicago: University of Chicago Press, 1968), p. 72n.

17. T. S. Eliot, "The Waste Land," in *Selected Poems* (New York: Harcourt, Brace, and World, [1967]), l. 17. All further citations will be to this edition, by line number enclosed in parentheses.

18. Among others, Richard Ellmann has noted—what is really quite obvious—that *The Waste Land* is about the Great War. See Richard Ellmann, "The First *Waste Land*," in A. Walton Litz, ed., *Eliot in His Time* (Princeton: Princeton University Press, 1972), p. 61.

19. Douglas Goldring, *Life Interests* (London: Macdonald, 1948), p. 261.

20. James E. Miller, Jr., *T. S. Eliot's Personal Waste Land: Exorcism of the Demons* (University Park: Pennsylvania State University Press, 1978), p. 66.

21. T. S. Eliot, *After Strange Gods, A Primer of Modern Heresy* (London: Faber & Faber, 1934), p. 20; and T. S. Eliot, *Notes Towards the Definition of Culture* (London: Faber & Faber, 1958), p. 52.

22. Hassall, *Brooke*, p. 536.

23. Siegfried Sassoon, *The Weald of Youth* (New York: Viking, 1942), p. 208.

24. T. S. Eliot, "Reflections on Contemporary Poets," *The Egoist* 4 (September 1917): 119. Furthermore, it is only in a qualified sense that later war poets reacted against Brooke. So, in 1918, Robert Graves wrote to Edward Marsh that "we all look up to [Brooke] as our elder brother and have immense admiration for his work from any standpoint, especially his technique, on which we all build. I know it is fashionable to dislike him: but no one does really, least of all R. N. [Nichols], S. S. [Sassoon] or R. G. [Graves]." Quoted in Martin Seymour-Smith, *Robert Graves, His Life and Work* (New York: Holt, Rinehart & Winston, 1982), p. 106.

25. Arthur Waugh, *Tradition and Change, Studies in Contemporary Literature* (London: Chapman & Hall, 1919), p. 38.

26. George Bernard Shaw, *The Perfect Wagnerite* (New York: Dodd, Mead & Co., 1936), pp. vi and x.

27. Bernard Shaw, "What I Owe to German Culture," *Adam* 35 (1970): 5–6.

28. Bernard Shaw, *Sixteen Self Sketches* (New York: Dodd, Mead & Co., 1949), pp. 117 and 201. When Shaw met Strindberg, his German—mixed with French—was good enough to permit effective communication.

29. Quoted in Doris Arthur Jones, *The Life and Letters of Henry Arthur Jones* (London: Gollancz, 1930), p. 312.

30. Terence de Vere White, "An Irishman Abroad," in *The Genius of Shaw*, ed. Michael Holroyd (London: Hodder & Stoughton, 1979), p. 37. Shaw even became a "subscriber to the War Loan in 1915—to the tune of £20,000." See Allen Chappelow, *Shaw*, p. 359.

31. Bernard Shaw, *Essays in Fabian Socialism* (London: Constable & Co., 1961), pp. 305–6. Still, Shaw did not approve of pushing for a total victory that would destroy Germany. See Chappelow, *Shaw*, p. 348.

32. For the joint manifesto with Count Harry Kessler, see Bernard Shaw, *What I Really Wrote About the War* (New York: Brentano's, 1931), p. 4. According to Hesketh Pearson, Shaw, "like all sensible men . . . hated war." In two articles published in the *Daily Chronicle* (March 1913 and January 1914), he proposed a triple alliance between Great Britain, France, and Germany, whereby if one nation attacked another the remaining nation would join in resisting the aggressor. He also proposed "compulsory military service, mitigated by full civil rights and proper pay to the soldiers, together with a considerable increase in the national armaments." See Hesketh Pearson, *G. B. S., A Full Length Portrait* (New York: Harper & Bros., 1950), p. 289. On a more serious, though no more effective, level, Sir Max Waechter in 1913 founded the European Federation League in order to foster "an Anglo-German understanding" that would also be "the foundation and the keystone of the Federation of Europe." Waechter's idea came fifty years—and two world wars—too early. See Max Waechter, "England, Germany, and the Peace of Europe," *The Fortnightly Review* 93 (1 May 1913): 841.

33. Winston Churchill, *Great Contemporaries* (New York: Putnam's, 1937), p. 44. Shaw essentially agreed with Churchill's assessment. " 'I suppose,' he said, 'that I escape lynching solely because people treat everything I say as a huge joke; the point being that if a solitary word I uttered were taken seriously the social order would be endangered.' " Quoted in Pearson, *G. B. S.*, p. 303.

34. Bertrand Russell, *Portraits from Memory* (New York: Simon & Schuster, 1956), p. 78.

35. Huxley's unpublished letter is in the collection of the Humanities Research Center of the University of Texas at Austin. T. S. Eliot's identification of Crome with Garsington is made in the annotations of his copy of *Crome Yellow*, now in the Houghton Library at Harvard.

36. Quoted in Leonard Woolf, *Beginning Again, An Autobiography of the Years 1911–1918* (London: Harbrace, 1964), p. 126.

37. For different views on the connection between Carlyle and Shaw, see Julian B. Kaye, *Bernard Shaw and the Nineteenth Century Tradition* (Norman: University of Oklahoma Press, 1958), pp. 9–15. Georg Roppen's *Evolution and Poetic Belief* (Oslo: Oslo University Press, 1956), p. 355, sees *The Perfect Wagnerite* as an early example of Shaw's "consciously drawing on his spiritual heritage: it is as if the soul of Carlyle were reborn and rushes into a new crusade against the infidel century." Roppen does not, however, discuss the ultimately Hegelian origins of Carlyle's and Wagner's ideas of progress. Lewis Crompton also quotes, in *Shaw the Dramatist* (Lincoln: University of Nebraska Press, 1969), p. 157, from a letter to Shaw's German translator, Siegfried Trebitsch, in which Shaw explicitly rejects the more conventional (and sentimental) interpretations of "heartbreak" and explains that instead he "was using the word in the way Carlyle had used it when he referred to the blind faith of nineteenth-century liberalism in the beneficient effects of laissez faire as 'heartbreaking nonsense.' "

38. Bernard Shaw, *Heartbreak House* (Baltimore: Penguin, 1969), p. 11. All further references to this play will be included in the text, by page number enclosed in parentheses.

39. Shaw's choice of names for his characters reflects, among other concerns, his desire to identify Heartbreak House as well as Horseback Hall with the virtues and vices of the industrial revolution and the imperial expansion of Britain. This is obviously the case with Shotover and Carlyle's Undershot, or with Hastings Utterword and Warren Hastings, but it also applies to such seemingly innocuous names as William Dunn's. William Dunn was a Scottish mechanic and mill owner who died in 1849 leaving a fortune of £500,000. Alfred has a doubly Victorian name—and, ironically, doubly poetic. Alfred, as Hesione learns, derives from Alfred Lord Tennyson, and Mangan, from the Irish poet, James Mangan whose chronic dipsomania may have reminded Shaw of his father, another "little boy" who dabbled in business.

40. Margery M. Morgan, *The Shavian Playground* (London: Methuen & Co., 1972), p. 214.

41. Philip Wayne translates these lines in Goethe, *Faust* (Baltimore: Penguin, 1971), p. 87, as:

> If to the fleeting hour I say
> "Remain, so fair thou art, remain,"
> Then bind me with your fatal chain,
> For I will perish in that day. . . .

42. In the postscript to *Back to Methuselah*, Shaw writes in regard to Goethe's concept of the eternal feminine that it is the "first modern manifesto of the mysterious forces of creative evolution." Quoted in Kaye, *Shaw*, p. 110. That these ideas were shared by other members of Shaw's circle can be seen from William Archer's *The Great Analysis*, where a "great catastrophe" is postulated as a necessary precondition to changing the world. See Arthur Marwick, *Britain in the Century of War* (London: Bodley Head, 1968), p. 48.

43. Bernard Shaw, *Major Critical Essays* (London: Constable, 1955), p. 208.

44. D. H. Lawrence, *The Collected Letters*, ed. H. T. Moore (New York: Viking, 1962), p. 366.

45. D. H. Lawrence, *Phoenix II*, ed. Warren Roberts and H. T. Moore (New York: Penguin, 1978), p. 400. Further references to this work will be cited in the text, by page number enclosed in parentheses. Lawrence was, of course, a man of strong emotions rather than of systematic philosophy. Hence his attitude toward the war sometimes fluctuated. Though he consistently opposed the war as the culmination of mechanized mass man, he just as consistently desired that culmination as the simultaneous destruction of mass man and the harbinger of a new man. For an illuminating discussion of Lawrence's attitude toward the war, see Paul Delany, *D. H. Lawrence's Nightmare: The Writer and His Circle in the Years of the Great War* (New York: Basic Books, 1978).

46. Wilfred Owen, "Disabled," *War Poems and Others*, ed. D. Hibbard (London: Chatto & Windus, 1973), p. 78.

47. D. H. Lawrence, *Phoenix I*, ed. E. D. McDonald (New York: Penguin, 1978), p. 407. Further references to this work will be included in the text, by page number enclosed in parentheses.

48. D. H. Lawrence, *Aaron's Rod* (London: Heinemann, 1971), p. 288.

49. The principal references are to Wagner's *Ring* but there is also at least one allusion to the "Liebestod" of *Tristan and Isolde*. D. H. Lawrence, *The Trespasser* (London: Heinemann, 1935), p. 98. For a detailed analysis of Lawrence's use of Wagner in this novel, see Mitzi M. Brunsdale, *The German Effect on D. H. Lawrence and His Works, 1885–1912*. Utah Studies in Literature and Linguistics, vol. 13 (Berne: Peter Lang, 1978), pp. 243ff.

50. Lawrence's school and university studies had included French and German. It was, in fact, when Lawrence went to inquire of one of his former professors, Ernest Weekley, about the possibility of a lectureship at a German university that he met Frieda. Arnim Arnold's *D. H. Lawrence and German Literature* (Montreal: Mansfield Book Mart, 1963), p. 33, quotes Ford Madox Ford to the effect that Lawrence "was a well-read German scholar who had absorbed Nietzsche, Marx, and Wagner as his daily breakfast. . . . Lawrence's German was quite good, although far from correct grammatically. He had not much difficulty in reading or speaking the language; he had a rich vocabulary, if little formal background." Helen Corke, the original of Helena Verden in *The Trespasser*, recalls that Lawrence used to give her lessons in German. See Norman Page, ed., *D. H. Lawrence, Interviews and Recollections* (Totowa, N.J.: Barnes & Noble, 1981), p. 81. In *The Trespasser* itself Cecil Byrne teaches Helena German because "she wanted to understand Wagner in his own language" (p. 290).

51. Jennifer Michaels-Tonks, *D. H. Lawrence: The Polarity of North and South—Germany and Italy in His Prose Works*. Studien zur Germanistik, Anglistik und Komparatistik, vol. 42 (Bonn: Bouvier, 1976) also discusses a number of German influences on Lawrence, including Frobenius and Gross.

52. Lawrence, *Letters*, p. 340.

53. Martin Green, *The von Richthofen Sisters* (New York: Basic Books, 1974), p. 341.

54. Arnold, *Lawrence*, p. 34. According to Delany, *Lawrence*, p. 134, Lawrence had read Hegel while at the University.

55. Von Hube, despite his obviously German name, claimed to be a Polish patriot. See Brunsdale, *German*, p. 38. This connection between Germans and Poles in Lawrence's mind also emerges in "The Prussian Officer," where the title character has a Polish countess for a mother. The roots of this association may lie in Lawrence's awareness that the von Richthofens were also partly of Polish descent.

56. This pattern is further confirmed in the pregnancy of the "corrupt" and "perfected" Minette.

57. D. H. Lawrence, *Women in Love* (New York: Modern Library, 1950), p. 235.

Chapter 8. No Salvation for the Hun

1. Bertrand Russell, *Autobiography, 1914–44* (Boston: Little, Brown & Co., 1968), p. 7. So too, in *Race and Nationality* (London: Heinemann, 1919), p. 250, John Oakesmith recalls that in August 1914, "from that thrilling moment when we became conscious that the national ideals of the European States, so far from co-operating towards the peaceful permeation of the world with what was best in each of them, were to fight out their conflicting claims in the old crude way of war—from that moment the whole community was seized with a passionate fervour of devotion which can only be compared, for the intensity of its ardour, with a religious revival."

2. Bertrand Russell, "Some Psychological Difficulties in Wartime," in Julian Bell, ed., *We Did Not Fight, 1914–18* (London: Gobden-Sanderson, 1935), p. 329; Cecil Gray, *Musical Chairs or Between Two Stools* (London: Home & Van Thal, 1948), p. 38. That Russell's adamant opposition to the war did have some effect on the officer class is evident from his helping to shape Siegfried Sassoon's decision in July 1917 (later withdrawn) to leave the army. So too Arthur Graeme West concluded, after reading *Justice in Wartime*, that the courage of those who resisted the war was greater than that of those who fought in it. "Duty to country and King and civilisation!" he writes in *Diary of a Dead Officer* (London: Pelican Press, 1918), p. 58. "Nonsense! For none of these is a man to be forced to leave his humanity on one side and make a passionate beast of himself. I am a man before I am anything else, and all that is human in me revolts. I would fain stand beside these men I admire [the conscientious objectors], whose cause is the highest part of human nature, calm reason, and kindliness."

3. Compton Mackenzie, "From Naples to Calais," in George A. Panichas, ed., *Promise of Greatness, The War of 1914–1918* (New York: John Day & Co., 1968), p. 242.

4. John Viscount Morley, *Memorandum on Resignation, August 1914* (New York: Macmillan, 1928), pp. 3, 17, 15. All further references to this work will be contained in the text, by page number enclosed in parentheses.

5. Grey's letter to Sir William Edward Goschen, British Amabassador in Berlin, is reproduced, together with a number of other relevant documents, in the appendix to Morley, *Memorandum*, pp. 33–39.

6. From *Poems of the Great War* (London: Chatto & Windus, 1914), p. 11.

7. By 1915, even out-and-out patriots like Sir R. F. Payne-Gallway realized that the Kaiser had never spoken of the British or any other army in these terms, though most people used to believe it even well after the war. The Rt. Hon. Sir Robert Vansittart dusted it off again in *Black Record: Germans Past and Present* (Toronto: Musson, 1941), p. 4, for use in yet another war, but by that time there were few takers for this propaganda chestnut. According to Paul Fussell, *The Great War and Modern Memory* (New York: Oxford, 1977), p. 116, the phrase was deliberately foisted on the Kaiser by Sir Frederick Maurice of the War Office.

8. Henry James, *Within the Rim and Other Essays* (London: Collins, 1918); Austin Harrison, *The Kaiser's War* (London: Allen & Unwin, 1914), p. 215; Frederic Harrison, *The*

German Peril (London: T. Fisher Unwin, Ltd., 1915), p. 12; Hilaire Belloc, *Elements of the Great War, The First Phase* (New York: Hearst's, 1915), p. 33; Gilbert Murray, *The Foreign Policy of Sir Edward Grey, 1906–1915* (Oxford: Clarendon Press, 1915), p. 104.

9. Crane Brinton, *Nietzsche* (Cambridge: Harvard University Press, 1948), p. 202; William Archer, *Fighting a Philosophy* (London: Oxford, 1915), pp. 26 and 6.

10. William Archer, *The Villain of the World Tragedy: A Letter to Professor Ulrich v. Wilamovitz Moellendorf* (London: Fisher Unwin, [1916]), pp. 44–45.

11. Norman Angell, *Prussianism and Its Destruction* (London: Heinemann, 1914), pp. 8–9. and xviii.

12. P. Chalmers Mitchell, *Evolution and the War* (London: John Murray, 1915), p. 105; Roger Fry, *Letters*, ed. Denys Sutton (New York: Random House, 1972), 2: 615. One reason why Nietzsche was consistently preferred to Hegel as the chief "cause" of the war may be because, as Eric Halévy points out in *Imperialism and the Rise of Labour*, trans. E. I. Wattein (London: Ernest Benn, 1951), p. 140, "at the close of the nineteenth century, Hegel possessed a larger number of followers in England than in Germany." A curious variation of the theory of Hegelian guilt for the war is given by Kingsley Martin in "English Political Thought To-day," in Rolf Gardiner and Heinz Rocholl, eds., *Britain and Germany* (London: Williams & Norgate, [1929]), p. 159: "It is in this school [of Oxford Hegelians] that many of the English Imperialists were trained. By becoming Imperialists and leaving the traditions of the Liberal Party, whose individualist creed and programme was exhausted by 1885, a new generation of Liberals gained power in 1906. It is not without significance that Milner, Haldane and Asquith were all trained in the school of Oxford Hegelianism."

13. In Maurice Hussey, ed., *Poetry of the First World War* (London: Longmans, 1967), p. 104.

14. Eleanor Sidgwick et al., *The International Crisis in Its Ethical and Psychological Aspects, Lectures Delivered in February and March, 1915* (London: Humphrey Milford, 1915), p. 77.

15. H. G. Wells, *The War That Will End War* (London: Palmer, 1914), p. 15.

16. Ronald Gray's *The German Tradition in Literature* (Cambridge: Cambridge University Press, 1965), p. 15, for instance, sees in the great Prussian dramatist Kleist the embodiment of an "immoral" tradition and finds it "an oppressive thing to hear . . . that one of the most popular authors among sixth-formers in German schools today is Kleist." He hopes that someday the West Germans will turn away from "Kleist's insane and brutal nationalism" (p. 351).

17. Arnold Bennett, *Liberty, A Statement of the British Case* (London: Hodder & Stoughton, 1914), pp. 22–23; Vansittart, *Black Record*, pp. 40–42; *Why We Are At War: Great Britain's Case*, by Members of the Oxford Faculty of Modern History (Oxford: Clarendon Press, 1914), p. 114; R. W. Seton-Watson, ed., *The War and Democrary* (London: Macmillan, 1915), p. 94; Angell, *Prussianism*, p. 43; Rosebery, *War*, p. 24; Hobhouse, *Democracy*, p. 173.

18. Quoted in Julian Symons, *Horatio Bottomley* (London: Cresset Press, 1955), pp. 166–67.

19. Several of the *Poems of the Great War* (1914) take this view, including versified condemnations and exhortations by Robert Bridges, Henry Newbolt, William Watson, Alfred Noyes, and the Chesterton brothers.

20. Arthur Conan Doyle, *The German War* (London: Hodder & Stoughton, 1914), p. 80.

21. Janet Penrose Trevelyan, *The Life of Mrs. Humphry Ward* (New York: Dodd, 1923), pp. 264 and 279. According to Sir Thomas Cook's *The Mark of the Beast* (London: John Murray, 1917), p. 66, such persons "who were accepted as honourable guests have used our hospitality as a means of spying." Whereas when the British would visit German homes, so writes Hall Caine in *The Drama of Three Hundred and Sixty Five Days* (London: Heinemann, 1915), p. 36, these homes would become "scenes of prolonged duplicity."

22. Sir Walter Raleigh, *Might Is Right* (Oxford: Clarendon Press, 1917), p. 3. Some of Raleigh's sentiments are strikingly anticipated by British reactions to the Boer war. According to J. A. Hobson, *The Psychology of Jingoism* (London: Grant Richards, 1901), p. 40, "Kipling's 'Good killing at Paardeburg, the first satisfactory killing of the war,' and the phrase 'exterminate

the vermin' which, in spite of official disclaimers, did actually voice the general sentiment of the British at Natal at the outbreak of hostilities, express honestly the savage passion in the mob-mind in this country."

23. Rudyard Kipling, *Kim* (New York: Collier, 1966), p. 53; Joseph Conrad, *Heart of Darkness*, ed. Robert Kimbrough (New York: W. W. Norton & Co., 1963), p. 51, Quoted in Willis, *Holy War*, p. 179. On 4 August 1917 Lloyd George affirmed that Britain was fighting "to defeat the most dangerous conspiracy ever plotted against the liberty of nations, carefully, insidiously, clandestinely planned in every detail with ruthless, cynical determination." Quoted in Arthur Ponsonby, *Falsehood in Wartime* (New York: Dutton, 1928), p. 58. At the end of the war the Allies insisted on including Article 231 in the Versailles Treaty, charging Germany with sole responsibility for the war.

24. Quoted in Trevelyan, *Ward*, p. 271. As to British preparedness, J. A. Spender writes in *Life, Journalism and Politics* (New York: Stokes, [1926]), 2: 176, that on the evening of the British declaration of war, he walked with Winston Churchill to the Admiralty. " 'At midnight,' he said, 'we shall be at war. Think of it, if you can—the fleet absolutely ready, with instructions for every ship and the word going out from that [radio] tower, at midnight.' " Virtually all of the important British ministers and military leaders—with the exception of Kitchener—believed that the war would be over by Christmas 1914.

25. Shaw, *What I Really*, p. 104. In Bertrand Russell's mind, however, there was no doubt about Grey's malignity. In *Portraits from Memory* (London: Allen & Unwin, 1956), p. 30, he recounts how he heard Grey advocating the Entente (anti-German) policy as early as 1902. "I protested vehemently," Russell writes. "I did not like being aligned with Czarist Russia, and I saw no insurmountable obstacle to a *modus vivendi* with the Kaiser's Germany. I foresaw that a great war would mark the end of an epoch and drastically lower the general level of civilization." According to George Lansbury's *My Life* (London: Constable, 1918), p. 203, if Campbell-Bannerman "had lived till 1914 the Jingo Liberal Imperalists, Grey, Asquith, and Haldane, would not have been permitted to plunge Britain into the Great War, and all their secret plotting and planning between 1906 and 1914 would have been impossible." On the other hand, in *My Political Life* (London: Hutchinson, 1953), 1:227, L. S. Amery sees Grey as too stupid to evolve such a policy himself, "a policy which he took from the brilliant and remorselessly penetrating brain of Sir Eyre Crowe . . . But I always doubted whether he fully understood what was happening in international affairs, in the sense at least of divining the outlook and underlying purposes of the foreigners [*sic*] he had to deal with." Similarly, G. H. Perris, in *Our Foreign Policy and Sir Edward Grey's Failure* (London: Melrose, 1912), pp. 216–23, also comments on Grey's strong anti-German feeling and on his inability to understand "foreigners." According to Earl Loreburn's *How the War Came* (London: Methuen, 1919), pp. 208–9, Grey deliberately misled the Germans about British intervention in the war.

26. Arthur Conan Doyle, *Danger and Other Stories* (New York: A. L. Burt, 1916), p. 64.

27. Doyle, *German*, p. 92.

28. Lord Northcliffe, *At the War* (London: Hodder & Stoughton, 1917), p. 171. Before the war Northcliffe was frequently accused, both in Germany and in Britain, of fomenting a hate campaign against Germany. Even as late as 5 December 1914, A. G. Gardiner could write in *The Daily News:* "You say that we prophesied Peace, but we worked for Peace, just as you prophesied War and worked for War. We lost and you won."

If Northcliffe did not start the fire, he certainly helped fan the flames of the invasion scare. Northcliffe's journalistic warmongering helped increase the circulation of his newspapers, and besides, as Northcliffe observed, "the average Briton . . . liked a good hate." Quoted in Paul M. Kennedy, *The Rise of the Anglo-German Antagonism, 1860–1914* (London: Allen & Unwin, 1980), p. 362.

29. Caroline E. Playne, *The Pre-War Mind in Britain* (London: Allen & Unwin, 1928), p. 406.

30. Richard Burton Haldane, *An Autobiography* (Garden City, N.Y.: Doubleday, 1929), pp. 210, 301. Haldane had been educated in Germany and was a great admirer not only of the German Army but also (like Matthew Arnold) of the German educational system. In *Great Britain and Germany. A Study in National Characteristics* (New York: American Association for International Conciliation, 1912), p. 26, he writes that he "can think of few things more desirable for the world than that England and Germany should come to understand each other." Nevertheless, when the crisis actually arose, Haldane was eager for war.

31. William LeQueux, *Britain's Deadly Peril* (London: Stanley Paul, 1915), pp. 18–19; 98. According to Nesta H. Webster's *Spacious Days. An Autobiography* (London: Hutchinson, n.d.), pp. 182–85, the government was coddling German spies: "The thinnest excuses were made at the time for the laxity shown to German spies." Webster recounts an instance when "one spring evening Mr. William Le Queux, the novelist, who had been officially enlisted in the spy hunt" came by with some radio equipment in order to lay a trap for a German spy. "At about 11 p.m. they announced that they had been able to contact a German agent and reply to him in German code inviting him to meet them at a certain spot in the woods below the house." The spy, however, never showed up.

It is a curious and not insignificant fact that LeQueux's prolific German spies took over where the nest of French spies, centered in the French embassy, left off in LeQueux's *England's Peril* (1899). See I. R. Clarke, *Voices Prophesying War, 1763–1984* (London: Oxford, 1966), p. 124.

On a more serious but no less depressing level, two distinguished naturalized Englishmen, Sir Ernest Cassel and Sir Edgar Speyer, became victims of spy mania. Cassell was accused of being in touch with enemy aircraft that were careful to avoid bombing his house in Park Lane; and Speyer, it was noted, always happened to be out of town whenever aid raids took place and in addition was believed to be in radio contact with German submarines. Both men, "Privy Councillors" of the realm, were cut by virtually all of their prewar acquaintance, and Speyer was asked to resign from the chairmanship of a London hospital. His wife—an American of German descent—was requested to withdraw her daughters from school and told to keep out of war work societies and associations. In May 1915 Speyer had had enough and left with his family for the United States. See E. F. Benson, *As We Are: A Modern Revue* (London: Longmans, Green & Co., 1932), pp. 57 and 244–50.

32. Richard Aldington, *Life for Life's Sake* (New York: Viking Press, 1941), p. 164. No one was more surprised at the astonishing consequences of "The Bowmen" than Machen himself. In the introduction to *The Bowmen and Other Legends of the War* (London: Simpkin, 1915), pp. 54–55, Machen recounts how, after repeated protestations that the events described in his story were completely imaginary, he still continued to be charged by clergymen to be humble for having been made a "vessel" for this vision. "I cannot conceive," Machen concludes, "of anyone being foolish enough to take pride in the begetting of some of the silliest tales that have ever disgraced the English tongue."

33. Quoted in Arthur Ponsonby, *Falsehood in War-Time* (New York: Dutton, 1928), pp. 63–64. Unless otherwise indicated, all quotations from newspapers or journals are drawn from this work.

34. Aldous Huxley, *Letters*, ed. Grover Smith (London: Chatto & Windus, 1969), p. 62; see also Christopher Isherwood, *Kathleen and Frank* (New York: Simon & Schuster, 1971), p. 404.

35. Arnold Bennett, *Journals, 1911–1921*, ed. Newman Flower (London: Cassell, 1932), p. 104.

36. Ponsonby, *Falsehood*, p. 64.

37. James, *Within*, pp. 76–77 and 29–30. James reacted to the outbreak of war with stunned incredulity, feeling that it had undone everything he and his generation had believed in. Still, he tried "to think it will be *interesting*—but have only got so far as to feel it sickening." When he saw Desmond MacCarthy shortly before the latter joined a Red Cross Ambulance unit in France, James reflected that this experience "can only contribute hereafter to his powers of

conversation." Quoted in Leon Edel, *Henry James, The Master: 1901–1916* (Philadelphia: Lippincott, 1972), pp. 512 and 515. After seeing James in November 1914, Bennett came away with the impression that he was "strongly pro-English and comes to weeping-point sometimes." Bennett, *Journals*, p. 108. How profoundly the war unhinged James is evident from his delusions, as he lay on his deathbed, that he was Napoleon.

38. Viscount James Bryce, *Evidence and Documents Laid Before the Committee on Alleged German Outrages* (Ottawa: Government Printing Bureau, 1916), p. 12.

39. Ibid., pp. 25–26. There is another account in the *Evidence*, which is even more graphic, of a similar outrage committed on an English woman married to a Belgian in a small town not far from Antwerp.

40. See Fussell, *Great War*, pp. 117–20, for a more detailed account of crucifixion atrocities, together with a discussion of some of its literary implications.

41. See James Morgan Read, *Atrocity Propaganda, 1914–19* (New Haven: Yale University Press, 1941), pp. 36–48. The most horrible aspect of these atrocity stories is that they seem to have served as models for some of the genuine atrocities committed by the Germans in World War II. This is particularly true of the story spread by British propaganda about the so-called cadaver factories supposedly operated behind the German lines. As Arthur Marwick writes in *The Deluge: British Society and the First World War* (London: Bodley Head, 1965), p. 213, the existence of such a gruesome place "made a great impression at the time, and it left its odour behind it: when tales first came through early in the Second World War of Hitler's gas chambers, Fleet Street would not print them, saying that it wanted no more corpse-conversion stories."

42. Ponsonby, *Falsehood*, pp. 67–69.

43. James Morgan Read, *Atrocity Propaganda, 1914–1919* (New Haven: Yale University Press, 1941), pp. 210–11; Laurence Binyon, *The Four Years* (London: Elkin Matthews, 1919), p. 79.

44. If Edith Cavell had pleaded ignorance of the destination of the men she helped, as the Princesse de Croy, another principal in the case, did, then almost certainly her punishment would have been reduced to a prison sentence.

45. A. E. Clark-Kennedy, *Edith Cavell, Pioneer and Patriot* (London: Faber & Faber, 1965), p. 233; Keeling, *Keeling*, p. 248; *War Is War* (New York: Dutton, 1930), pp. 221–22.

46. Harold Picton, *Is It To Be Hate?* (London: Allen & Unwin, [1915]), p. 17; George Bernard Shaw, *Plays* (New York: Wise, 1930), 15:201.

47. Louis L. Cornell, *Kipling in India* (London: Macmillan, 1966), p. 163. In E. O. Morel's *King Leopold's Rule in Africa* (London: Heinemann, 1904), there are photographs of children without hands. Conrad's "Heart of Darkness," it should be remembered, is set in the Belgian Congo.

48. Caroline E. Playne, *The Pre-War Mind in Britain* (London: Allen & Unwin, 1928), p. 194; Norman Angell, *The Public Mind: Its Disorder, Its Exploitation* (New York: Dutton, 1927), p. 105. See also Hobson, *Psychology*, p. 59 and *passim*, for various atrocity legends, including one which has Paul Kruger sawing a young girl in half because she refused to divulge military secrets.

49. H. E. Barnes, *The Genesis of the World War* (New York: Knopf, 1926), p. 557. See also Philip Gibbs, *Now It Can Be Told* (New York: Harper, 1920), for a variety of British atrocities supposedly committed against Germans.

50. Stephen McKenna, *While I Remember* (New York: Doran, 1921), p. 154. See also Fussell, *Great War*, p. 316, for the tragic relation between the atrocity stories of the First World War and the all too real atrocities of the Second.

Conclusion

1. Oswald Mosley is unquestionably the most notorious of this group. The political movement that he founded—the British Union of Fascists—was not neglible but neither was it

primarily oriented toward Germany. Indeed, at the time it was established, Hitler had not yet seized power. See Robert Skidelsky's *Oswald Mosley* (New York: Holt, 1975). More to the point is the Anglo-German Fellowship, an organization supported by the German government and with a membership that included a number of influential political and business figures. Eccentric but nevertheless symbolic of pro-German and pro-Nazi English feeling is the story of Unity Mitford, who became a personal friend of Hitler's. See David Pryce-Jones's *Unity Mitford: A Quest* (London: Weidenfeld & Nicolson, 1976). In the late 1930s there was a flurry of prominent visitors to Hitler's Germany, visitors who often returned full of enthusiasm for Hitler and what he had done to Germany. Lloyd George was the most notable of these "Berchtesgaden Pilgrims," though George was no longer a real power in British politics at this time. More significant, perhaps, was the visit of the Air Minister, the Marquess of Londonderry, who remarked on the "racial connection which in itself establishes a primary friendly feeling between us which cannot be said to exist between us and the French." See his *Ourselves and Germany* (London: Robert Hale, 1938), p. 13.

2. D. H. Lawrence, *Kangaroo* (New York: Seltzer, 1923), p. 253.

3. C. H. C. Thomas, "Germany, German Literature and Mid-Nineteenth Century British Novelists," in R. W. Lacy, ed., *Affinities, Essays in German and English Literature* (London: Oswald Wolff, 1971), p. 34.

4. Laurence Housman, *A. E. H.* (London: Cape, 1937), p. 77.

5. John Maynard Keynes, *Two Memoirs* (London: Rupert Hart-Davis, 1949), p. 19.

6. More in line with the general British response to Germany at this time is Margaret McCarthy's experience, as recounted in *Generation in Revolt* (London: Heinemann, 1953), p. 139. Like Auden and his friends, McCarthy was involved with the German Communist Party, but unlike them she found them not much better than the Nazis: both were German. "The fear, the imbalance," she writes, "the burning hatred, the brutality and blood lust which were so shockingly evident were not confined to the Nazis; they were equally obvious among the Communists. . . ."

7. Stephen Spender was later to discover traces of the German propensity toward evil in the landscape itself. In *European Witness* (New York: Reynal & Hitchcock, 1946), pp. 6–7, he writes that "the landscape of Germany is as varied as that of any other country, yet much of it has in common a mental quality, less sensuous and luminous than France, less earthy than England. It is possible to think of it abstractly and it is possible to imagine it as full of intentions, moods. It doesn't suggest the gods and nymphs of Greece, nor is it haunted with the sense of individuals like England or France, but it is full of impulses, some warm and friendly, some sinister." Even those rare writers actually still interested in Germany, like John Mander, seem to feel that they must hedge their sympathies with ironies, protestations, and qualifications. So, for instance, in Mander's "Must We Love the Germans?" *Encounter* 33 (December 1969): 36–44, the titular question already suggests that the German bores are once again obtruding themselves—with their tiresome nimiety and *Schwaermerei*—on a much-tried British patience.

8. George Orwell, "Rudyard Kipling," in *A Collection of Essays* (Garden City, N.Y.: Doubleday, 1954), p. 124. Orwell's view is still quite acceptable, as we can see from Michael Edwards's identical misreading of the poem in *Rudyard Kipling, The Man, His Work and His World*, ed. John Gross (London: Weidenfeld & Nicolson, 1972), p. 44.

9. D. C. Watt, *Britain Looks to Germany: British Opinion and Policy Towards Germany Since 1945* (London: Wolff, 1965), p. 7.

Works Cited in the Text

Aldington, Richard. *Life for Life's Sake.* New York: Viking, 1941.

Alpers, Anthony. *Katherine Mansfield.* New York: Viking, 1954.

———. *The Life of Katherine Mansfield.* New York: Viking, 1980.

Amery, L. S. *My Political Life.* London: Hutchinson, 1953.

Angell, Norman. *After All.* New York: Farrar, Straus & Young, [1951].

———. *The Great Illusion.* New York: G. P. Putnam's Sons, 1911.

———. *Prussianism and Its Destruction.* London: Heinemann, 1914.

———. *The Public Mind: Its Disorder, Its Exploitation.* New York: Dutton, 1927.

Archer, William. *Fighting a Philosophy.* London: Oxford, 1915.

———. *The Villain of the World Tragedy: A Letter to Professor Ulrich v. Wilamovitz Moellendorf.* London: Fisher Unwin, [1916].

Arnold, Arnim. *D. H. Lawrence and German Literature.* Montreal: Mansfield Book Mart, 1963.

Aubry, G. Jean. *Joseph Conrad: Life and Letters.* New York: Doubleday, 1927.

Bagehot, Walter. *Physics and Politics.* New York: Knopf, 1948.

Baines, Jocelyn. *Joseph Conrad: A Critical Biography.* New York: McGraw-Hill, 1967.

Barker, Ernest. *National Characteristics and the Factors in Its Formation.* London: Methuen, 1927.

Barker, J. Ellis. *Modern Germany.* 5th ed. London: Smith, Elder & Co., 1915.

Barnes, H.E. *The Genesis of the World War.* New York: Knopf, 1926.

Bazley, Basil M. "Kipling's Opinion of the Germans," *The Kipling Journal* (July 1945), 3–5.

Beerbohm, Max. "P. C., X, 36," in *Kipling and the Critics,* ed. Elliott L. Gilbert. New York: New York University Press, 1965.

Bell, Julian, ed. *We Did Not Fight, 1914–1918.* London: Cobden-Sanderson, 1935.

Belloc, Hilaire. *Cautionary Tales.* London: Duckworth, 1939.

———. *Elements of the Great War: The First Phase.* New York: Hearst's, 1915.

———. *Emmanuel Burden, Merchant.* London: Methuen, 1927.

———. *Letters,* ed. Robert Speaight. London: Hollis & Carter, 1958.

———. *The Modern Traveller.* London: Edward Arnold, 1898.

Bennett, Arnold. *Journals, 1911–1921.* Edited by Newman Flower. London: Cassell, 1932.

———. *Letters.* Edited by James Hepburn. London: Oxford, 1968.

———. *Liberty, A Statement of the British Case.* London: Hodder & Stoughton, 1914.

Benson, E. F. *As We Are: A Modern Revue.* London: Longmans, Green & Co., 1932.

Bergson, Henri. *The Meaning of the War: Life and Matter in Conflict.* New York: Macmillan, 1915.

Berkman, Sylvia. *Katherine Mansfield.* New Haven: Yale University Press, 1951.

Bodelsen, C. A. *Aspects of Kipling's Art.* Manchester: University Press, 1964.

Bradley, R. N. *Racial Origins of the British Character.* London: Allen & Unwin, 1926.

Brie, Friedrich. *Imperialistische Stroemungen in der englischen Literatur.* Halle: Niemeyer, 1928.

Brinton, Brane. *Nietzsche.* Cambridge: Harvard University Press, 1948.

Brooke, Rupert. *The Letters.* Edited by Geoffrey Keynes. London: Faber, 1968.

———. *The Poetical Works.* Edited by Geoffrey Keynes. London: Faber, 1974.

———. *The Prose.* Edited by Christopher Hassall. London: Sidgwick & Jackson, 1956.

Brower, Reuben, ed. *On Translation.* New York: Oxford, 1966.

Brunsdale, Mitzi M. *The German Effect on D. H. Lawrence and His Works, 1885–1912.* Utah Studies in Literature and Linguistics, vol. 13. Berne: Peter Lang, 1978.

Bryce, Viscount James. *Evidence and Documents Laid Before the Committee on Alleged German Outrages.* Ottawa: Government Printing Bureau, 1916.

Buchan, John. *Adventures of Richard Hannay.* Cambridge, Mass.: Riverside Press, n.d.

———. *The Clearing House.* London: Hodder & Stoughton, 1946.

———. "The German Mind," *Land and Water* 5 (6 November 1915): 17–19.

————. *Greenmantle*. London: Nelson, n.d.

Buckley, Arabella. *History of England for Beginners*. London: Macmillan, 1887.

Buitenhuis, Peter. "Writers at War: Propaganda and Fiction in the Great War," *University of Texas Quarterly* 45 (September 1976): 277–94.

Butler, E.M. *Paper Boats*. London: Collins, 1959.

Caine, Hall. *The Drama of Three Hundred and Sixty Five Days*. London: Heinemann, 1915.

Carlyle, Thomas. *Past and Present*. London: Chapman & Hall, 1897.

Carrington, C. E. *The Life of Rudyard Kipling*. Garden City, N.Y.: Doubleday, 1955.

Carswell, John. *Lives and Letters*. New York: New Directions, 1978.

Chappelow, Allen. *Shaw—"The Chucker-Out."* London: Allen & Unwin, 1969.

Charms, Leslie de. *Elizabeth of the German Garden*. London: Heinemann, 1958.

Chesterton, Cecil. *The Prussian Hath Said in His Heart*. London: Chapman & Hall, 1914.

Chesterton, G. K. *The Crimes of England*. New York: John Lane, 1916.

————. *The Paradoxes of Mr. Pond*. New York: Dodd, Mead & Co., 1945.

Churchill, Winston. *Great Contemporaries*. New York: Putnam's, 1937.

Clark, Ronald W. *The Life of Bertrand Russell*. New York: Knopf, 1976.

Clark-Kennedy, A. E. *Edith Cavell, Pioneer and Patriot*. London: Faber & Faber, 1965.

Clarke, I.E. *Voices Prophesying War, 1763–1914*. London: Oxford, 1966.

Coghill, Nevill. "The Unfading Memory of Rudyard Kipling," *The Kipling Journal* 32 (December 1965): 65–70.

Cohn, Norman. *Warrant for Genocide*. New York: Harper & Row, 1967.

Collett, Anthony. *The Changing Face of England*. London: Nisbet, 1927.

Conrad, Jesse. *Joseph Conrad As I Knew Him*. London: Heinemann, 1926.

Conrad, Joseph. *Falk*. New York: Doubleday, 1914.

————. *Heart of Darkness*. Edited by Robert Kimbrough. New York: Norton, 1963.

————. *Lord Jim*. Edited by R. B. Heilman. New York: Holt, Rinehart & Winston, 1967.

————. *Notes on Life and Letters*. New York: Doubleday, 1925.

————. *A Personal Record*. New York: Doubleday, 1925.

————. *Victory, An Island Tale*. New York: Doubleday, 1927.

Conway, Sir Martin. *The Crowd in Peace and War*. London: Longmans, 1915.

Cook, Sir Thomas. *The Mask of the Beast.* London: John Murray, 1917.

Cornell, Louis L. *Kipling in India.* London: Macmillan, 1966.

Cramb, J. A. *Germany and England.* London: John Murray, 1914.

Crompton, Lewis. *Shaw the Dramatist.* Lincoln: University of Nebraska Press, 1969.

Crookshank, F. G. *The Mongol in Our Midst: A Study of Man and His Three Faces.* London: Kegan Paul, 1924.

Dance, E. H. *History the Betrayer, A Study in Bias.* London: Hutchinson, 1960.

Dangerfield, George. *The Strange Death of Liberal England.* New York: Capricorn, 1961.

Dawson, A. J. *The Message.* Boston: Dana Estes & Co., 1907.

Delany, Paul. *D. H. Lawrence's Nightmare.* New York: Basic Books, 1978.

Dobrée, Bonamy. *The Lamp and the Lute.* New York: Barnes & Noble, 1964.

————. *Rudyard Kipling, Realist and Fabulist.* London: Oxford, 1967.

Doyle, Sir Arthur Conan. *The Annotated Sherlock Holmes.* Edited by W. S. Baring-Gould. New York: Clarkson Potter, 1967.

————. *Danger and Other Stories.* New York: A. L. Burt, 1916.

————. *The Exploits of Brigadier Gerard.* New York: Appleton, 1896.

————. *The Firm of Girdlestone.* New York: A. L. Burt, n.d.

————. *The German War.* London: Hodder & Stoughton, 1914.

Dyserinck, Hugo. *Komparatistik: Eine Einführung.* Aachener Beiträge zur Komparatistik. Band I. Bonn: Bouvier Verlag, 1981.

————. "Zum Problem de 'images' und 'mirages' und ihrer Untersuchung im Rahmen der Vergleichenden Literaturwissenschaft," *Arcadia* 1 (1966): 108–20.

Edel, Leon. *Henry James, The Master: 1901–1916.* Philadelphia: Lippincott, 1972.

Eliot, T. S. *After Strange Gods, A Primer of Modern Heresy.* London: Faber & Faber, 1934.

————. *Notes Towards the Definition of Culture.* London: Faber & Faber, 1958.

————. "Reflections on Contemporary Poets," *The Egoist* 4 (September 1917): 118–19.

————. *Selected Poems.* New York: Harcourt, Brace & World, [1967].

Ellis, Havelock. *The New Spirit.* New York: Boni & Liveright, n.d.

————. *A Study of British Genius.* London: Constable, 1914.

"Events of the Week," *The Nation* 15 (1 August 1914): 653.

Faber, Richard. *The Vision and the Need: Late Victorian Imperialist Aims.* London: Faber & Faber, 1966.

Fitch, Sir Joshua. *Thomas and Matthew Arnold.* New York: Scribners, 1898.

Fleure, H. J. *The Peoples of Europe.* London: Oxford, 1925.

———. *The Races of Mankind.* London: Benn, 1927.

Ford, Ford Madox. *The Good Soldier.* London: The Bodley Head. 1962.

———. *Parade's End.* London: The Bodley Head, 1963

———. *Return to Yesterday.* New York: Liveright, 1932.

Forster. E. M. *Aspects of the Novel.* New York: Harcourt, Brace & World, 1966.

———. *Goldsworthy Lowes Dickinson.* London: Edward Arnold, 1962.

———. *Howards End.* New York: Vintage, n.d.

———. *The Longest Journey.* London: Oxford, 1960.

———. *The Manuscripts of 'Howards End.'* Edited by Oliver Stallybrass. London: Edward Arnold, 1973.

———. *Marianne Thornton.* New York: Harcourt, Brace & Co., 1956.

———. *Nordic Twilight.* London: Macmillan, 1940.

———. "Recollections of Nassenheide," *The Listener* (1 January 1959), 214.

———. "Revolution at Bayreuth," *The Listener* (4 November 1954), 755–57.

———. *Two Cheers for Democracy.* London: Edward Arnold, 1972.

Fraenkel, Heinrich. *Deutschland im Urteil des Auslandes Frueher und— Jetzt.* Munich: Georg Mueller, 1916.

Freeman, Edward. *The Chief Periods of European History.* London: Macmillan, 1886.

Fromm, Gloria G. *Dorothy Richardson.* Urbana: University of Illinois Press, 1977.

Fry, Roger. *Letters.* Edited by Denys Sutton. New York: Random House, 1972.

Furbank, P. N. *E. M. Forster: A Life.* London: Secker & Warburg, 1977.

———. "John Bull in the German Garden." *Encounter* 22 (April 1964): 85–91.

Fussell, Paul. *The Great War and Modern Memory.* New York: Oxford, 1977.

Gadd, David. *The Loving Friends: A Portrait of Bloomsbury.* New York: Harcourt Brace Jovanovich, 1974.

Galton, Francis. *Hereditary Genius.* London: Macmillan, 1914.

Gardiner, Ralf and Heinz Rocholl, eds. *Britain and Germany.* London: Williams & Norgate, [1929].

Gardner, Philip, ed. *E. M. Forster: The Critical Heritage*. London: Routledge & Kegan Paul, 1973.

Garnett, David. *Great Friends*. London: Macmillan, 1979.

George, W. L. "The Price of Nationality," *English Review* 20 (1915): 184–96.

"The German Peril," *Blackwood's* (January 1898), 107–22.

Gibbs, Philip. *Now It Can Be Told*. New York: Harper, 1920.

Gilbert, Elliott. *The Good Kipling: Studies in the Short Story*. [Athens]: Ohio University Press, [1971].

————, ed. *Kipling and the Critics*. New York: New York University Press, 1965.

Goethe, Johann Wolfgang von. *Faust*. Translated by Philip Wayne. Baltimore: Penguin, 1971.

————. *Werke*, ed. Josef Kunz. Hamburg: Christian Wegner Verlag, 1960.

Goldring, Douglas. *Reputations*. New York: Thomas Seltzer, 1920.

————. *South Lodge: Reminiscences of Violet Hunt, Ford Madox Ford and the English Review Circle*. London: Constable, 1943.

Gordon, E. V. *An Introduction to Old Norse*. London: Oxford, [1927].

Graves, Robert. *Fairies and Fuseliers*. New York: Knopf, [1919].

————. *Good-bye to All That*. Garden City, N. Y.: Doubleday, 1957.

Gray, Cecil. *Musical Chairs or Between Two Stools*. London: Home & Van Thal, 1948.

Gray, Ronald. *The German Tradition in Literature*. Cambridge: Cambridge University Press, 1965.

Green, Martin. *The von Richthofen Sisters*. New York: Basic Books, 1974.

Green, Robert. *Ford Madox Ford: Prose and Politics*. Cambridge: Cambridge University Press, 1981.

Green, Roger Lancelyn. *A. E. Mason*. London: Max Parrish, 1952.

Green, R. L., ed. *Kipling: The Critical Heritage*. London: Routledge & Kegan Paul, 1971.

Greene, Graham. *The Old School*. London: Jonathan Cape, 1934.

Gross, John, ed. *Rudyard Kipling: The Man, His Work and His World*. London: Weidenfeld & Nicholson, 1972.

Gurko, Leo. *Joseph Conrad, Giant in Exile*. New York: Macmillan, 1962.

Haddon, A. C. *Races of Man and Their Distribution*. New York: Macmillan, 1925.

Haines, George. *Essays on German Influence upon English Education and Science, 1850–1919*. Hamden: Archon Books, 1969.

Haldane, Richard Burton, An Autobiography. Garden City, N. Y.: Doubleday, 1929.

————. *Great Britain and Germany: A Study in National Characteristics.* New York: American Association for International Conciliation, 1912.

Hale, Orton James. *Publicity and Diplomacy, with Special Reference to England and Germany, 1890–1914.* New York: Appleton-Century, 1940.

Halévy. Eric. *Imperialism and the Rise of Labour.* Trans. E. I. Wattein. London: Ernest Benn, 1951.

Hardy, Thomas. *The Writings of Thomas Hardy in Prose and Verse.* Anniversary Edition. New York: Harper, n.d.

[Harris, Frank.] "England and Germany," *Saturday Review* 84 (11 September 1897): 278–79.

Harrison, Austin. *The Kaiser's War.* London: Allen & Unwin, 1914.

Harrison, Frederic. *The German Peril.* London: Fisher Unwin, 1915.

Harrison, Jane. *Alpha and Omega.* London: Sidgwick & Jackson, 1915.

Hassall, Christopher. *Rupert Brooke: A Biography.* London: Faber & Faber, 1964.

Hegel, Georg Wilhelm Friedrich. *The Philosophy.* Edited by C. J. Friedrich. New York: Modern Library, 1954.

Heller, Erich. *The Disinherited Mind.* Cambridge: Bowes & Bowes, 1952.

Henley, William. *The Song of the Sword and Other Verses.* London: David Nutt, 1892.

Herder, Johann Gottfried von. *Outlines of a Philosophy of the History of Man.* Translated by T. Churchill. New York: Bergman, [1966].

Hewlett, Maurice. *Letters,* ed. Laurence Binyon. London: Methuen, 1926.

Hirst, F. W. *The Six Panics and Other Essays.* London: Methuen, 1913.

Hobhouse, L. T. *A World in Conflict.* London: Fisher Unwin, 1915.

Hobson, J. A. *The Psychology of Jingoism.* London: Grant Richards, 1901.

Holroyd, Michael, ed. *The Genius of Shaw.* London: Hodder & Stoughton, 1979.

————. *Lytton Strachey, A Critical Biography.* New York: Holt, Rinehart & Winston, 1968.

Housman, Laurence. *A.E.H.* London: Jonathan Cape, 1937.

Howard, Michael. *War and the Liberal Conscience.* New Brunswick, N.J.: Rutgers University Press, 1978.

Hueffer, Ford Madox. "High Germany—I: How It Feels to Be Members of Subject Races," *The Saturday Review* 112 (7 October 1911): 421–22.

————. "High Germany—II: Utopia," *The Saturday Review* 112 (7 October 1911): 454–56.

————. *When Blood Is Their Argument: An Analysis of Prussian Culture.* New York: Hodder & Stoughton, 1915.

Hunt, Violet. *The Desirable Alien: At Home in Germany.* London: Chatto & Windus, 1913.

————. *I Have This to Say: The Story of My Flurried Years*. New York: Boni & Liveright, [1926].

————. *The Last Ditch*. London: Stanley Paul & Co., 1926.

Hunt, Violet and F. M. Hueffer. *Zeppelin Nights*. London: John Lane, 1916.

Hussey, Maurice, ed. *Poetry of the First World War*. London: Longmans, 1967.

Huxley, Aldous. *Letters*. Edited by Grover Smith. London: Chatto & Windus, 1969.

Hynes, Samuel. *The Edwardian Turn of Mind*. Princeton: Princeton University Press, 1968.

Inge, William Ralph. *Outspoken Essays*. London: Longmans, 1923.

Isherwood, Christopher. *Kathleen and Frank*. New York: Simon & Schuster, 1971.

James, Henry. *Within the Rim and Other Essays*. London: Collins, 1918.

Jerome, Jerome K. *My Life and Times*. London: Hodder & Stoughton, [1926].

Jeshuran, Chandran. "Lord Lansdowne and the 'Anti-German Clique' at the Foreign Office," *Journal of Southeast Asian Studies* 3 (September 1972): 229–46.

Johnston, Sir Harry. *Common Sense in Foreign Policy*. New York: Dutton, 1913.

Jones, Alun R. *The Life and Opinions of T. E. Hulme*. London: Gollancz, 1960.

Jones, Doris Arthur. *The Life and Letters of Henry Arthur Jones*. London: Gollancz, 1930.

Joseph, Bernard. *Nationality: Its Nature and Its Problems*. London: Allen & Unwin, 1929.

Karl, Frederick. *Joseph Conrad: A Reader's Guide*. Rev. ed. New York: Farrar, Straus & Giroux, 1969.

————. *Joseph Conrad: The Three Lives*. New York: Farrar, Straus & Giroux, 1979.

Kaye, Julian B. *Bernard Shaw and the Nineteenth Century Tradition*. Norman: University of Oklahoma Press, 1958.

Kayser, Walter. *Das Groteske, Seine Gestaltung in Malerei und Dichtung*. Oldenburg: Stallung Verlag, 1957.

Keane, A. H. *Ethnology*. Cambridge: Cambridge University Press, 1909.

Keeling, Frederick H. *Letters and Recollections*. Edited by E. T. New York: Macmillan, n.d.

Kennedy, Paul M. *The Rise of the Anglo-German Antagonism, 1860–1914*. London: Allen & Unwin, 1980.

————, ed. *The War Plans of the Great Powers, 1880–1914*. London: Allen & Unwin, 1978.

Kenworthy, J. M. *Peace or War?* New York: Boni & Liveright, 1927.

Keynes, J. M. *The Economic Consequences of the Peace.* London: Macmillan, 1920.

———. *Two Memoirs.* London: Rupert Hart-Davis, 1949.

King Albert's Book. New York: Hearst International [1915].

Kingsley, Charles. *The Roman and the Teuton.* London: Macmillan, 1875.

Kingsmill, Hugh. *Frank Harris.* London: Cape, 1932.

Kipling, Rudyard. *The Eyes of Asia.* Garden City, N.Y.: Doubleday, 1918.

———. *France at War.* London: Macmillan, 1915.

———. *The Fringes of the Fleet.* London: Macmillan, 1915.

———. *Kim.* New York: Collier, 1966.

———. *The Writings in Prose and Verse.* New York: Scribners, 1917.

Koch-Hillebrecht, Manfred. *Das Deutschenbild: Gegenwart, Geschichte, Psychologie.* München: C. H. Beck Verlag, 1977.

Kohn, Hans. *The Idea of Nationalism.* New York: Macmillan, 1948.

Kunitz, Stanley, ed. *Twentieth Century Authors.* New York: Wilson, 1942.

Lacy, R. W., ed. *Affinities, Essays in German and English Literature.* London: Oswald Wolff, 1971.

Lansbury, George. *My Life.* London: Constable, 1918.

Larkin, Philip. *Required Writing.* New York: Farrar, Straus & Giroux, 1984.

Lawrence, D. H. *Aaron's Rod.* London: Heinemann, 1971.

———. *The Collected Letters.* Edited by H. T. Moore. New York: Viking, 1962.

———. "England, My England," *The English Review* 21 (Aug.-Dec. 1915): 238–52.

———. *Kangaroo.* New York: Seltzer, 1923.

———. *Phoenix I.* Edited by E. D. McDonald. New York: Penguin, 1978.

———. *Phoenix II.* Edited by Warren Roberts and H. T. Moore. New York: Penguin, 1978.

———. *The Trespasser.* London: Heinemann, 1935.

———. *Women in Love.* New York: Modern Library, 1950.

Lea, Homer. *The Day of the Saxon.* New York: Harper & Bros., 1912.

Leonard, R. M. *Patriotic Poems.* London: Oxford, 1914.

Le Queux, William L. *Britain's Deadly Peril.* London: Stanley Paul, 1915.

Litz, A. Walton, *Eliot in His Time.* Princeton: Princeton University Press, 1972.

Londonderry, The Marquess of. *Ourselves and Germany.* London: Robert Hale, 1938.

Loreburn, The Earl of. *How the War Came.* London: Methuen, 1919.

Loti, Pierre. *The Trail of the Barbarians.* Translated by F. M. Hueffer. London: Longmans, 1917.

McCarthy, Margaret. *Generation in Revolt.* London: Heinemann, 1953.

McDougall, William. *Is America Safe for Democracy?* New York: Scribner's, 1921.

Machen, Arthur. *The Bowmen and Other Legends of the War.* London: Simpkin, 1915.

McKenna, Stephen. *While I Remember.* New York: Doran, 1921.

MacNamara, Nottidge Charles. *Origin and Character of the British People.* London: Smith, Elder & Co., 1900.

MacShane, Frank, ed. *Ford Madox Ford: The Critical Heritage.* London: Routledge & Kegan Paul, 1972.

Madariaga, Salvador de. *Portrait of Europe.* London: Hollis & Carter, 1952.

Mander, John. "Must We Love the Germans?" *Encounter* 33 (December 1969): 36–44.

————. *Our German Cousins.* London: John Murray, 1974.

Mansfield, Katherine. *In a German Pension.* New York: Knopf, 1926.

————. *The Short Stories.* New York: Knopf, 1954.

Martin, Albert. *The Last Crusade: The Church of England in the First World War.* Durham, N.C.: Duke University Press, 1974.

Marwick, Arthur. *Britain in the Century of War.* London: Bodley Head, 1968.

————. *The Deluge: British Society and the First World War.* London: Bodley Head, 1965.

Masterman, C. F. G. *England After War.* New York: Harcourt, Brace & Co., 1923.

Maugham, W. Somerset. "Introduction" to *A Choice of Kipling's Prose.* London: Macmillan, 1952.

[Maxse, Leo.] "The German Jew and the German Empire," *National Review* 64 (October 1914): 229–42.

Meine, Kurt. *England und Deutschland in der Zeit des Ueberganges vom Manchestertum zum Imperialismus, 1871 bis 1876.* Berlin: Ebering, 1937.

Members of the Oxford Faculty of Modern History. *Why We Are at War: Great Britain's Case.* Oxford: Clarendon Press, 1914.

Meredith, George. *The Letters.* Edited by L. L. Cline. Oxford: Clarendon Press, 1970.

Michaels-Tonks, Jennifer. *D. H. Lawrence: The Polarity of North South— Germany and Italy in His Prose Works.* Studien zur Germanistik, Anglistik und Komparatistik. Vol. 42. Bonn: Bouvier, 1976.

Miller, James E., Jr. *T. S. Eliot's Personal Waste Land: Exorcism of the Demons.* University Park: Pennsylvania State University Press, 1978.

[Mitchell, P. C.] "A Biological View of Our Foreign Policy," *Saturday Review* 82 (1 February 1896): 118–20.

Mitchell, P. Chalmers. *Evolution and the War.* London: John Murray, 1915.

Mizener, Arthur. *The Saddest Story.* New York: World, 1971.

Montague, C. E. *Disenchantment.* New York: Brentano's, 1922.

Moon, Parker Thomas. *Imperialism and World Politics.* New York: Macmillan, 1926.

Morel, E. O. *King Leopold's Rule in Africa.* London: Heinemann, 1904.

Morgan, Margery M. *The Shavian Playground.* London: Methuen & Co., 1972.

Morley, John. *Memorandum on Resignation, August 1914.* New York: Macmillan, 1928.

Moser, Thomas. *The Life in the Fiction of Ford Madox Ford.* Princeton: Princeton University Press, 1980.

Muir, Ramsay. *Nationalism and Internationalism.* London: Constable, 1917.

Muir, Willa. "Translating from German," in *On Translation,* edited by Reuben Brower. New York: Oxford, 1966.

Munro, H. H. *When William Came, A Story of London under the Hohenzollerns.* New York: Viking, 1929.

Murray, Gilbert. *Ethical Problems of the War.* London: Nelson, 1915.

————. *Faith, War, and Policy: Addresses and Essays on the European War.* Boston: Riverside Press, 1917.

————. *The Foreign Policy of Sir Edward Grey, 1906–1915.* Oxford: Clarendon Press, 1915.

————. *Gilbert Murray: An Unfinished Autobiography,* ed. Jean Smith and Arnold Toynbee. London: Allen & Unwin, 1960.

————. "National Ideals: Conscious and Unconscious," *International Journal of Ethics* 11 (October 1900), 1–22.

————. *The Ordeal of This Generation.* New York: Harper & Bros., 1929.

————. *Then and Now.* Oxford: Clarendon Press, 1935.

————. *Thoughts on the War.* Oxford: Clarendon Press, 1914.

Newsome, David. *On the Edge of Paradise: A. C. Benson, The Diarist.* London: John Murray, 1980.

Nicholas, Thomas. *Pedigree of the English People.* London: Longmans, 1868.

Nichols, Robert. *Anthology of War Poetry, 1914–1918.* London: Nicholson & Watson, 1943.

Nicholson, Ivor. "An Aspect of British Official Wartime Propaganda," *Cornhill Magazine* 70 (June 1931), 593–606.

Nisbet, Robert. *The Social Philosophers.* Frogmore: Paladin, 1976.

Northcliffe, Lord. *At the War.* London: Hodder & Stoughton, 1917.

Oakesmith, John. *Race and Nationality.* London: Heinemann, 1919.

Oppenheim, E. Phillips. *The Double Traitor.* New York: A. L. Burt Co., [1915].

Orwell, George. *A Collection of Essays.* Garden City, N.Y.: Doubleday, 1954.

Owen, Wilfred. *War Poems and Others.* Edited by D. Hibberd. London: Chatto & Windus, 1973.

Page, Malcolm. "The Nationality of the Airman in 'Mary Postgate,'" *The Kipling Journal* 37 (June 1970): 14–15.

Page, Norman. *D. H. Lawrence, Interviews and Recollections.* Totowa, N.J.: Barnes & Noble, 1981.

Page, William, ed. *A History of Hertfordshire.* London: Constable, 1912.

Peake, Harold. *The English Village: The Origin and Decay of Its Community.* London: Benn Brothers, 1922.

Panichas, George A. *Promise of Greatness: The War of 1914–1918.* New York: John Day & Co., 1968.

Pearsall, Robert Brainerd. *Rupert Brooke: The Man and the Poet.* Amsterdam: Rodopi, 1974.

Pearson, C. H. *National Life and Character: A Forecast.* London: Macmillan, 1894.

Pearson, Hesketh. *G. B. S., A Full Length Portrait.* New York: Harper & Bros., 1950.

Pearson, Karl. *National Life and Character from the Standpoint of Science.* Cambridge: Cambridge University Press, [1905].

Percy, The Earl of. "Military Policy and the War," *National Review* 57 (August 1911): 954–68.

Perris, G. H. *Our Foreign Policy and Sir Edward Grey's Failure.* London: Andrew Melrose, 1912.

Phillips, Lady. *A Friendly Germany: Why Not?* London: Constable, 1913.

Picton, Harold. *Is It To Be Hate?* London: Allen & Unwin, [1915].

Pike, Luke Owen. *The English and Their Origin.* London: Longmans, 1886.

Playne, Caroline E. *The Pre-War Mind in Britain.* London: Allen & Unwin, 1928.

Poems of the Great War. London: Chatto & Windus, 1914.

Ponsonby, Arthur. *Falsehood in Wartime.* New York: Dutton, 1928.

Pound, Ezra. "At Last the Novel Appears," in *James Joyce, A Portrait of the Artist as a Young Man,* ed. Chester Anderson. New York: Viking, 1968.

Powys, John Cowper. *The Menace of German Culture.* London: W. Ridder, 1915.

Pryce-Jones, David. *Unity Mitford: A Quest.* London: Weidenfeld & Nicholson, 1976.

Radclyffe, Raymond. "The Germans in the City," *English Review* 21 (Aug.–Dec., 1915): 521–26.

Raffel, Burton. *Poems from the Old English.* Lincoln: University of Nebraska Press, 1964.

Raleigh, Sir Walter. *Might Is Right.* Oxford: Clarendon Press, 1917.

———. *Some Gains of the War.* [New York]: Doran, 1918.

———. *The War of Ideas.* London: Oxford, 1917.

Raphael, Alice. *Goethe the Challenger.* New York: Jonathan Cape, 1932.

Read, James Morgan. *Atrocity Propaganda, 1914–1919.* New Haven: Yale University Press, 1941.

Retinger, J. H. *Conrad and His Contemporaries.* New York: Roy Publishers, 1943.

Richardson, Dorothy. *Pointed Roofs.* New York: Knopf, 1919.

Robertson, J. M. *The Germans.* London: Williams & Norgate, 1916.

Robson, W. W. "Kipling's Later Stories," in *Kipling's Mind and Art*, ed. Andrew Rutherford. Stanford: Stanford University Press, 1964.

Roby, Kinley E. *A Writer at War: Arnold Bennett, 1914–1918.* Baton Rouge: Louisiana State University Press, 1972.

Rogers, Timothy. *Rupert Brooke: A Reappraisal.* London: Routledge & Kegan Paul, 1971.

Rolfe, Frederick [Baron Corvo]. *Hadrian the Seventh.* London: Chatto & Windus, 1950.

Roppen, Georg. *Evolution and Poetic Belief.* Oslo: Oslo University Press, 1956.

Rosebery, Lord Archibald. *War! A Fight to the Finish.* Stirling: Eneas Mackay, [1914].

Rosenberg, John. *Dorothy Richardson: The Forgotten Genius.* London: Duckworth, 1973.

Ruskin, John. *The Works.* Library Edition, ed. E. T. Cook and A. Wedderburn. London: George Allen, 1905.

Russell, Bertrand. *The Autobiography of Bertrand Russell, 1914–1944.* Boston: Little, Brown & Co., 1968.

———. *History of Western Philosophy.* London: Allen & Unwin, 1945.

———. *Portraits from Memory.* New York: Simon & Schuster, 1956.

Santayana, George. *Three Philosophical Poets.* Cambridge: Harvard University Press, 1947.

Sassoon, Siegfried. *Memoirs of an Infantry Officer.* New York: Collier, 1969.

———. *Siegfried's Journey.* London: Faber, 1945.

————. *The Weald of Youth.* New York: Viking, 1942.

Seton-Jackson, R. W., ed. *The War and Democracy.* London: Macmillan, 1915.

Seymour-Smith, Martin. *Robert Graves, His Life and Work.* New York: Holt, Rinehart & Winston, 1982.

Shaw, George Bernard. *Essays in Fabian Socialism.* London: Constable, 1961.

————. *Heartbreak House.* Baltimore: Penguin, 1969.

————. *The Perfect Wagnerite.* New York: Dodd, Mead & Co., 1936.

————. *Plays.* New York: Wise, 1930.

————. *Sixteen Self Sketches.* New York: Dodd, Mead & Co., 1949.

————. "What I Owe to German Culture," *Adam,* 35 (1970): 5–6.

————. *What I Really Wrote About the War.* New York: Brentano's, 1931.

Sherry, Norman. *Conrad's Eastern World.* Cambridge: Cambridge University Press, 1966.

————. *Conrad's Western World.* Cambridge: Cambridge University Press, 1971.

Sidgwick, Eleanor et al. *The International Crisis in Its Ethical and Psychological Aspects, Lectures Delivered in February and March, 1915.* London: Humphrey Ward, 1915.

Skidelsky, Robert. *Oswald Mosley.* New York: Holt, 1975.

Smith, Grover. *T. S. Eliot's Poetry and Plays: A Study in Sources and Meaning.* Chicago: University of Chicago Press, 1968.

Sontag, R. J. *Germany and England: Background of Conflict, 1848–1894.* New York: Russell & Russell, 1964.

Sorley, Charles Hamilton. *Letters.* Cambridge: Cambridge University Press, 1919.

————. *Marlborough and Other Poems.* Cambridge: Cambridge University Press, 1919.

Southam, B. C. *A Student's Guide to the Selected Poems of T. S. Eliot.* London: Faber & Faber, 1968.

Spender, J. A. *Life, Journalism, and Politics.* New York: Stokes, [1926].

Spender, Stephen. *European Witness.* New York: Reynal & Hitchcock, 1946.

Spottiswoode, Sybil. *Her Husband's Country.* New York: Duffield & Co., 1911.

Squires, J. D. *British Propaganda at Home and in the United States from 1914 to 1917.* Cambridge: Harvard University Press, 1935.

Stead, W. T. "The Lord Chief Justice of Europe," *The Contemporary Review* 71 (April 1897): 595–603.

Stewart, J. I. M. *Eight Modern Writers.* Oxford: Oxford University Press, 1963.

———. *Rudyard Kipling.* London: Gollancz, 1966.

Steiner, George. *In Bluebeard's Castle.* New Haven: Yale University Press, 1973.

Steiner, Zara S. *The Foreign Office and Foreign Policy, 1898–1914.* Cambridge: Cambridge University Press, 1969.

Symons, Julian. *Horatio Bottomley.* London: Cresset Press, 1955.

Taylor, Isaac. *The Origin of the Aryans.* London: Scott, 1914.

Taylor, P. B. and W. H. Auden, eds. and trans. *The Elder Edda.* London: Faber & Faber, 1969.

Tennyson, Alfred Lord. *Complete Poetical Works.* Boston: Riverside Press, 1898.

Thompson, Laurence. *Robert Blatchford, Portrait of an Englishman.* London: Gollancz, 1951.

Tompkins, J. M. S. *The Art of Rudyard Kipling.* London: Methuen, 1959.

Toynbee, Arnold. *Nationality and War.* London: J.M. Dent, 1915.

Treitschke, Heinrich von. *Politics.* New York: Macmillan, 1916.

Trevelyan, Janet Penrose. *The Life of Mrs. Humphry Ward.* New York: Dodd, 1923.

Trilling, Lionel. *E. M. Forster.* Norfolk, Conn.: New Directions, 1943.

Trotter, W. B. *Instincts of the Herd in Peace and War.* New York: Macmillan, 1916.

Tuchman, Barbara. *The Guns of August.* New York: Macmillan, 1962.

Turner, E. S. *Boys Will Be Boys.* London: Michael Joseph, 1948.

Turville-Petre, E. O. G. *Myth and Religion of the North.* London: Weidenfeld & Nicolson, 1964.

Vansittart, Peter. *Voices from the Great War, 1870–1914.* London: Jonathan Cape, 1981.

Vansittart, Sir Robert. *Black Record: Germans Past and Present.* Toronto: Musson, 1941.

Waechter, Max. "England, Germany, and the Peace of Europe." *The Fortnightly Review* 93 (1 May 1913): 829–841.

Wagner, Richard. *The Rhine Gold.* Mainz: Schotts Soehne, [1897].

Watt, D. C. *Britain Looks to Germany: British Opinion and Policy Towards Germany Since 1945.* London: Wolff, 1965.

Waugh, Arthur. *Tradition and Change: Studies in Contemporary Literature.* London: Chapman & Hall, 1919.

Wells, H. G. *Mr. Britling Sees It Through.* Chicago: Donolme & Co., 1917.

———. *An Englishman Looks at the World.* London: Cassell, 1914.

————. "The Liberal Fear of Russia," *The Nation* (22 August, 1914).

————. *The Outline of History.* New York: Macmillan, 1920.

————. *The War in the Air.* London: Bell, 1908.

————. *The War That Will End War.* London: Palmer, 1914.

————. *What Is Coming? A European Forecast.* New York: Macmillan, 1916.

West, Arthur Graeme. *Diary of a Dead Officer.* London: Pelican Press, 1918.

Weston, Jessie L. *The Legends of the Wagner Drama: Studies in Mythology and Romance.* London: David Nutt, 1896.

White, Terence de Vere. "An Irishman Abroad," in *The Genius of Shaw,* ed. Michael Holroyd. London: Hodder & Stoughton, 1979.

Willis, Irene Cooper. *England's Holy War: A Study of English Liberal Idealism During the Great War.* New York: Knopf, 1928.

Wilson, Edmund. *The Wound and the Bow.* New York: Oxford University Press, 1965.

Wodehouse, Thomas [Lord Newton]. *Lord Lansdowne: A Biography.* London: Macmillan, 1929.

Woolf, Leonard. *Beginning Again: An Autobiograpy of the Years 1911–1918.* London: Harbrace, 1964.

Woolf, Virginia. "Letters to Angus Davidson," *Adam* 37 (1972): 28.

[Woolf, Virginia.] "Review of *The Collected Poems of Rupert Brooke,*" TLS (8 August 1918), 371.

"A World at Stake!" *The Magnet* 9 (31 October 1914): 1–4.

Wylie, I. A. R. *All Sorts.* London: Mills & Boon, 1919.

————. *Dividing Waters.* Indianapolis: Bobbs-Merrill, 1911.

————. *Eight Years in Germany.* London: Mills & Boon, 1914.

————. *The Germans.* Indianapolis: Bobbs-Merrill, 1911.

————. *My Life with George.* New York: Random House, 1940.

Index